T0373702

Lacan and Deleuze

Lacan and Deleuze

A Disjunctive Synthesis

EDITED BY BOŠTJAN NEDOH
AND ANDREJA ZEVNIK

EDINBURGH
University Press

Edinburgh University Press is one of the leading university presses in the UK.
We publish academic books and journals in our selected subject areas across the
humanities and social sciences, combining cutting-edge scholarship with high
editorial and production values to produce academic works of lasting importance.
For more information visit our website: www.edinburghuniversitypress.com

© editorial matter and organisation Boštjan Nedoh and Andreja Zevnik, 2016, 2018
© the chapters their several authors, 2016, 2018

Edinburgh University Press Ltd
The Tun – Holyrood Road
12(2f) Jackson's Entry
Edinburgh EH8 8PJ

First published in hardback by Edinburgh University Press 2016

Typeset in Adobe Garamond Pro by
Servis Filmsetting Ltd, Stockport, Cheshire
and printed and bound by CPI Group (UK) Ltd
Croydon, CR0 4YY

A CIP record for this book is available from the British Library

ISBN 978 1 4744 0829 5 (hardback)
ISBN 978 1 4744 3227 6 (paperback)
ISBN 978 1 4744 0830 1 (webready PDF)
ISBN 978 1 4744 0831 8 (epub)

The right of Boštjan Nedoh and Andreja Zevnik to be identified as the editors of
this work has been asserted in accordance with the Copyright, Designs and Patents
Act 1988, and the Copyright and Related Rights Regulations 2003 (SI No. 2498).

Contents

Acknowledgements

Jacques Lacan and Gilles Deleuze are probably two of the most prominent figures of twentieth-century continental philosophy. As this volume aims to show, the life of these two minds is polluted with their intellectual (and personal) quarrels, and yet those should not prevent (or in fact discourage) us from trying to put the two in a kind of a dialogue. It might well not be a dialogue of agreement, but neither is it one of complete disagreement and dismissal. A rather positive engagement with the two thinkers that does justice to their work and acknowledges any intellectual cross-fertilisation is perhaps the main contribution of the presented volume.

The idea came about in the summer of 2014. It did not take long before we had gathered together an excellent group of scholars from philosophy, cultural studies and politics. We have been privileged to work with this group of contributing authors who have all generously given their time to produce these chapters, and have shown patience and enthusiasm throughout the production of the book. Their encouragement and remarkable skills in keeping to the deadline (even if it was the 'final final final one') are greatly appreciated. For invaluable help and support we would also like to thank Ersev Ersoy, Michelle Houston and Carol Macdonald at the publishers, Edinburgh University Press. They were a pleasure to work with.

Numerous individuals and academic environments have influenced this volume. We would like to thank our respective institutions, the Politics Discipline Area at the University of Manchester and the Institute of Philosophy, Scientific Research Centre of the Slovenian Academy of Sciences and Arts in Ljubljana for their support and intellectual inspiration. In addition, we are particularly grateful to Lorenzo Chiesa, Guillaume Collett, Adrian Johnston, Marco Piasentier, Laurent de Sutter and Samo Tomšič for their help in the peer-review process, discussion

viii marker

of ideas, support for the project, assistance when that extra push was needed and always invaluable critique. There are many others who played an important yet not all that visible role in the preparation of this book or who have angered us enough to begin thinking about this project. We are also exceptionally lucky to be part of some truly special relationships and share our everyday life with some amazing individuals who never cease to surprise and inspire. Neither of us could do without them; *dream attack* comes to mind.

On this note Boštjan would in particular like to acknowledge the selfless support of his family and especially thank his wife Jerneja and son Oskar.

This volume is more than just an exposition of the disjunctive synthesis between Lacan's and Deleuze's respective thoughts. It also offers insights and important developments in the two respective theoretical fields. Moreover, this book is a political intervention, perhaps a statement to those who are still reluctant to think Deleuze with Lacan or Lacan with Deleuze, or as we explain later in the book, of the *Lacanuze*. The book is offered with this in mind.

Introduction: On a Disjunctive Synthesis between Lacan and Deleuze

Boštjan Nedoh and Andreja Zevnik

In the history of the late twentieth-century continental philosophy an intellectual controversy between Gilles Deleuze and Jacques Lacan is one that is perhaps known best. It is often said that Lacan is the most radical representative of structuralism, a thinker of negativity and alienation, of lack and subjective destitution. Deleuze, in contrast, is pictured as a great opponent and critic of the structuralist project in general and of Lacanian psychoanalysis in particular, as one of the key twentieth-century thinkers of vitalism and a philosopher of positivity, creative potentialities of desire and production. Nowadays it seems impossible not to choose sides: to either opt for Deleuze (against Lacan) or for Lacan (against Deleuze). Structuralism and negativity versus vitalism and positivity, the lack of the subject versus the fold of subjectivation. Lacan and Deleuze, it seems, cannot be further apart. Yet, this common opinion is in many ways misleading, made in the absence of any serious intellectual engagement with the two thinkers, and one which overemphasises their biographical anecdotes (associated notably with the quarrel surrounding the publication of Deleuze and Guattari's *Anti-Oedipus* in 1972), of which, no doubt, there were many.[1]

The past two decades have seen a number of attempts that aimed at creating a productive dialogue between the works of Deleuze and Lacan;[2] yet most of these attempts fall short in reaching their goal as they at least implicitly buy into the previously established two-sided opposition with Lacanians and psychoanalysis on the one end and Deleuzians and schizoanalysis on the other end. In other words, contemporary debates addressing the difference between the two authors are largely still structured around the most irreconcilable moments, such as the negativity of castration compared with the positivity of desire.

Precisely these prejudices which often hinder if not stop short the debate about and between Deleuze and Lacan can overshadow what is interesting in this irreconcilable dialogue between the two. When the aforementioned personal quarrels are put aside, there are different ways in which one might wish to approach this conversation. A path that emerged on the back of the different chapters in this book investigates their relationship to structuralism. While they maintained their differences, Lacan and Deleuze also share a very similar position in relation to the structuralist project in a period prior to the events of 1968 in France. Assuming they both contributed to the structuralist project, it must be stressed that their contributions are quite specific. They both started outside what was considered in the early 1960s to be an intellectual core of structuralism, namely Louis Althusser's 'Reading Capital' group. The starting point of the latter was the study of Marx's *Capital*, in relation to which the members of the group, including Althusser as the leader, developed a new epistemological framework commonly termed 'structural Marxism'. It is a reading which distinctly broke with the previous essentialist readings of Marx's 'critique of political economy'. Although Marx is far from being foreign to either Deleuze's or Lacan's work, in their contributions to the structuralist project, Marx certainly did not represent their point of departure. On the one hand, Deleuze, after a rather unproductive period between 1953 (*Empiricism and Subjectivity*) and 1962 (*Nietzsche and Philosophy*), only gradually approached structuralist issues; they are most directly considered in 'How Do We Recognize Structuralism?' (1967) and in *The Logic of Sense* (1969) where he goes through the readings of the two vitalist philosophers par excellence, Nietzsche and Bergson.[3] On the other hand, Lacan influenced the structuralist project not simply by his 'return to Freud', but also by including in this return the conceptual and scientific innovations of structural linguistics (Saussure and Jakobson). If '*the unconscious is structured like a language*',[4] it is so because the two basic mechanisms that operate in dream work, namely condensation and displacement, correspond to the linguistic concepts of metaphor and metonymy.[5]

However, compared with the work of Althusser's circle, the peculiarity of Deleuze's and Lacan's structuralisms lies in their non-Marxist reading, which in turn opens the space for a somewhat different definition of structuralism itself. In other words, Lacan's and Deleuze's structuralism is from the outset *another* structuralism, also referred to as post-structuralism, but one which in Lacan turns into a 'hyper-structuralism', to use Jean-Claude Milner's expression,[6] and in Deleuze into 'hyper-idealism'.[7] In both instances the paradoxical status of structuralism implies that the structure itself is not sufficient in representing the totality of the theoretical framework – an additional element, which produces internal exclusions, is introduced. In other words, the structure is lacking or can only actualise itself in relation to or as a product of an element outside. This inevitably poses a question about the relationship between the structure and its immanent otherness, which in Lacan's case appears in the form of a subject while in Deleuze's as something he defines as the 'non-personal singularity'.

In Deleuze's work the relationship between the structure and its otherness is first and foremost realised in his understanding of immanence. Surprisingly to some, Deleuze's immanence appears as a rather controversial concept. Commonly, it is understood as Deleuze's critique and a turn away from (post-)Kantian – or perhaps even (post-)Cartesian – philosophies of representation. Notwithstanding their differences, they all share the presupposition of the transcendental subject as the condition that makes the thought possible. The starting premise of these philosophies is that, if the object ought to be thought, the thought itself must be located in the domain of reason (as the guarantor of the truth), instead of being located in the domain of the senses (which can often deceive). In other words, if reason has access to truth, then it must be seen as transcendental or external in relation to sensations or the immanence of the object. And yet, as Levy R. Bryant stresses, a depiction of Deleuze's philosophy as anti-representational wrongly implies the antinomy between immanence and transcendence. In fact, as he puts it, Deleuze's philosophy or more precisely the ontology of immanence does not emerge as a critique or a response to all other philosophies of representation because they are transcendental, but because *they are not transcendental enough*.[8] In other words, following Bryant's statement closely, Deleuze's ontology of immanence could be defined as hyper-transcendental. If the philosophies of representation separated the subject from the object as final entity, Deleuze displaces the subject into the object itself, or, better, it is the object, which transcends itself into thought and becomes infinite. Such an object is what Deleuze calls the 'event' and it is inextricably connected to the 'undetermined infinite' form of the verb as 'the event of language'.[9] This displacement of the subject into an object, or better the failure of their reciprocal distinction, is at the basis of Deleuze's philosophy. Further, it sets the foundations for Deleuze's thought, which relies on the overturning of common metaphysical pairs – such as action–thought; sensible–intelligible; copy–simulacrum, and so on – into forms where the two poles are no longer distinguishable; in this way Deleuze creates the 'univocity of being'.

In Lacan's context the above-mentioned relation between the structure and its otherness is inseparable from Freud's theory of repression and in particular with what Freud calls the primary repression (*Urverdrängung*).[10] Unlike most common readings where repression is read as something caused by trauma – as repetition of the primal trauma of birth – the theorem of primary repression turns this picture on its head. As Alenka Zupančič states:

> The 'primary repressed' marker or representative of the drive is something that has never been conscious, and has never been part of any subjective experience, but constitutes its ground. The logic of repression by association is the logic of what Freud calls the repression proper, whereas the primal repression is precisely not a repression in this sense. In it the causality usually associated with the unconscious is turned upside down: it is not that we repress a signifier because of a traumatic experience related to it, it is rather because this signifier is repressed that we can experience something as traumatic (and not simply as painful, frustrating etc.) and repress it.[11]

The structure in the Lacanian sense is formed by the aforementioned primal repression of the representative of the drive (or the signifier), which appears as repressed from the very beginning. The metaphor, the symptom or the signifying chain (as well as the subject as the effect of the signifying chain), which occupies the space emptied by the signifier, emerges only after or under the condition of the primary repressed signifier. It constitutes the hole around which the drive revolves.

Although it may seem that the relationship between structural conditions of the symbolic order (within which the subject exists) is transcendental, in the sense that the condition pre-exists what steps into the place emptied by the primary repressed signifier, Lacan explicitly states that we should grasp this logic of causality not as one of genesis but as one of immanent synchrony:

> The primal repressed is a signifier, and we can always regard what is built on this as constituting the symptom qua a scaffolding of signifiers. Repressed and symptom are homogeneous, and reducible to the functions of signifiers. Although their structure is built up step by step like any edifice, it is nevertheless, in the end, inscribable in synchronic terms.[12]

However, as Jean-Claude Milner points out, such a conception of the structure in Lacan can still be seen as being part of a stronger type of structuralism, while the 'weak structuralism' or 'hyper-structuralism' arises only in Seminar XVII (1968, indeed!) with the so-called 'theory of discourses'. According to Milner, the axiom of Lacan's stronger structuralism is on the position within the structure; or better the position in the structure gives all determinations to the element occupying that position; in contrast, the definition of 'weak structuralism' or 'hyper-structuralism' says that the elements maintain some of their properties or determinations even when they change the position within the structure. In other words, the elements in the discourses (object a, $\$$, S_1, S_2) maintain some of their characteristics even when they change their structural position in the discourse.[13]

And yet, while in Lacan the relationship between the structure and its otherness also appears as immanent, there is a crucial difference from how Deleuze conceptualises this very relation: on the one hand, Deleuze associates it with the univocity of being, giving the ontological status to both structure and its excess, whilst Lacan, on the other hand, considers the primal repression as a negative condition of being itself. A condition which is irreducible to the status of both being and non-being but should instead be grasped as 'unrealized'.[14]

This collection of chapters attempts to draw out precisely this paradoxical irreducibility of Lacan and Deleuze to a common ground or better to a paradoxical status of the common ground itself. Rather than opting for one side against the other, their relationship appears to be an enigmatic one. Perhaps the two thinkers offer an esoteric debate: one of responses and reservations without naming names; one in which the reader can be often left in doubt whether Deleuze and Lacan really talk to each other when they *are* talking to each other and, simultaneously, a conviction that they talk to each other precisely and only when they do not name each other.

The problematics of this impossible or a failed relationship between Deleuze and Lacan is introduced by Peter Klepec's chapter 'For Another Lacan–Deleuze Encounter'. By discussing the question of 'encounter', it gives the encounter a conceptual value: what does it mean to encounter oneself or something, and with what kind of encounter are we dealing in the relationship between Deleuze and Lacan? Has this encounter anything to do with what Lacan called the 'encounter with the [traumatic] real'? In an attempt to give a conceptual value to the notion of encounter itself, this chapter succeeds in displacing the standard picture of their relation on a conceptually much more productive terrain, arguing for 'another' encounter' between Deleuze and Lacan.

Laurent de Sutter's chapter 'Reciprocal Portrait of Jacques Lacan in Gilles Deleuze' complements Klepec's chapter. It locates the debate about their relationship in the terrain of the ambiguous relation between perversion and law in (Sade's) sadism and (Sacher-Masoch's) masochism. When Deleuze wrote his 'Presentation of Sacher-Masoch', he intended it as a sort of an intervention into the then flourishing discussion about Sade's *oeuvre* – to which Lacan had contributed with his famous article on 'Kant with Sade'. The question about the perversion of law, which was anchored in Kant's idea of the moral law, which interested Lacan greatly (but also Roland Barthes or Pierre Klossowski), was suddenly reshaped. It turned from causes to consequences, from the impossible foundation of law to its self-destruction which is produced by its very application. It is this very turn that de Sutter's chapter proposes to explore, by retelling the story of the love triangle that destroyed the law.

In Boštjan Nedoh's 'Does the Body without Organs Have Any Sex at All? Lacan and Deleuze on Perversion and Sexual Difference' the discussion about Lacan's and Deleuze's respective views on perversion is further elaborated through a discussion of the problematic status of sexual difference within the structure of perversion. On the one hand, this chapter attempts to show how the master concept in Deleuze's late philosophy, which is that of the 'body without organs' linked to the 'absolute Outside' or 'field of immanence', does not differ from but rather fits with Deleuze's early analysis of perversion and fetishistic disavowal as 'beyond the Other' (with the Other meaning the symbolic order of differences). Moreover, contrary to the widespread belief, Deleuze's understanding of perversion as 'beyond the Other' is made through an affirmative reading of and a reference to Lacanian theory of perversion. Although it may seem that Deleuze in his work tries to oppose affirmative fetishistic disavowal to neurotic repression, a close reading of Lacan shows how these two clinical structures cannot be opposed but instead share a common condition of possibility: a primary repressed signifier which stands for the famous inexistence of the sexual relationship and is located on the feminine side of Lacan's formulas of sexuation. In this respect, Lacan's engagement with feminine *jouissance* as one 'beyond the phallus' may be seen as his answer to Deleuze's problem of the topology of the Outside, which cannot be thought without the phallus and is in turn immanent to it.

Scott Wilson's 'Gnomonology: Deleuze's Phobias and the Line of Flight between Speech and the Body' looks closely at how Deleuze's concepts of the 'line of flight' and 'becoming' find definition in a creative rethinking of Lacan's understanding of phobia as neither exactly a structure nor a symptom but a 'gnomon' or pointer that marks a gate or threshold (*phobos* is both fear and flight), especially with regard to Deleuze's own philosophical creativity and the politics of escape. Beginning with a Lacanian reading of Deleuze's own phobias – we find from François Dosse's biography that Deleuze had a phobia of both milk products and schizophrenics – the chapter offers a different way of understanding the dynamic genesis and development of Deleuze's philosophy and schizoanalysis. In addition, it looks at the political efficacy of notions of 'ex-sistence' and 'becoming' in Lacan and Deleuze with reference to the various cultural, 'gnomonological' figures of flight and phobia that in often terrifying ways indicate the path to the exit (from the state, capitalism, humanism, (post)modernity, and so on): the [under erasure] woman, the animal and the 'anomalous'.

In 'Lacan, Deleuze and the Politics of the Face' Andreja Zevnik aims to discuss Lacan's and Deleuze's attempts to break away from signification or from the image the face gives to the subject in the scopic realm and in the structure of language. Perhaps countering Deleuze's attack on Lacan and his 'fixation' on the gaze, Zevnik aims to show that both thinkers have a similar endeavour in mind. While Deleuze might indeed pursue the break away from sovereign discourses of signification and subjectivation with a turn to the body, Lacan in contrast maintains the tension internally, either in the form of a returned/anxious gaze or through the linguistic form, which does away with meaning. The chapter proceeds in two ways: first the focus is on Lacan's conceptualisation of the gaze and how 'the subject' or face emerges on the back of it. This notion is then taken apart with a reference to the anxious gaze (in Lacan) and deterritorialisation (in Deleuze). To highlight the politics of the face and de-facialisation, in the final part the chapter returns to Lacan and highlights three moments in Lacan's thought which counter Deleuze's critique and in fact bring the two thinkers closer together: the politics, the body and the unconscious. In doing so, the chapter aims to put in discussion these two thinkers and shows how one perhaps less significant concept mobilises almost the entirety of their respective thoughts, and how despite differences and different terminology, the two are closer than they (or the respective schools of thought) made them appear.

In his '*Denkwunderkeiten*: On Deleuze, Schreber and Freud' Tadej Troha offers a unique analysis of the role and mode of the 'verb' at the intersection of Deleuze's *The Logic of Sense*, Freud's analysis of Schreber's case and a close reading of Schreber's *Memoirs of My Nervous Illness* [*Denkwürdigkeiten eines Nervenkranken*] itself. The chapter departs from *The Logic of Sense*, in which Deleuze develops a theory of the verb, which in his conception represents a category of language and further points to its inner paradox. On the one hand, language consolidates boundaries, denotes identities and properties, while on the other hand, it transcends these very same boundaries and features as a moment of becoming. This pair of consolidation and transcendence first appears as a difference between a noun, an adjective and a verb and is later translated into a difference between the two poles of the verb, the present tense and the infinitive, with only the latter denoting the moment of becoming. At this point, the theoretical construction of the role of the verb *wundern*, 'to miracle', in Schreber becomes focal for the analysis. The theory of the verb *wundern* brings to light the intricacies of Schreber's own specific use of this verb and their implications for a materialist radicalisation of Deleuze's thesis on the undetermined infinitive while it, alongside, amends the linguistic formulas in Freud's analysis of Schreber.

Guillaume Collett in his chapter 'Snark, Jabberwock, Poord'jeli: Deleuze and the Lacanian School on the Names-of-the-Father' traces the development of Lacan's idea of the Names-of-the-Father from its origins in the 1950s to its further elaboration by Lacan's disciples, such as Serge Leclaire and Gilles Deleuze. Already by the end of Seminar X Lacan had put in place a project – a never realised seminar – to expand on a new conception, that of the *Names*-of-the-Father. This conception went hand in hand with core shifts in Lacan's understanding of the relation between structure and the body in its material singularity (partial object, erogenous zone, drive). By the time we reach the seminars of the mid-1970s, the Name-of-the-Father is to be understood as knotted together with it to produce a singular configuration of the Real, Symbolic and Imaginary, as an 'event' (names as singular knots). In this new configuration, the maternal imaginary is given greater importance and no longer unilaterally subjected to the universality of structure. It is at this point, as Collett argues, that first Leclaire and later Deleuze advance Lacan's work. Building on his famous case study 'Poord'jeli' (or the dream with the unicorn) and on his interpretation of Freud's Wolf Man case, Leclaire developed his own conception of the letter – or more precisely, of the body of the letter. Through it, not only was he able to articulate a systematic theory of structure's anchoring to the material singularity of the erogenous body; he also worked these insights into a new reading of the Oedipus complex. In sum, Leclaire conceived of each Name-of-the-Father in terms closer to a *genesis* of sense from the body's nonsense. By explicitly defining Leclaire's 'Poord'jeli' as an 'esoteric word' in his 1969 *Logic of Sense*, Deleuze reiterates his aim to bring together the work of the Lacanian school with a new 'esoteric' or nonsensical formalism. The function of the esoteric word is to construct a 'surface', to let the body's 'depths' articulate with the ideal 'heights' of linguistic form, entailing a bilateral or immanent knotting of the maternal (depths) and paternal (heights), producing an 'event' or disjunctive synthesis. Collett's chapter discusses what is probably the strongest moment of disjunctive synthesis in Lacan's and Deleuze's work.

In his 'Baroque Structuralism: Deleuze, Lacan and the Critique of Linguistics', Samo Tomšič puts the established cultural perceptions of Deleuze and Lacan and the apparent unsurpassable contradiction between the two under question by examining the encounter between Lacan's radicalisation of structuralism and Deleuze's exploration of vitalism on the terrain of topology. This mathematisation is understood as the minimal common ground, where the actual philosophical dialogue between Deleuze and Lacan can take place. In doing so, the chapter explores Lacan's and Deleuze's references to the baroque; Lacan's ground-breaking Seminar XX and Deleuze's study of *Foucault* and *The Fold*. In both cases the baroque serves as the privileged point of entry in the discussion of the structural dynamics and of the peculiar materiality of linguistic effects in the living body: a body of *jouissance* (Lacan) and the curviness of matter (Deleuze). By referring to the baroque, both Lacan and Deleuze move beyond the classical structuralist frames of representation and address the problem of linguistic production, a problem that Lacan most notably discussed in reference to Marx, and Deleuze in his outstanding analyses of unconscious machines. Deleuze's introduction of the fold, on the one hand, and Lacan's constant reference to aspheric topology, on the other hand, displace the accent from the lack to the void. In this move, Deleuze and Lacan indicate a different understanding of structure, which fits more accurately with the topology of the unconscious and with the space introduced by the modern scientific paradigms such as linguistics.

Lorenzo Chiesa's 'Exalted Obscenity and the Lawyer of God: Lacan, Deleuze and the Baroque' takes Tomšič's chapter further, by focusing on the still very much overlooked debate about the status of the baroque in both thinkers. In his 1973 Seminar XX, Lacan states that his discourse partakes of the baroque and that the art of this period is crucial in order to understand what he means by *jouissance* and sexual difference. Fifteen years later, Deleuze consecrates one of his last books to an investigation of the influence the same artistic style had on Leibniz's notion of the fold. Deleuze develops it further, placing it at the centre of a new kind of philosophy of difference. In this chapter, Chiesa aims to show how Lacan's and Deleuze's apparently distant treatments of the baroque form a dialogue around the notion of difference. The lecture in which Lacan speaks about the baroque stands out as one of the most blatant anti-philosophical moments in his *oeuvre*. In fewer than ten pages he outlines a new ontology in which being does not think. Chiesa shows how a para-ontology of in-difference can derive from Lacan's thought and how such a stance on being converges and contrasts with Deleuze's ontology of the fold presented as a relationship of difference in itself.

In her chapter 'The Death Drive' Alenka Zupančič continues the discussion started by Chiesa, which addresses the relationship between Lacan and Deleuze from the perspective of their respective ontological projects, confronting in more detail Lacan's concept of the *One* (as developed in Seminar XIX) and placing it in discussion with Deleuze's discussion of the univocity of Being (from *Difference and Repetition*). The point of departure is the unconventional reading of Freud's *Beyond the Pleasure Principle*, a text with which both thinkers engaged and which challenges the established understandings of the notion of the death drive. Lacan and Deleuze both firmly reject the idea that the psychic apparatus strives toward homeostasis and links 'surplus pleasure' with repetition. The debate between both thinkers turns interesting on the level of ontological consequences and in a discussion about the production of the *One in* and *through* repetition. Deleuze's name for this *One* is 'univocity of Being', whereas Lacan develops an original and philosophically polemical theory summed up in the enigmatic statement *Il y a de l'Un* (there is something of *One*). Lacan's *One* is caught in a pulsating place between movement and stagnation. Stained with negativity, it does not get fully constituted, and its understanding relies on the logic of the signifier and the paradoxes of aspheric topology. This chapter's discussion delves into the philosophy of Lacan's topology and his mathematical formalisations, which, in opposition to Deleuze's vitalistic understanding of the *One*, opt for a somewhat different path of thinking about the production of surplus and which situate *jouissance* as the limit of the classical philosophical ontology; an ontology to which Deleuze arguably remains inscribed.

Adrian Johnston's 'Repetition and Difference: Žižek, Deleuze and Lacanian Drives' brings to a close the discussion about Deleuze's and Lacan's respective ontological projects with reference to the Freudian concept of death drive. Johnston displaces the concept in reference to the contemporary debate between him and Žižek concerning the question of 'transcendental materialism'. After a close and systematic approach to Žižek's reading of Hegel's articulation of the subject alongside Lacan's theory of drive, Johnston further develops the Lacanian distinction between drive and desire (one also adopted by Deleuze) and proposes a systematic framework of arguments for an affirmation rather than a rejection (made by Žižek in his last work, *Absolute Recoil*) of transcendental materialism and acknowledges its responsibility for contemporary scientific breakthroughs.

Finally, Paul M. Livingston's chapter 'Lacan, Deleuze and the Consequences of Formalism' focuses on Deleuze's and Lacan's specific uses of formalism and shows how in a period around 1970 (Deleuze's publication of *Difference and Repetition* and of *The Logic of Sense*; Lacan's Seminars XVII, XIX and XX) both thinkers developed very similar positions with respect to formalism and formalisation in philosophy and in psychoanalysis. Moreover, in the last section, this chapter distinguishes these from other contemporary uses of formalism in the wake of Deleuze and Lacan, specifically ones which either miss the specific level on which formalism bears witness to the passage of the Lacanian real by substituting it for a direct ontologisation of mathematics, or relapses to what is essentially a *pre-*formal thought of the logic of contradiction under the mandate of a (post-) structuralist renewal of the Hegelian dialectic.

After reading the chapters offered here, one can no doubt be left with different impressions and one's own interpretations of the relationship between the two thinkers who probably most strongly marked the landscape of contemporary twentieth-century philosophy. The relationship between the two theoretical projects probably aligns itself best with Deleuze's own expression: a disjunctive synthesis of which the best example is portmanteau words. As he put it, regarding the contracting word 'frumious':

Thus, the necessary disjunction is not between fuming and furious, for one may indeed be both at once; rather, it is between fuming-and-furious on the one hand and furious-and-fuming on the other. In this sense, the function of the portmanteau word always consists in the ramification of the series into which it is inserted. This is the reason why it never exists alone.[15]

Perhaps, we could conclude on a similar note when considering the relationship between Deleuze and Lacan: although the supremacy of one side over the other is often claimed, in the last instance neither can exist without the other. And if this relation of disjunctive synthesis might be seen by Deleuzians as the relationship between Deleuze-and-Lacan and by Lacanians as the relationship between Lacan-and-Deleuze, the disjunction forces us to step in the exact middle and invent a new contracting word: *Lacanuze*.

Notes

1. In contrast to the rather hostile atmosphere that surrounded the relationship between Deleuze and Lacan in the 1970s, it is worth mentioning one anecdote from 1967. After a conference in Lyon, Deleuze and Lacan were allegedly sharing a friendly drink, a bottle of vodka each. This was around the time when Deleuze published his essay on Sacher-Masoch 'Coldness and Cruelty' (just prior to his 1968 and 1969 masterpieces *Difference and Repetition* and *The Logic of Sense*) for which Lacan explicitly expressed admiration in his (unpublished) seminar *The Logic of Phantasy* (1966–7). In this seminar Lacan states: 'Someone who is not a psychoanalyst, M Deleuze to name him, presents a book by Sacher Masoch: *Présentation de Sacher Masoch*. He writes on masochism undoubtedly the best text that has ever been written! I mean the best, compared to everything that has been written on the theme in psychoanalysis' (Lacan, Jacques, *The Logic of Phantasy* (unpublished seminar), Lecture from 19 April 1967, trans. Cormac Gallagher from unedited French manuscripts, available at <http://www.lacaninireland.com/web/wp-content/uploads/2010/06/14-Logic-of-Phantasy-Complete.pdf> (last accessed 24 March 2016)).
2. See, for instance, de Bolle, Leen (ed.), *Deleuze and Psychoanalysis: Philosophical Essays on Deleuze's Debate with Psychoanalysis* (Leuven: Leuven University Press, 2010); Žižek, Slavoj, *Organs without Bodies: On Deleuze and Consequences* (London: Routledge, 2003); Smith, Daniel W., 'The Inverse Side of the Structure: Žižek on Deleuze on Lacan', *Criticism*, 46: 4 (Fall 2004), pp. 635–50. Regarding the question of 'the baroque' in Deleuze and Lacan, see also Lahiji, Nadir Z. 'The Baroque Idea: Lacan contra Deleuze, and Žižek's Unwritten Book', *International Journal of Žižek Studies*, 5: 2 (2011).
3. See especially Deleuze, Gilles, *Nietzsche et la philosophie* (Paris: Presses universitaires de France, 1962) and *Le Bergsonisme* (Paris: Presses universitaires de France, 1966).
4. Lacan, Jacques, *The Seminar of Jacques Lacan, Book XI: The Four Fundamental Concepts of Psychoanalysis* (London and New York: W. W. Norton, 1998), p. 20; original emphasis.
5. See Lacan, Jacques, 'The Instance of the Letter in the Unconscious or Reason Since Freud', in *Écrits* (London and New York: W. W. Norton, 2006), pp. 412–41.
6. Milner, Jean-Claude, *Le périple structural: figures et paradigme* (Paris: Seuil, 2002), pp. 141–68.
7. For the explanation of this term, see further discussion below.

8. Bryant, Levy R., *Difference and Givenness: Deleuze's Transcendental Empiricism and the Ontology of Immanence* (Evanston: Northwestern University Press, 2008), p. 22; original emphasis.

9. Deleuze, Gilles, *The Logic of Sense* (London: The Athlone Press, 1990), p. 185.

10. 'We have reason to assume that there is a primal repression, a first phase of repression, which consists in the psychical (ideational) representative of the drive [*die psychische (Vorstellungs-) Repräsentanz des Tribes*] being denied entrance into the conscious. With this a *fixation* is established; the representative in question persists unaltered from then onwards and the drive remains attached to it' (Freud, Sigmund, 'Repression', in *The Standard Edition of the Complete Psychological Works of Sigmund Freud, Vol. XIV*, ed. and trans. James Strachey (London: Vintage, 2001), p. 148).

11. Zupančič, Alenka, 'Ponavljanje' [Repetition], *Filozofski vestnik* 28: 1 (2007), p. 69.

12. Lacan, *Four Fundamental Concepts*, p. 176.

13. See again Milner, *Le périple structural*, pp. 141–9.

14. Ibid. p. 30.

15. Deleuze, *The Logic of Sense*, pp. 46–7.

Chapter 1

For Another Lacan–Deleuze Encounter

Peter Klepec

How does one encounter something or someone? What happens? What is the logic of encounter as such? What if the 'Lacan–Deleuze encounter' is all about *these* questions? What if the questions regarding the nature and logics of an encounter are intrinsically bound with the theoretical/practical projects and central notions of Deleuze and Lacan, if there are any: the event (philosophy) in the former and the unconscious (psychoanalysis) in the latter? For Lacan (and to a certain degree for Deleuze, too) an encounter is necessary and unavoidable for a human being: an encounter with language and speech. For Lacan, the human being is a speaking being, whereas for him the unconscious is nothing but the 'effects of speech on the subject'.[1] One could say then that for Lacan an encounter is necessary, whereas *how* one deals with it is *always singular* and *contingent* (or how one encounters one's own image in the mirror, the Other, one's own sexuality, desire, fantasy, drive, *jouissance*, one's own symptoms and unconscious, *objet petit a*, psychoanalysis, transference, partner, love, etc.). However, if Lacan were to claim only that, he would be a nominalist claiming that there are only individual encounters and only differences. For him there is also logic here, the logic of a certain deadlock, which has its own inner limits, inconsistencies and antagonisms, which Lacan calls the real, the real as impossible. It is here at the point where things by definition do not work out that Lacan meets Deleuze and it is here that *another* Lacan–Deleuze encounter and, more generally, *another* encounter between philosophy and psychoanalysis is on the agenda today. This is a vast topic, though, and we will limit ourselves here to only its basic outline.

There is a general consensus that the encounter between Deleuze and Lacan turned out badly. It would be interesting to delve more deeply into the details, but due to the lack of space we will limit ourselves to a couple of remarks. It is well known that there was a brief period of proximity between Deleuze and Lacan in the years 1967–9, but with Guattari entering the picture things first changed[2] and then came to a close with the publication of *Anti-Oedipus* in 1972. While Lacan according to Dosse wanted to meet with Deleuze and discuss the work, Deleuze declined and talked to Lacan only once over the phone, while Guattari did meet with him, but only for that last time. But already at the biographical level the story told by Dosse is not completely accurate. Didier Eribon in 1995[3] published Deleuze's recollection of a meeting with Lacan at the latter's home several months after the publication of *Anti-Oedipus*. Deleuze waited a long time in the antechamber ('a little too long', he says). When Lacan finally received him, he rolled out a list of all his disciples, said that they were all worthless (except Jacques-Alain Miller), then looked at Deleuze and finally said to him: 'What I need is someone like you!' This, together with the words he supposedly said to Guattari at their last meeting ('What counts for me is that analysis exist'), puts the supposed closure in a slightly different light. That does not mean that psychoanalysis was not criticised rather heavily by both until the end. Deleuze, for instance, in 1977 claims that psychoanalysis 'stifles the production of desire', 'all of psychoanalysis is designed to keep people from speaking and to take away the conditions of true expression', and that it 'is based on the liberal-bourgeois form of the contract',[4] yet he speaks of Lacan in the same period rather approvingly: 'Only Lacan has kept a certain sense of laughter, but he admits he is forced to laugh alone.'[5] Regardless of the harshness of their critique, it seems that Deleuze and Guattari were still interested in what Lacan had to say. According to Scott Wilson, Deleuze did not himself attend Lacan's seminars, but 'in the aftermath of the publication of *Anti-Oedipus* it is reported that he and Guattari asked Deleuze's wife Fanny Deleuze to attend to see what reaction, if any, Lacan would make to their book'.[6] And although Lacan devoted his Seminar XXI *Les non-dupes errent* (1973–4) partly to Deleuze and Guattari's critique, in his lesson from 12 February 1974 he refers to Deleuze rather approvingly, although he does not mention his name ('a person who has read Sacher-Masoch'). So there are, in short, facts omitted by the prevailing story about the Lacan–Deleuze encounter. But even these facts cannot really change the predominant view thereof: first there was mutual love at first sight, but then there came another, true love (Guattari for Deleuze as 'two streams coming together to make a "third stream"') and the seductions of 'the old man', Lacan ('What I need is someone like you!'), were finally turned down, rebuffed. Love, hatred, indifference, that is the story.

But what if it is simply false? False, not in the sense that things did not quite happen that way, but in the sense that it puts us on the wrong track.

It is true that Deleuze and Lacan do not share the same view on many things.[7] They indeed come from very different theoretical backgrounds, assumptions, theses, problems and last but not least, from very different disciplines: philosophy (Deleuze) is not psychoanalysis (Lacan), and vice versa. But exactly the same also holds for the Deleuze–Guattari encounter. Their story, told by Dosse, begins at exactly the same point:

> In 1968, Gilles Deleuze and Félix Guattari inhabited very different worlds, and there was little chance that they would ever meet. Deleuze was a recognized philosopher who had by then already published a large body of work; Guattari was a militant psychoanalyst, the director of a psychiatric clinic, the author of several articles, and a social scientist. While we might agree with Robert Maggiori that they were destined to meet, there was no historical necessity in the meeting. How their two worlds came into contact with each other remains an open question.[8]

Does that not hold for every encounter in the strict sense of the word? Is not encounter as such surrounded by a kind of mystery, is it not an open question, a surprise, a shock even? Not only missed or traumatic encounters, but also the beginning of something beautiful like love – 'love is nothing but the encounter'[9] – entail paradoxes, enigmas, open questions.

In this sense, one could say that an encounter is an event in a more philosophical sense. Here many numerous contemporary philosophers come to mind (Badiou, Žižek, Althusser, Heidegger, Derrida, etc.), but we will limit ourselves to Deleuze,[10] for whom first and foremost nobody can master the effects of an event. This is not far from Lacan's basic understanding of communication: the essence of every communication is misunderstanding, since 'the sender [. . .] receives from the receiver his own message in an inverted form'.[11] Every dialogue, discussion or encounter has its (comical) effects, and although Deleuze does not share Lacan's view on language, he is very much against discussion or communication:

> It is already hard enough to understand what someone is trying to say. Discussion is just an exercise in narcissism where everyone takes turns showing off. [. . .] Discussion has no place in the work of philosophy. The phrase 'let's discuss it' is an act of terror.[12]

Because of that, 'every philosopher runs away when he or she hears someone say "Let's discuss this."'[13] All one should do, for Deleuze, is not to discuss what someone is saying, but to explore it, play around with the terms, add something, and relate it to something else. Movement always happens either behind the thinker's back or, as Deleuze puts it in another context: 'You think you've got to port, but then find yourself thrown back out onto the open sea.'[14] This holds even when you take an author from behind and give him a child that would be his own offspring, yet monstrous, which nonetheless happened in the case of *Anti-Oedipus*, which Lacan even recognised as his '*progéniture délirante*'.[15] And is not Lacan's complaint,[16] by the way, encountered here in an inverted form?

This turning on its head, this topsy-turvy, is the gist of what Lacan tells us about the 'encounter with the real' and other encounters as well. Take love, for instance, which for Lacan supplements the non-existent sexual relationship, yet it does not bring harmony or peace. What love will bring about is simply not predictable: 'to know what your partner will do is not a proof of love'.[17] Thus for Lacan the encounter always involves a dimension of the unexpected and of surprise and it is here that he introduces the 'encounter with the real' in his Seminar XI, where he uses, as is well known, Aristotle's famous example of encounter as *tyche* (chance, happening, fortune, luck) from his *Physics* (196a, 3–5): 'if a man comes to market and there chances on someone he has been wishing to meet but was not expecting to meet there'. But while for Aristotle this accidental encounter is a rather nice surprise, for psychoanalysis even happy encounters are never simple. That is why Lacan proposes a certain courage, even courage in love, which

> has to do with what he called the contingency of the encounter – an encounter, in the partner, with their symptoms, their solitude and everything that constitutes their own exile from the relation that, between the sexes, does not exist. [. . .] the courage of love involves facing up to the impasse and 'going through' anxiety. A capacity for invention, a 'will to chance' [*volonté de chance*], as Georges Bataille put it, a desire to be in the game that is being played, which, as everyone knows, makes oneself believe one is capable of anything – it 'gives one wings', as we say in French.[18]

Yet love is not simply pure bliss, happiness or harmony. It always involves 'turning on one's head'. Using Aristotle's example we may say that we want to meet someone, we may even set off on a date with the explicit intention of finding ourselves a 'partner', but this never happens in the way we expect. We may 'fall in love', but this still always surprises us, since it necessarily happens 'elsewhere' than where we expected it, or intended it:

> This is why a love encounter can be quite upsetting, and is never simply a moment of pure happiness (where everything finally 'adds up'). It is always accompanied by a feeling of perplexity, confusion, a feeling that we've got something that we don't know exactly what to do with, and yet something rather pleasant. [. . .] What happens in a love encounter is not simply that the sexual nonrelation is momentarily suspended with an unexpected emergence of a (possible) relation, but something rather more complex: it is that the nonrelation itself suddenly emerges as a mode (as well as the condition) of a relation.[19]

A certain aspect of this mode of relation as nonrelation reminds one of Deleuze's '"between-the-two" of solitudes',[20] which comes to the fore when one writes or creates: 'When you work, you are necessarily in absolute solitude. [. . .] But it is an extremely populous solitude. Populated not with dreams, phantasms or plans, but with encounters.'[21] We never think or write alone: 'Even when you think you're writing on your own, you're perhaps doing it with someone else you can't always name.'[22] But sometimes you can name them and then they are called 'conceptual personae'. The role of the latter for Deleuze is not only to show thought's territories, but to think in us, to play a part in the very creation of the author's concepts. In this sense 'Lacan' is undoubtedly a conceptual persona for Deleuze at least for two reasons: because 'it is possible that the conceptual persona only rarely or allusively appears for himself' and because even when conceptual personae are 'antipathetic',

> they are so while belonging fully to the plane that the philosopher in question lays out and to the concepts he creates. They then indicate the dangers specific to this plane, the bad perceptions, bad feelings, and even negative movements that emerge from it, and they will themselves inspire original concepts whose repulsive character remains a constitutive property of that philosophy.[23]

One encounters 'conceptual personae' by chance in the same manner as one 'falls in love' or as one encounters psychoanalysis (transference). And it is here that Deleuze encounters in Lacan the *objet petit a*:

> Debt, the letter, the handkerchief or the crown, the nature of this object is specified by Lacan: it is always displaced in relation to itself. Its peculiar property is not to be where one looks for it, and conversely, also to be found where it is not.[24]

Here, at this point of 'to be found where one is not' we can also measure the ultimate irony of the Lacan–Deleuze encounter: Deleuze is not the philosopher that Lacan thinks he is and Lacan is not the psychoanalyst that Deleuze thinks he is. While there is no doubt that Deleuze is interested in nothing but philosophy, Lacan is clear: 'I am not a philosopher at all.'[25] The story of Lacan and philosophy[26] is a complex one, but one thing is for certain: for Lacan philosophy goes together with the master's discourse, while psychoanalysis is on the 'other side'. But here Lacan is perhaps at least regarding one point close to Deleuze – philosophy, that is, a certain form of philosophy, the history of philosophy, is for the latter bound with the repressor's role. One could even speak in this vein of 'state philosophy': 'Philosophy is shot through with the project of becoming the official language of a Pure State.'[27] It is perhaps against this philosophy that Lacan rebels: 'I rebel, if I can say, against philosophy.'[28] And there are some other points as well where we could speak of the general proximity between Deleuze and Lacan. While Lacan focuses on the gaps and holes of discourse or knowledge, also Deleuze is interested in 'the cracks', 'holes' or 'gaps', since he accentuates the dissolution of the subject, the disintegration of the body, the destruction of the world, the 'minorisation' of politics and the 'stuttering' of language:

> Thought is primarily trespass and violence, the enemy, and nothing presupposes philosophy: everything begins with misosophy. Do not count upon thought to ensure the relative necessity of what it thinks. Rather, count upon the contingency of an encounter with that which forces thought to raise up and educate the absolute necessity of an act of thought or a passion to think. [. . .] Something in the world forces us to think. This something is an object not of recognition but of a fundamental *encounter*. What is encountered may be Socrates, a temple or a demon. It may be grasped in a range of affective tones: wonder, love, hatred, suffering.[29]

The truth of Deleuze depends on an encounter with something that forces us to think, and while it begins for Deleuze in the sensible and in intensity, for Lacan this 'range of affective tones' would be nothing but transference. Lacan would also agree that 'nothing presupposes philosophy' or Freud's *Wissentrieb*, there is namely always a certain 'I don't want to know anything about it.' That is why Deleuze, on the other hand, is so interested in everything that goes counter to or against clichés, models, habits, norms, generality, rules and laws. He is convinced that philosophy creates new concepts and in this way resists opinion. His opposition to common sense and his critique of representational[30] thinking goes together to a certain degree with Lacan's claim that we learn only from something that does not fit our fantasies. Understanding is basically intertwined with recognition, or as Lacan has put it, 'one never understands anything but one's fantasies'. But here, as soon as we pass from generality to detail, already some important differences start to occur. They are visible already on the orthographical level (Deleuze never writes 'fantasy', but 'phantasm', and he almost never uses Lacan's term for drive, *pulsion*, but stubbornly uses the term 'instinct') and concern concepts that are important for later Lacan such as *jouissance*,[31] *lalangue* and the real, as well as 'classical' Lacanian notions such as desire. Instead of going too deeply into the details, we will limit ourselves here briefly to the problematics of interpretation, language and the real, which is at the centre of the critique of psychoanalysis in *Anti-Oedipus*. Besides well-known points concerning desire, lack, signifier and structure, the general argument against psychoanalysis of Deleuze and Guattari is that in its interpretation it proceeds too quickly while knowing in advance what the interpretation will be: an Oedipal family structure. It seems here that for Deleuze in general cases in psychoanalysis are always illustrations, *Beispiels*, rather than *Falls*, cases that follow their own logic, start from scratch, and which often question and redefine so-called general theory. Concerning the Oedipal scheme, it seems that Deleuze and Guattari are knocking here, so to speak, on open doors since at that time Lacan was already beyond Oedipus; for instance in his Seminar XVII he proposes 'to analyze the Oedipus complex as being Freud's dream'.[32] The same holds for interpretation, which for Deleuze and Guattari always ends in transcendence and religion: 'Interpretation is our modern way of believing and of being pious.'[33] But already from Seminar XI on Lacan explicitly links interpretation and hermeneutics with religion: 'hermeneutics, on the other hand, makes ready use of interpretation. In this respect, we see, at least, a corridor of communication between psychoanalysis and the religious register.'[34] Not only in *Triumph of Religion*, where he accentuates that religion is designed so that men would not perceive what is going wrong or not going well, but also elsewhere Lacan accentuates that: 'religious sense will have a boom you have no idea of. Religion is namely the original site of sense.'[35] Psychoanalysis is, again, on the other side, since it holds on to what does not make sense and what does not go well[36] (symptom): 'When the space of a lapsus no longer carries any meaning (or interpretation), then only is one sure that one is in the unconscious.'[37] It is here at this point of lapsus that Lacan introduces his 'real-unconscious', while in his Seminar XX he accentuates *jouis-sense* and introduces *lalangue* (llanguage):

> Language is, no doubt, made up of llanguage. It is knowledge's hare-brained lucubration *(élucubration)* about llanguage. [. . .] Llanguage affects us first of all by everything it brings with it by way of effects that are affects. If we can say that the unconscious is structured like a language, it is in the sense that effects of llanguage, already there qua knowledge, go well beyond anything the being who speaks is capable of enunciating.[38]

If for quite some time Lacan saw linguistics as a scientific ally of psychoanalysis, he now labels it as 'linguistricks', showing its limitations. If he continues to define the human being as a speaking being and if he knows that 'what dominates society is the practice of language', he now accentuates that it is the signifier that 'is the cause of jouissance. Without the signifier, how could we even approach that part of the body?'[39] In other words, if every reality is founded and defined by a discourse as a social link, every reality is approached also with apparatuses of *jouissance*. Lacan does redefine here the signifier, which is now not only stupid, but first and foremost imperative; however, he continues to give priority to language and continues to emphasise the link between the unconscious and language.

It is here that Deleuze and Guattari intervene and cut Lacan's theory into two:

> Lacan's admirable theory of desire appears to us to have two poles: one related to 'the object small a' as a desiring-machine, which defines desire in terms of a real production, thus going beyond both any idea of need and any idea of fantasy, and the other related to the 'great Other' as a signifier which reintroduces a certain notion of lack.[40]

This warding off of big Other from the strictly Lacanian perspective does not make sense. It has many consequences we cannot go into here, but the bottom line is that it perhaps represents an attack on Lacan's conceptions of language and desire ('desire is the desire of the Other'). It seems that later Deleuze still insists on one of its aspects:

> People's dreams are always all-consuming and threaten to devour us. What other people dream is very dangerous. Dreams are terrifying will to power. Each of us is more or less a victim of other people's dreams. [. . .] Beware of the dreams of others, because if you are caught in their dream, you are done for.[41]

So on the one hand we have here Sartre's view ('Hell is other people'), malicious Other, while on the other hand it seems that for Deleuze there is no Other, which is, to cut a long story short, simply wrong. Not only in *The Logic of Sense* and *Difference and Repetition*, but also later Deleuze knows very well that a kind of mediation is necessary: 'Mediators are fundamental. Creation's all about mediators.'[42] For that reason philosophy needs conceptual personae, it can occur 'between friends', it always begins 'in-between', and that is also why it was 'so compromised with God'.[43] In short, Deleuze knows in a way, as Lacan would put it, that one has 'to be duped', though, and this complicates things further, this is for him a construction – 'you have to form your mediators'. But does one have to be duped by language? If Lacan in Seminar XVII insisted: 'Language is the condition of the unconscious – that's what I say',[44] five years later, in *Television* and perhaps until the very end as well, he is categorical: 'There is no unconscious except for the speaking being.'[45]

And as for Deleuze and Guattari, what is their general stance towards language? Both seem to struggle with it. Guattari in his own words embraced the *objet petit a* precisely for being an escape from language – 'I'm not at all sure that the object "a" in Lacan is anything other than a vanishing point, a leak, an escape from the despotic character of signifying chains.'[46] In his *Machinic Unconscious* from 1979 he even proclaimed a programme of exiting language and later continued to struggle with it, while Deleuze's project, as Jean-Jacques Lecercle has brilliantly shown, is characterised by an *anti-linguistic* turn, too. And yet for Deleuze language remains the problem up to the point where the 'problematic of language tends to absorb the whole of Deleuze's first philosophy, that in Deleuze language is everywhere'.[47]

Here we come back to the problematics of encounter and event, since for Deleuze 'events make language possible'.[48] If events are something that we encounter and if there is no law as to how they are to be encountered, this goes in the direction of Lacan's later introduction of *lalangue*. Even one of Deleuze's central tenets presented from his early work on Bergson until the very end, that is, that 'there must be at least two multiplicities, two types, from the outset',[49] brings him closer to psychoanalysis even there where he himself might not have admitted or been aware of. When he is developing his notion of repetition in *Difference and Repetition* (every repetition brings about something new, not in the sense of forecast, regularity, lawfulness, but in the sense of something unique, singular, unforeseeable, 'object = x'), the conception of quasi-cause as a short-circuit between two series in *The Logic of Sense* or the notion of the event in 'May '68 Did Not Take Place', he is not only close to Lacan, but also to Freud's presentation of lapsus: 'even these obscurer cases of slips of the tongue can be explained by a convergence, a mutual "interference", between two different intended speeches'.[50] It is this interference of two wills, two causalities, that interests Deleuze, too:

> In historical phenomena such as the revolution of 1789, the Commune, the revolution of 1917, there is always one part of the *event* that is irreducible to any social determinism, or to causal chains. Historians are not very fond of this aspect: they restore causality after the fact. Yet the event is itself a splitting off from [*décrochage*], or a breaking with causality; it is bifurcation, a deviation with respect to laws, an unstable condition which opens up a new field of the possible. [. . .] The possible does not pre-exist, it is created by the event.[51]

It is here that one encounters the real as developed by Lacan in his conceptualisation between cause and law in Seminar XI: 'Cause is to be distinguished from that which is determinate in a chain, in other words the law.'[52] Lacan here presents us a cause that is not as inscribed in the laws of regularity and continuity, but rather presents a break with them, a discontinuity. The cause as rupture or break with causality is on the side of contingency and encounter, of surprise, of something that lies beyond four Aristotelian causes (*tyche* and *automaton*), of something that does not work ('il n'y a de cause que ce qui cloche', says Lacan[53]). Such a cause for Lacan opens a gap, a hole, and 'Freudian unconscious is situated at that point, where, between cause and that which it affects, there is always something wrong. [. . .] For what the unconscious does is to show us the gap [. . .].'[54] What happens here when a gap is opened, what happens, as Deleuze would put it, 'in-between'? A couple of lines further Lacan claims that 'in this gap, something happens', 'something of the order of the *non-realized*',[55] and this something that one encounters will later become 'real-unconscious' modelled upon lapsus:[56] 'the unconscious, I would say, is real'.[57] There is then development in Lacan from cause against law in Seminar XI to 'I believe that the real is without law' and the 'real does not have an order' in Seminar XXIII.[58] It is a strange development, indeed:

> Well, it must be acknowledged that the first Lacan (and here I am calling the first Lacan everything that precedes the cut introduced by *Seminar VI*, which denies the existence of the Other of the Other, namely the Lacan of the 'Rome Report' and the five first Seminars) was constantly fixed on, constantly striving to determine what the laws of language are, the laws of discourse, the laws of speech, the laws of the signifier – this is something that strikes me, looking back. One can make a list of these laws [. . .] to such an extent that one can say that here there is something of a passion – the passion of the first Lacan for finding laws. [. . .] It is this same Lacan who will come to announce in his last teaching that *the real is without law*.[59]

What is the real Lacan is talking about? Undoubtedly Deleuze and Lacan would not agree what the real is. And without a doubt the real for Lacan has, as he himself openly admits, 'more than one sense'. It is neither easy to grasp nor easy to present, since 'it is at the limits of our experience'.[60] Throughout Lacan's teachings we find passages like 'the real always returns to the same place', 'the real is impossible', however, the real never forms a whole; there are always only 'pieces of the real'. The real is always thought in connection with the symbolic or discourse, it is always a remainder, an excess: 'When discourse runs up against something, falters, and can go no further, encountering a "there is no" [*il n'y a pas*] – and that by its own logic – that's the real.'[61]

But what kind of encounter is the 'encounter with the real'? Is it only an ill-timed, missed, failed encounter, or as Lacan puts it in Seminar XI: 'The function of the *tyche*, of the real as encounter – the encounter in so far as it may be missed, in so far as it is essentially the missed encounter'?[62] Here a recent self-critique of Žižek may be of some help to see what was perhaps bothering Deleuze and Guattari in *Anti-Oedipus*, too. In his 'Foreword to the second edition' of *For They Know Not What They Do* Žižek presented a self-critique concerning the stance he adopted in the first edition of the book (1989). According to him, his basic philosophical weakness is that he endorses that there is

> a quasi-transcendental reading of Lacan, focused on the notion of the real as an impossible Thing-In-Itself; in so doing, it opens the doors to the celebration of failure: to the idea that every act ultimately misfires, and that the proper ethical stance is heroically to accept this failure.[63]

So, does the real in Lacan always involve only failed or missed encounters? To present perhaps a 'more optimistic view', in *Anti-Oedipus* Deleuze and Guattari openly affirm: 'The real is not impossible; it is simply more and more artificial.'[64] Although this is directed contra Lacan, we saw already in the previous paragraph that Lacan was not a poet of failure, since for him 'the real happens',[65] however, *when* and *where* remains always contingent and always a surprise. So, the real as impossible for Lacan is not transcendent, somewhere beyond; on the contrary, it is here manifest all the time in the guise of the real-unconscious, which might seem again close to another thesis of Deleuze and Guattari, that is, that 'the unconscious is the real in itself'.[66] Does not the thesis on the real-unconscious mean that 'you haven't got hold of the unconscious, you never get hold of it'?[67]

The answer here is more ambiguous than it might seem at first sight. First, for Lacan in a certain sense you do get hold of the real. At the very beginning of *Television* Lacan speaks about impossibility: saying all truth is literally impossible, words fail, and yet through this very impossibility truth holds onto the real, *'tient au réel'*[68]. But not in the sense that Deleuze seems to suggest that one must 'reverse' 'Freud's formulation': 'You *must* produce the unconscious. Produce it, or be happy with your symptoms, your ego, and your psychoanalyst.'[69] If later Lacan might agree that the end of analysis involves identification with one's own sinthome as one's own mode of enjoyment and as one's own production (sinthome = synt-hetic + saint = symptom, Saint Thomas), he also adds that this operation also has to produce a certain waste, *déchet*, of the psychoanalyst, which for Lacan precisely as *saint* 'acts as trash'. While it is true that all the work in analysis is the work of the free association of the patient, this work has to be done in the presence of an analyst, via transference and in analysis. It seems that in Deleuze's above words all this is omitted as one can do a sort of self-analysis, or something that does not even remotely resemble a psychoanalytic session. While for Lacan the unconscious speaks, *ça parle* and while he adds to it later that *ça jouit*, Deleuze seem to go in the same direction since he accentuates happiness, but happiness is neither *jouissance* nor *bonheur*, which for Lacan is a matter of an encounter[70] and yet it is in a way also everywhere – the 'subject is happy-go-lucky'.[71] But for Lacan there are always troubles with happiness since we find ourselves exiled from it, which is perhaps best illustrated in Seminar VII by the story of the individual who emigrated from Germany to America and who was asked, 'Are you happy?' 'Oh, yes, I am very happy,' he answered, 'I am really very, very happy, *aber nicht glücklich*!' Deleuze who, as we see prefers to speak about ego, not of subject as Lacan does, would not agree on this point with Lacan, and he does not agree in the cited passage with Freud ('the unconscious has nothing to do with Freudian slips'[72]), since for him the 'unconscious is substance which must be created, placed, made to flow; it is a social and political space which must be won'.[73] That could not be further from Freud and Lacan, since for them the unconscious cannot be won, we cannot have control over the unconscious, it has no master. It produces by itself, it cannot be produced at will. And if for Deleuze this production is linked with Spinoza ('we don't even know what a body can do'[74]), for Freud and Lacan this body is a speaking body. The unconscious speaks, whereas for Deleuze and Guattari the unconscious 'engineers, it is machinic'.[75] And while for them this is linked with desire itself, which produces, this production is not what Lacan has in mind. In his Seminar XX he accentuates that the speaking body does not produce symptoms, a pathology and formations of the unconscious, but what is usually called culture as such: the speaking body, 'when one leaves it all alone, it sub-limates with all its might, it sees Beauty and the Good – not to mention Truth, and it is there, as I just told you, that it comes closest to what is at stake'.[76] For Lacan the unconscious works in a slightly different way:

> as knowledge that does not think, or calculate, or judge – which doesn't pre-vent it from being at work (as in dreams, for example). Let's say that it is the ideal worker, the one Marx made the flower of the capitalist economy in the hope of seeing him take over the discourse of the master; which, in effect, is what happened, although in an unexpected form. There are surprises in these matters of discourse; that is, indeed, the point of the unconscious.[77]

These surprises are surprises of the real, of the real-unconscious, which produces formations of the unconscious, symptoms, or even better: sinthomes.

So, the real is not impossible for Lacan, it does happen. Even more, it is not where one expects it, it changes itself rather unexpectedly, it is without laws. Jacques-Alain Miller has recently presented his latest view on this real in his text 'The Real in the 21st Century'.[78] Let us briefly review his main points here. Miller first states that Lacan's gradual abandonment of the Name-of-the-Father has certain clinical consequences since it brings with it the extension of madness to everyone who speaks or *tout le monde est fou*. This abandonment should go together with another one, namely that of the claim that 'there is knowledge in the real', since the latter still relies on the illusion of regularity, prediction and the very existence of laws. If there are no laws of the real, the real does not, as early Lacan was convinced, always return to the same place. This real still supposes nature and natural laws as always the same; however, the real that does not have laws has broken free from nature. If there are no laws that the real is obeying, if 'there is great disorder in the real', as Miller puts it, this real as unbearable goes together with the nostalgia for the lost order and tradition. Hence calls for '*noli me tangere*' concerning nature and tradition 'do not mess with (human) nature' in the age of ethical committees. This, by the way, is a great temptation in today's science and in the contemporary materialism of neuroscience trying to find out 'ultimate' laws that the real is obeying. The claim that 'there is no knowledge in the real' redefines the Freudian unconscious, the 'unconscious structured like a language'. Later Lacan's introduction of *lalangue*, which goes together with the claim that there is no law of dispersion and diversity of languages, put an emphasis on

> the pure encounter with *lalangue* and its effects of jouissance in the body. It is sketched as a pure shock of the drive. The real, understood in this way, is neither a cosmos nor a world; it is also not an order: it is a piece, an a-systematic fragment, separated from the fictional knowledge that was produced from this encounter. And this encounter of *lalangue* and the body does not respond to any prior law, it is contingent and always appears perverse – this encounter and its consequences – because this encounter is translated by a deviation of jouissance with respect to that which jouissance ought to be, which remains in force as a dream.[79]

All this demands a redefinition of psychoanalysis as a practice that relies on transference and on a subject supposed to know: on this basis one constitutes knowledge not in the real but about the real. Instead of interpretation, one has to underscore the defence against the real without law and without meaning.

Although it is a brief text, which does not develop things or present them in detail, it nonetheless presents a couple of misunderstandings. First, although for Lacan the real always returns to the same place, one could hardly speak of nature in the usual sense. It is true, though, that sometimes Lacan presents a loss, as in Seminar XI, as a natural loss, but he knows very well that for psychoanalysis, and for him too, neither nature nor culture is the point of departure, but their excess as a product of their intersection and of encounter, as Lacan himself pointed out numerous times.[80] Miller himself knows very well that for Lacan the human being is deeply denaturalised simply by being a speaking being. He knows very well too that his thesis that 'there is no knowledge in the real' means that Freud's *Trieb* is not instinct, but drive and that, last but not least, 'there is no sexual relationship'. An oversimplified presentation of the change between Lacan's different notions of the real might miss the point that Miller himself wants to underline that Lacan's psychoanalysis is to be thought against the background of the break introduced by modern science with its infinite universe. And while Lacan for a long time tried to align psychoanalysis with (modern) science and claimed that the real does not lie, cheat or deceive, he has now, with the real-unconscious and the claim that the 'real is without laws', come to the point where this is in complete opposition to his earlier thesis: 'the notion that the real, as difficult as it may be to penetrate, is unable to play tricks on us', he says in his Seminar III and claims that this supposition of the real as a non-deceiver (Descartes, Einstein) is 'essential to the constitution of the world of science'.[81] In short, one cannot speak about laws of the real as natural, scientific laws, despite Freud's or Lacan's occasional temptation to do so. Lacan in general sees the real as a limit point, a deadline for these laws, or sees in the real, starting with Seminar XI, something that goes against these laws. Basically one could say that there are no laws of the real in Lacan, even before he introduced his claim that the 'real is without laws'. So, why did he do it anyway? To underscore that there is a different real than the real of science. It is against science that Lacan in his Seminar XVIII affirms:

> What is real is what opens up a hole in this semblance, in this articulated semblance which is the scientific discourse. The scientific discourse progresses without even worrying if it is a discourse of semblance or not. [. . .] The only reference reached by its deductions is the impossible. This impossible is the real. In physics, we aim at something which is real with the help of the discursive apparatus which, in its crispness, encounters the limits of its consistency.[82]

The very expression 'réel sans loi' obeys the same logic as the joke about 'coffee without cream' from Lubitsch's movie *Ninotchka* or as Alenka Zupančič has pointed out: 'when something is denied, what was denied does not disappear completely, but stays as its own trace and subsists within negation'.[83] So, when Lacan says that the real is without laws, he simply underlines that the real in psychoanalysis should be understood as different from the real of science and yet against its background.

But what about the many distinctions that Miller introduces in the above-mentioned text? The distinction between order–disorder and between cyclical nature and nature-out-of-joint reminds us of Deleuze's distinction between time as Chronos and time as Aion. This, however, is not the only point where Miller approaches Deleuze or, better stated, where he enters into a debate with Deleuze without perhaps even realising it. Do not these two prevalent discourses of modernity with which he begins his text and which have begun to destroy the traditional structure of human experience – the discourse of science and the discourse of capitalism – also lie at the centre of the project of capitalism and schizophrenia of Deleuze and Guattari? Does he not elsewhere speak about 'caprice as a will beyond law', which puts him in the discussion about Deleuze's above-mentioned Sartrean vision of the Other? Has he not recently spoken about the body-event, and does not his approach to Lacanian biology address the same topics as Deleuze's *Difference and Repetition*?[84] Does he not speak recently about henology instead of ontology and does he not give priority to the '*clinamen* of *jouissance*', which puts him willy-nilly not only with Deleuze, but also with Althusser, who in his thesis on the underground current of the materialism of encounter included Deleuze among its proponents precisely because of a certain primacy of positivity, swerve, *clinamen* and disorder in Deleuze's opus,[85] and so on? In short, it seems that *another* encounter between contemporary psychoanalysis and contemporary philosophy is on the agenda today.

This seems also to be Lacan's view. In his *Triumph of Religion*,[86] when he mentions the idea of '*la loi qui bouge*', 'law that moves/changes', he also says:

> I happened to come across a short article by Henri Poincaré regarding the evolution of laws. You surely haven't read it as it is out of print, something only bibliophiles can find. Émile Boutroux, who was a philosopher, raised the question whether it was unthinkable that laws themselves evolve. Poincaré, who was a mathematician, got all up in arms at the idea of such evolution, since what a scientist is seeking is precisely a law insofar as it does not evolve. It is exceedingly rare for a philosopher to be more intelligent than a mathematician, but here a philosopher just so happened to raise an important question. Why, in fact, wouldn't laws evolve when we conceive of the world as having evolved? [. . .] But, after all, why not also think that maybe someday we will be able to know a little bit more about the real? [. . .] Thus we must be wary – things get developed, thoroughfares open up that are completely insane, that we surely could not have imagined or in any way have foreseen. Things will perhaps be such that we will one day have a notion of the evolution of laws.
>
> In any case, I don't see how that makes the real any more transcendent. It is a very difficult notion to handle, a notion that people have thus far approached only with extreme caution.[87]

Why is it interesting that Lacan mentions here the evolution of laws? Because at the centre of Deleuze's entire opus there are notions of evolving and change: becoming and deterritorialisation. And it is not unimportant for us here that becoming is for Deleuze linked with an encounter: 'An encounter is perhaps the same thing as a becoming, or nuptials.'[88] In other words, becoming is 'an encounter between two reigns, a short-circuit, the picking up of a code where each is deterritorialised'.[89] So, it is here at the point of the real, of the real-unconscious, that another encounter between Lacan and Deleuze is 'on the table'. And not only with Deleuze, with Badiou perhaps (is not his notion of truth that of a law which moves? Does not truth make holes in knowledge?), Kripke (his 'Wittgenstein's sceptical paradox' implies capricious shifts from *plus* to *quus*), Žižek, Dolar, Zupančič, and so on. Or, as Lacan put it: yes, 'it is a philosophical problem, that's true. There are, in fact, little domains where philosophy might still have something to say.'[90]

Notes

1. Lacan, Jacques, *The Seminar of Jacques Lacan, Book XI: The Four Fundamental Concepts of Psychoanalysis* (London and New York: W. W. Norton, 1998), pp. 128, 149.
2. See Dosse, François, *Gilles Deleuze and Félix Guattari: Intersecting Lives* (New York: Columbia University Press, 2010), pp. 183–222. This is also Deleuze's own story: 'My encounter with Félix Guattari changed a lot of things.' Deleuze, Gilles and Parnet, Claire, *Dialogues II* (London and New York: Continuum, 2006), p. 12.
3. 'Le "Je me souviens" de Gilles Deleuze' (interview by Didier Eribon), *Le Nouvel Observateur*, 1619 (16–22 November 1995), pp. 50–1. See also Roudinesco, Elisabeth, *Jacques Lacan* (Cambridge: Polity Press, 1997), p. 347; Smith, Daniel W., 'The Inverse Side of the Structure: Žižek on Deleuze on Lacan', *Criticism*, 46: 4 (Fall 2004), pp. 635–50.
4. Deleuze, Gilles, *Two Regimes of Madness: Texts and Interviews 1975–1995* (Los Angeles: Semiotext(e), 2007), pp. 79–88.
5. Deleuze and Parnet, *Dialogues II*, p. 60.
6. Wilson, Scott, *The Order of Joy. Beyond the Cultural Politics of Enjoyment* (New York: State University of New York Press 2008), p. 166.
7. See Hallward, Peter, 'You Can't Have it Both Ways: Deleuze or Lacan', in de Bolle, Leen (ed.), *Deleuze and Psychoanalysis: Philosophical Essays on Deleuze's Debate with Psychoanalysis* (Leuven: Leuven University Press, 2010), pp. 33–50.
8. Dosse, *Intersecting Lives*, p. 1.
9. Lacan, Jacques, *Autres écrits* (Paris: Seuil, 2001), p. 288.
10. 'I've tried in all my books to discover the nature of events; it's a philosophical concept.' Deleuze, Gilles, *Negotiations* (New York: Columbia University Press, 1995), p. 141.
11. Lacan, Jacques, *Écrits* (London and New York: W. W. Norton, 2006), p. 30.
12. Deleuze, *Two Regimes*, p. 384.
13. Deleuze, Gilles and Guattari, Félix, *What is Philosophy?* (London and New York: Verso, 2009), p. 28. See also Deleuze, *Negotiations*, p. 139; Deleuze and Parnet, *Dialogues II*, p. 1.
14. Deleuze, *Negotiations*, p. 94. 'Things never pass where you think, nor along the paths you think' (Deleuze and Parnet, *Dialogues II*, p. 3).
15. Miller, Jacques-Alain, 'Une histoire de la psychanalyse', *Magazine Littéraire*, 271 (November 1989), pp. 20–6.
16. 'Lacan himself says "I'm not getting much help"' (Deleuze, *Negotiations*, p. 14). For the relationship between Deleuze and Lacan and for a philosophical approach to complaint and complaining as such, see the brilliant book by Schuster, Aaron, *The Trouble with Pleasure: Deleuze and Psychoanalysis* (Cambridge, MA, and London: MIT Press, 2016).
17. Lacan, Jacques, *The Seminar of Jacques Lacan, Book XX: Encore* (London and New York: W. W. Norton, 1998), p. 146.
18. Naveau, Laure, 'A Clinic of Love Disorder', *Hurly-Burly: The International Lacanian Journal of Psychoanalysis*, 11 (May 2014), pp. 117, 120.
19. Zupančič, Alenka, *The Odd One In: On Comedy* (Cambridge, MA, and London: MIT Press, 2008), p. 134.
20. Deleuze and Parnet, *Dialogues II*, p. 7.
21. Ibid. p. 5.
22. Deleuze, *Negotiations*, p. 141.
23. Deleuze and Guattari, *What is Philosophy?*, p. 63.
24. Deleuze, Gilles, *Desert Islands and Other Texts 1953–1974* (Los Angeles: Semiotext(e), 2004), p. 185.
25. Lacan, Jacques, *The Triumph of Religion Preceded by Discourse to Catholics* (Cambridge: Polity Press, 2013), p. 96.

26. 'I've been doing nothing but that since I was twenty, exploring the philosophers on the subject of love' (Lacan, *Encore*, p. 75).
27. Deleuze and Parnet, *Dialogues II*, p. 10.
28. Lacan, Jacques, 'Monsieur A.', *Ornicar?*, 21–2 (Summer 1980), p. 17. But is Lacan against philosophy as such, or against a particular philosophy? Žižek claims that Lacan here has Deleuze's thought in mind as a philosophical stance epitomising a 'false subversive radicalization that fits the existing power constellation perfectly in the climate of post-May '68 Paris' (Žižek, Slavoj, *The Ticklish Subject: The Absent Centre of Political Ontology* (London and New York: Verso, 1999), pp. 250–1).
29. Deleuze, Gilles, *Difference and Repetition* (London and New York: Continuum, 2004), p. 176.
30. Here one should delineate a line of division between Deleuze and Lacan that I cannot follow here and which concerns an entire new conception of representation implied in Lacan's dictum 'a signifier represents a subject for another signifier'. See Zupančič, Alenka, 'The Fifth Condition', in Hallward, Peter (ed.), *Think Again: Alain Badiou and the Future of Philosophy* (London and New York: Continuum, 2004), pp. 199–200.
31. For more on this, see Schuster, *The Trouble with Pleasure*.
32. Lacan, Jacques, *The Seminar of Jacques Lacan, Book XVII: The Other Side of Psychoanalysis* (London and New York: W. W. Norton, 2007), p. 117. See also Lapeyre, Michel, *Au-delà du complexe d'Oedipe* (Paris: Economica, 1997).
33. Deleuze, Gilles and Guattari, Félix, *Anti-Oedipus: Capitalism and Schizophrenia* (London and New York: Continuum, 2009), p. 187.
34. Lacan, *Four Fundamental Concepts*, p. 8.
35. Lacan, 'Monsieur A.', p. 19.
36. It is here that another problematic of the real arises that I cannot go into here: 'it is *in order to function* that a social machine must *not function well* [. . .] The dysfunctions are an essential element of its very ability to function, which is not the least important aspect of the system of cruelty' (Deleuze and Guattari, *Anti-Oedipus*, p. 166). This problem concerns not only psychoanalysis, but also technology, revolution, change, capitalism, and so on. In this sense, 'one is tempted to say that Capital itself is the Real of our age' (Žižek, *Ticklish Subject*, p. 276).
37. Lacan, *Four Fundamental Concepts*, p. vii.
38. Lacan, *Encore*, p. 139.
39. Ibid. p. 24.
40. Deleuze and Guattari, *Anti-Oedipus*, p. 27.
41. Deleuze, *Two Regimes*, p. 323.
42. Deleuze, *Negotiations*, p. 125.
43. Gilles Deleuze, Seminar on 25 November 1980, available at <http://www.webdeleuze.com/php/texte.php?cle=17&groupe=Spinoza&langue=2> (last accessed 2 March 2016). See also Goodchild, Philip, 'Why is Philosophy so Compromised with God?', in Bryden, Mary (ed.), *Deleuze and Religion* (Abingdon: Routledge, 2001), pp. 156–66.
44. Lacan, *Other Side of Psychoanalysis*, p. 41.
45. Lacan, Jacques, *Television: A Challenge to the Psychoanalytic Establishment* (New York and London: W. W. Norton, 1990), p. 5.
46. Deleuze, *Desert Islands*, p. 224.
47. Lecercle, Jean-Jacques, *Deleuze and Language* (Basingstoke and New York: Palgrave Macmillan, 2002), p. 255.
48. Deleuze, Gilles, *The Logic of Sense* (London and New York: Continuum, 2004), p. 208.
49. Deleuze and Guattari, *What is Philosophy?*, p. 152.
50. Freud, Sigmund, *Introductory Lectures on Psychoanalysis* (Harmondsworth: Penguin, 1973), p. 58.
51. Deleuze, *Two Regimes*, pp. 233–4.
52. Lacan, *Four Fundamental Concepts*, p. 22.

53. Lacan, Jacques, *Le séminaire, livre XI: Les quatre concepts fondamentaux de la psychanalyse* (Paris: Seuil, 1973), p. 25.
54. Lacan, *Four Fundamental Concepts*, p. 22.
55. Recently philosophy has showed that it has something to say about the nature of this 'something', not in the sense of ontology, but rather of disontology. See Zupančič, Alenka, *Seksualno in ontologija [Sexual and Ontology]* (Ljubljana: DTP, 2011); Žižek, Slavoj, *Less Than Nothing: Hegel and the Shadow of Dialectical Materialism* (London and New York: Verso, 2012); Dolar, Mladen, 'Tyche, clinamen, den', *Continental Philosophy Review*, 46: 2 (August 2013), pp. 223–39.
56. See Soler, Colette, *Lacan, l'inconscient réinventée* (Paris: Presses universitaires de France, 2009), pp. 52–3.
57. Lacan, *Four Fundamental Concepts*, p. vii.
58. Lacan, Jacques, *Le séminaire de Jacques Lacan, livre XXIII: Le sinthome* (Paris: Seuil, 2005), p. 137. See also Miller, Jacques-Alain, 'Le réel est sans loi', *Cause freudienne*, 49 (2001), pp. 7–19.
59. Miller, Jacques-Alain, 'Other without Other', *Hurly-Burly: The International Lacanian Journal of Psychoanalysis*, 10 (December 2013), pp. 15–30.
60. Lacan, Jacques, *Le séminaire de Jacques Lacan, livre IV: La relation d'objet* (Paris: Seuil, 1994), p. 31. The problematics of the real in Lacan is complex and well elaborated in the now already vast literature on it.
61. Miller, Jacques-Alain, 'Microscopia', in Lacan, *Television*, p. xxiii.
62. Lacan, *Four Fundamental Concepts*, p. 55.
63. Žižek, Slavoj, *For They Know Not What They Do: Enjoyment as a Political Factor*, 2nd edn (London and New York: Verso, 2008), p. xii.
64. Deleuze and Guattari, *Anti-Oedipus*, p. 37.
65. Zupančič, Alenka, *Ethics of the Real: Kant, Lacan* (London and New York: Verso, 2000), p. 234.
66. Deleuze and Guattari, *Anti-Oedipus*, p. 60.
67. Deleuze and Parnet, *Dialogues II*, p. 58.
68. Lacan, *Autres écrits*, p. 509.
69. Deleuze, *Two Regimes*, p. 81.
70. 'Certainly Freud leaves no doubt, any more than Aristotle, that what man is seeking, his goal, is happiness. It's odd that in almost all languages happiness offers itself in terms of an encounter – *tyche*. Except in English and even there it's very close. A kind of favourable divinity is involved. *Bonheur* in French suggests to us *augurum*, a good sign and a fortunate encounter. *Glück* is the same as *gelück*. "Happiness" is after all "happen"; it, too, is an encounter, even if one does not feel the need to add the prefix, which strictly speaking indicates the happy character of the thing' (Lacan, Jacques, *The Seminar of Jacques Lacan, Book VII: The Ethics of Psychoanalysis* (London: Routledge, 1992), p. 13).
71. Lacan, *Television*, p. 22.
72. Deleuze, *Two Regimes of Madness*, p. 81.
73. Deleuze and Parnet, *Dialogues II*, p. 58.
74. Deleuze, Gilles, *Spinoza: Practical Philosophy* (San Francisco: City Lights Books, 1988), pp. 17–18.
75. Deleuze and Guattari, *Anti-Oedipus*, p. 60.
76. Lacan, *Encore*, p. 120.
77. Lacan, *Television*, p. 14.
78. Miller, Jacques-Alain, 'The Real in the 21st Century', *Hurly-Burly: The International Lacanian Journal of Psychoanalysis*, 9 (2013), pp. 199–206.
79. Ibid. p. 205.
80. See, for instance, Lacan, *Television*, p. 6.
81. Jacques Lacan, *The Seminar of Jacques Lacan, Book III: The Psychoses* (London and New York: W. W. Norton, 2003), p. 64.

82. Lacan, Jacques, *Le séminaire de Jacques Lacan, livre XVIII: D'un discours qui ne serait pas de semblant* (Paris: Seuil, 2006), p. 28.
83. Zupančič, Alenka, 'Med dvema ne' ['Between Two "No"s'], *Problemi*, 48: 8–9 (2010), p. 63. See also Žižek, Slavoj, *Absolute Recoil: Towards a New Foundation of Dialectical Materialism* (London and New York: Verso, 2014), pp. 404–5.
84. See Miller, Jacques-Alain, 'Théorie du caprice', *Quarto*, 71 (December 2000), pp. 6–12; 'The Symptom and Body-Event', *Lacanian Ink*, 19 (Fall 2001), pp. 4–47; 'Lacanian Biology and the Event of Body', *Lacanian Ink*, 18 (Spring 2001), pp. 6–29; Chiesa, Lorenzo, 'The World of Desire: Lacan between Evolutionary Biology and Psychoanalytic Theory', *Filozofski vestnik*, 30: 2 (2009), pp. 83–112; Pearson, Keith Ansell, *Germinal Life: The Difference and Repetition of Deleuze* (Abingdon: Routledge, 1999).
85. Althusser, Louis, *Philosophy of the Encounter: Later Writings 1978–1987* (London and New York: Verso, 2006), p. 189.
86. Lacan, Jacques, 'La troisième', *Cause freudienne*, 79 (2011), pp. 1–33.
87. Lacan, *The Triumph*, pp. 81–2.
88. Deleuze and Parnet, *Dialogues II*, p. 5.
89. Ibid. p. 33.
90. Lacan, *The Triumph*, pp. 82–3.

Chapter 2

Reciprocal Portrait of Jacques Lacan in Gilles Deleuze

Laurent de Sutter

Once upon a time, there was the Marquis de Sade

No one was really surprised by the appearance of the 1967 winter issue of the journal *Tel Quel* – an important special issue on the work of the Marquis de Sade, in which one found the names of Pierre Klossowski, Roland Barthes, Hubert Damisch, Michel Tort and Philippe Sollers.[1] Twenty years had passed since Klossowski's *Sade, My Neighbour*, published by Seuil, had inaugurated the lengthy process resulting in Sade being seen by the era's intelligentsia as the paragon of subversion.[2] This process had consisted of numerous stages, the main one being the publication of the first modern edition of the marquis's *oeuvre*, which Jean-Jacques Pauvert had brought to the public's attention between 1947 and 1955 (this edition had led to numerous court cases, which he finally won through an appeal in 1957).[3] In the meantime, Maurice Blanchot had published *Lautréamont et Sade*, Simone de Beauvoir 'Must We Burn de Sade?' in *Les temps modernes*, Georges Bataille *Literature and Evil* and the chapter 'De Sade's Sovereign Man' in *Eroticism*, and Foucault had dedicated numerous passages from his *History of Madness* and *The Order of Things* to the marquis.[4] When the special issue of *Tel Quel* consecrated to 'Sade's Thought' was published, it had become evident to all those who kept abreast of the period's intellectual developments that the name Donatien Alphonse François de Sade numbered among those most able to produce the new in thought. The fact that this came from a dynamic of subversion – or rather, as Bataille put it, from a 'transgressive' one[5] – only gave it more value. This is what gave it its modernity, insofar as modernity wanted above all to call into question all established order, as well as the foundations on which it claimed to rest, in order to reconcile it with the real.[6] Moreover, this was the thesis of one of the most significant texts on Sade during this period: Jacques Lacan's article 'Kant with Sade', which was intended to serve as the preface to an edition of *Philosophy in the Bedroom*, and ultimately appeared in *Critique* in 1963, before being republished three years later in *Écrits*.[7] The radicalism of Lacan's interpretation was unprecedented: he explained that Sade is subversive only to the extent that he incarnates the 'truth', the concrete implementation, of modernity's purest ethical apparatus – the one described by Immanuel Kant in *Critique of Practical Reason*, from 1788.[8] Contrary to what one might have imagined, Sade's 'thought' constituted the negation not of Kant's but of that which the latter concealed by resorting to a moral argument grafted onto the category of the Good, namely Evil, insofar as Evil has the Good's final say – it is its truth, its *law*.

Update and modernity

Like all of Lacan's '*écrits*', 'Kant with Sade' was a curious text, its difficulty – made almost painful thanks to its dead ends and jumps – making it sometimes difficult to isolate from the surrounding noise what made it all worth it: the brilliant power of its witticisms, its 'rockets', through which he shifted age-old truths in a single breath. Yet, despite its difficulties, one could see how much this text wanted to follow on from what Bataille and the others had inaugurated in regards to Sade under the rubric of 'transgression' and, *at the same time*, how much it rejected it with all its strength. For Bataille, as for Foucault, Klossowski, Blanchot, Beauvoir or Barthes, it was agreed that the marquis's *oeuvre* ranked him amongst the heralds of modernity – and that it was necessary both to align oneself with his work and to update it for the era of late capitalism or of disciplinary society.[9] Yet, Lacan proposed the reverse: rather than attempting to update Sade's thought, one should return to its more or less avowed source in order to understand what it was itself updating, both in the sense of 'updating' (*l'update*) and in the sense of the obscure revelation of a hidden meaning.[10] For Lacan, Sade was not modern; at the most he helped shine a light on what modernity tried in vain to cover up, but which came vividly to light each time one of its seams burst, which often happened. What was this, then? In his article, Lacan used an enigmatic expression to answer this question: 'the desire of the Other'; what Sade helped make sense of was how much the moral law described by Kant was haunted by a desire made all the more monstrous by its having no object, by its being pure desire.[11] Lacan explained that this pure desire was nothing else than the desire by which an authority (which he called the Other) haunted, parasitised, what dull rationality considered as the singular desires of subjects with more or less self-mastery over themselves, over their fantasms, and over their *jouissance*. In reality, subjects are never masters of anything; if they desire, it is only under the gaze of the Other, under the obscure menace of this Other's desire, since it is thanks to this desire that they are free to abandon themselves – and to derive from it a little *jouissance*, and thus suffering. This was indeed the truth of Kant's moral law: the monstrous desire of the Good, authorising everyone's *jouissance* by delegating their desire to a foreign and inaccessible authority which desires instead of them, which formulates for them the sense of their desire – in other words this Good which Sade, sniggering, suddenly came to tell us was in fact Evil.

The mad dream of a philosopher

In truth, it was not the first time that Lacan had been interested in the authority of the law as prefigured by the thought of Kant; a large part of his 1959–60 Seminar, *The Ethics of Psychoanalysis*, had been devoted to it.[12] Compared with the lessons of 'Kant with Sade', however, this seminar struck a different balance: if the notion of moral law was presented here as a monstrous authority, almost obscene in its formalistic demand, this obscenity was not yet put into a relation with the literal one which bore Sade's mark. The monstrosity of the law was the monstrosity of what always turns out to be impossible to satisfy but whose satisfaction one is nonetheless required to attempt, namely the monstrosity of pure, excessive demand, which unceasingly refers subjects back to their own moral hopelessness (*nullité morale*). As such during the period of the seminar only the strict aspect of this monstrosity was shown; what was not yet displayed was its contorted grimace, which Sade had demonstrated was masked by strictness as the acceptable mask of the wearer's obscene *jouissance*. What was missing was the *jouissance* of the Other – of the legislator, imposing his law on lost subjects who are only capable of desiring if they are assured that this desire will be *recognised* by an omnipotent external authority, even if it is only a fiction. In the seminar of 1959–60, Lacan had nevertheless still not drawn this conclusion from what he was strongly (*de fou*), almost perversely, aware of in Kant's moral thought, and which he knew was the very environment or ecology in which human subjects' moral lives unfolded. To do this, what was missing was the hermeneutic operator that was Sade – as well as, perhaps, the recognition of what Sade had prompted Lacan's contemporaries to think and to which, with the exception of Klossowski, he had curtly given short shrift.[13] It was with Sade that the referent of the perverse monstrosity of Kant's moral law suddenly found its true name – 'Evil', and thus in opposition to the Good of which Kant believed he provided the ground (*fondement*), one that was as pure as it was inaccessible to the process of intellectual construction of which he had made himself the champion. In Sade, Evil was the real incarnation of that of which the Good in Kant was the fantasm; it was the nightmare lying at the heart of Kant's cherished ethical dream – at the heart of the very possibility that this dream could one day become a reality, whatever it may be, rather than remaining only the mad dream of a philosopher.

Sacher-Masoch arrives on stage

The moment when Lacan returned anew to Sade – in 1969 at the beginning of his seminar on *The Other Side of Psychoanalysis* – other publications had further expanded the literature elicited by the works of the marquis – although this time they took a kind of step to one side.[14] Perhaps tired of the attention Sade's work received in intellectual circles, in 1967 Gilles Deleuze had written a substantial preface to a new edition of *Venus in Furs*, the most celebrated of Leopold von Sacher-Masoch's novels. This preface grew out of a short article titled 'From Sacher-Masoch to Masochism', published in 1961 in the journal *Arguments*.[15] In his preface, Deleuze had attempted to develop something like a psychopolitics of perversion, weighing up Sade's and Sacher-Masoch's respective undertakings. In his attempt, he arrived at the original discovery that their respective works balanced out as equal corresponding halves. Several times, in the form of footnotes, Deleuze acknowledged his debt to Lacan: a first time in regards to the notion of the symbolic; and a second time in regards to the 'elusive character of the object of [Kant's moral] law' – as described by Lacan in 'Kant with Sade'.[16] As the latter had stated, the pure formalism of the moral law in Kant led to its being not only without object, but also without matter and without specification, such that it was impossible to know in what it consisted and even what its content was – besides the form of the law itself.[17] It was a law which, by this very fact, Deleuze added, was able to exceed its instances of conditioning – a law which defined 'a realm of transgression where one is already guilty, and where one oversteps the bounds without knowing what they are'.[18] *One is always-already guilty* faced with Kant's moral law, because the purity of its formalism prevents us from ever satisfying its demands – and particularly since its demands are without content, substance, reality, since they do not exist outside this very formalism. It was this lemma which Lacan had not perceived in the encounter he had orchestrated between the thought of Kant and of Sade. He had failed to understand the extent to which Sade's thought remained unthinkable if one did not think it together with the thought of Sacher-Masoch, which complemented it from the viewpoint of the critique of the consequences of the law. By reading Sade one could put one's finger on the obscene character of what the law claimed to be its ground; by reading Sacher-Masoch one could put one's finger on the obscene character of what the law could attain if correctly exercised (*de son bon exercise*).

When one conforms to the law

For Deleuze, invoking the figure of Sacher-Masoch was not only a way of forcefully differentiating himself from the latest intellectual fad; it was also a way of suggesting that there was more to the thought of Sade than a more or less avowed will to *wipe one's arse* with the law, in the pure form Kant had attempted to produce. As with Lacan, what interested him was not so much the ruin of the ethical figure of the law as the manner in which this ruin called for subjects who thought their desire otherwise – which is to say who redefined their relation to the Other once it (as guarantor of the ground (*bien-fondé*) of the law) had found itself ruined along with the law itself. Moreover, one had to be more precise: what the ruin of the law allowed one to perceive was the extent to which the Other – which was presumed to guarantee it, be it in the form of the Father, God, the State, Nature, Destiny, and so on – did not actually exist; or, at least, not otherwise than as the face of Evil to which Sade had dedicated his *oeuvre*, as the inaccessible view of the law's descent into Evil. If the moral law functioned, we would in effect be always-already guilty in the eyes of an authority which would know our guilt better than we could ever claim to – since it would also know our desire, to the extent that our desire would be no different from the one which we believe to be that of this very authority. *The desire of the Other is the site of our guilt*; it is the point where the moral law designates us as guilty in the eyes of what guarantees this law, all the while incarnating our desire. The latter is nothing else than the desire to which the law applies itself in us, thus finding us to be excellent reasons to be guilty in the eyes of the Other and hence to exist for it. To conform to the categorical imperative Kant formulated boils down to making one's desire conform to a desire ascribable to an always too powerful (*trop grand*) Other, one that is always too pure and too perfect. In fact, this Other sustains itself by means of a desire for ethical perfection on the basis of which it is possible to *judge* all those who attempt to submit themselves to it and who fail in doing so. This was, at least, the lesson which Lacan was able to extract from his reading of Sade – a lesson which, according to Deleuze, redoubled itself as long as one was interested in Sacher-Masoch. The latter highlighted what was produced when one ended up truly answering something like a pure ethical imperative: what else is a masochistic contract than the artistic implementation (*mise en oeuvre littérale*) of the law extending to the point where the perfection of its realisation flips the wise and sovereign face over to reveal the grimace of *jouissance* and of humiliation constituting the very expression of desire animating it? If any attempt to ground the law pertains to the obscene, the will to obey it to the letter pertains to an obscenity that is even greater.[19]

The irony of theory, humour of practice

Even though Lacan consecrated numerous incidental commentaries to the category of 'masochism', he never attempted with Sacher-Masoch what he attempted with Sade – even if, in a lesson from *From an Other to the Other*, he indirectly mentioned Deleuze's *Presentation of Sacher-Masoch*.[20] Yet, for those who followed his seminar on *The Other Side of Psychoanalysis*, held two years before the appearance of Deleuze's book, it must have been obvious that Lacan's position regarding Sade had once again evolved, pushing him in a direction which now included what one could decipher as discrete winks at the philosopher's work. In *From an Other to the Other*, the psychoanalyst had insisted anew on the strange game which could be played, at the heart of masochism, with the desire of the Other, as the latter operated the recognition of the subject's desire. In reality, this game entailed the cancelling of this Other, conceived as the owner of the desire which holds the key to the subject's desire.[21] In *The Other Side of Psychoanalysis*, by contrast, he left the domain of cold reflection to come back to a word which already appeared in 'Kant with Sade', but from which he had only drawn a few hasty conclusions, and without any link to what he could first have said about 'witticism' (*du mot 'd'esprit'*): 'humour' (*le mot 'humour'*).[22] There is a Sadien 'humour' which, Lacan wrote in his article, pertains to 'black' humour, which consists in showing to what extent the King is naked, God powerless, the Master in reality a slave – to what extent the Other is an authority that is weak and whose tyranny can be reversed by he who *truly* desires.[23] In *The Other Side of Psychoanalysis*, Lacan decided to amend this qualification – and declared to his audience that, in reality, humour, rather than being on the side of Sade, was situated on the side of Sacher-Masoch, insofar as the masochist, he explained, does not even need a God, a King, or a Master.[24] As Lacan put it:

> The masochist is a fine humorist. He has no need of God, his lackey will do. He gets his kicks by enjoying within limits that are moreover discreet, naturally, and like any good masochist, as you can see, you just have to read him, he finds it funny. He is a humorous master.[25]

This reversal was the direct consequence of the psychoanalyst's reading of Deleuze, who had been the first to insist on the difference between the irony of Sade (aimed at an impossible foundation) and the humour of Sacher-Masoch (created by the strict application of a law impossible to apply).[26] For Lacan, this difference turned out to be crucial: it allowed one to distinguish between the theorist and the practitioner.[27]

The Other is a practical joke (*une farce*)

What is a theorist? It is he who never ceases looking toward the foundation, to perceive to what extent it is holed – to what extent what presents itself as a foundation is in fact but a vacillating plaster throne, incapable of receiving the Master who is supposed to sit there. On the contrary, what is a practitioner? He who draws the strictest consequences from a given state of affairs – he who respects what he observes so scrupulously that only their own impossibility, their own absurdity leads to this respect giving rise to a new state of affairs, yet one that is opposed to the one that was supposed to ensue from this respect. If respecting the law to the very end turns out to be impossible, it is not because this impossibility results from a subject's carelessness (as Kant put it, with a tired expression), but rather because it is the law itself which is impossible, in the sense that it is also a nasty kid, a spoiled child, an immature tyrant. It was this distinction which Lacan was confirming, in *The Other Side of Psychoanalysis*, while, in the wake of Deleuze, he was highlighting the extent to which the masochist was a humorist – which is to say the extent to which he was aware that the *jouissance* of the Other is a pitiful *jouissance* and the desire founded on it a rubbish desire (*un désir nul*). *The Other is a (practical) joke* (*une farce*), and it is hilarious that we continue to act as if it were not the case; it is a doubtful joke, onto which we hold for fear of having to face up to how alone we are in constructing our desire – and to the *jouissance* by which it is liable to be marked. Such was the teaching that Sacher-Masoch added to Sade's: where the latter had pointed with a cruel irony, the dimension of the obscenity proper to the Other's desire, the former, with a wry smile, suggested that in reality this obscenity was nothing more than what we indeed wanted it to be. From this viewpoint, it was necessary to conclude that the position of the masochist in the order of discourse is strongly equivalent to that of the hysteric, who searches for a 'Master over whom to reign' – and who invariably finds only a windbag made all the more ridiculous by the fact that, following the example of the frog in the fable, it tends to pass itself off as something it is not.[28] As with the hysteric, the masochist is he who makes it possible to understand that the Master does not exist, that there is not an Other – or, in any case, that no authority exists that can in any way guarantee something like a desire. Desire is without guarantee and without guarantor; it unfolds itself in the enigmatic singularity of the collapse (*effondrement*) (as Deleuze put it: un/grounding ('*effondement*')) of its guarantee and of its guarantor – a collapse which offers it the only possible ethical principle.[29]

Introduction to the ethics of subjects

Lacan's long dialogue with Kant's *oeuvre* agreed on one point: the necessity of affirming the possibility of something like an ethics of subjects – although unlike Kant's, this ethics did not unfold itself on the basis of a logic of principles but of an algebra of structure. The paradox of the Sadian reading of Kant which Lacan proposed was indeed that it amounted to a reading that resulted, in the final instance, in the reversal of all that Kant believed – with the sole exception of empty, hollow structure, devoid of all content, which Kant could grasp. *Something had to hold*: this was the conviction on which rested Lacan's half-ironic, half-humoristic undertaking – something which, contra Kant, could not take on the form of a maxim liable to be integrated by subjects from outside. Rather than a maxim offering, as a final blow, a substantial content to an ethics wishing itself to be formal through and through, Lacan offered an injunction, a call or a cry, which claimed to offer subjects no safeguard against their own collapse, no mastery of their own becoming: 'do not compromise your desire'.[30] This injunction was not a maxim to the extent that it did not propose a way to behave. On the contrary, it pertained to a kind of enigma, a challenge which if it contained a threat also amounted to a shrugging of the shoulders – *do what you want; if you give up, you will see what happens.* When, in 1969, Lacan incorporated into his seminars Deleuze's remarks on masochistic humour, the figure of the law which continued to appear there was no more than a powerless puppet; it would have been a joke, a sinister form of slapstick, to have brought it back in through the window after having chased it out the front door. In fact, the injunction addressed to each subject not to 'renounce their desire' no longer partook of the law;

it only partook of the possibility of unfolding oneself as subject outside of any logic of mastery – except to recognise the structural place of the Master insofar as it is responsible for the structural place of the subject. What remained of the law was not so much the injunction as such as the manner, as frivolous as arbitrary, in which it continued to make the structure of which it constituted the linguistic articulation function – without anybody knowing in the end whether this structure had the least importance for Lacan. At the end of the 1960s, Lacan's structuralism had become a kind of game; the injunction 'do not give up on your desire' tried to push one to participate in this game – even if everyone knew very well how little, in truth, there was to be gained by playing it.[31]

The ambiguous pragmatism of structure

For Lacan, there was an important difference between the formalism of the moral law and the formalism of structure: the vanity of one of them inevitably led to a farcical collapse at the point where the whim of the other led to an invitation to a game resembling above all an invitation to cheat. Everything happened as if Lacan could advance one category only by subtracting it from itself, only by removing from itself any possibility of self-affirmation. Everything happened as if he could only conceive of concepts at the moment of the ruin of their institution (*instauration*) as concepts – and indeed in the very *movement* of this collapse. Likewise for the category of structure, which underpinned all his work but which, it seems, he nonetheless could not accept constituted a guiding model, an epistemological system to which he would have had to subscribe while making only a few minor criticisms. When Lacan seized a category, it was rather to twist it in the same manner as his Punch Culebras cigar – which is to say in order to make it unable to carry out the task it had been designed for, and to make it capable of carrying out an entirely different task to which it seemed foreign. It was hence in this way that the category of structure allowed him to nullify the category of the law all the while conserving it at the level of the empty word. This empty word played the role of perficient ghost in the curious machinery that structure was supposed to constitute, yet precisely only as self-annulment or self-collapse. The emptiness (*nullité*) of the law, and of the Other as its supposed guarantor, is a useful emptiness. It plays a structural role in the subject: *managing* the impossible, which unfolds in the guise of abandoning one's desire or, on the contrary, in the guise of refusing to renounce it, since it unfolds outside coordinates fixed by the Other's desire. *There is a pragmatism of structure* which rejoins the one Deleuze wished for: a pragmatism of the point of desire on to which a subject can hold to construct their own desiring assemblage (*agencement*) – by playing the slightly ridiculous game of not renouncing one's desire, in the absence of the even more ridiculous game of the law and of the Other. Of course, this pragmatism was an ambiguous one. Still, we know how much Lacan valued ambiguity, especially in the domain of the law from which – as he put it in *The Other Side of Psychoanalysis* in regards to the ambiguous relation between law and justice – the latter derives all its value while wearing out its truth.[32] It is impossible to determine precisely what Lacan believed (*tenait*) – indeed, he believed precisely one thing: that one can know nothing (*que rien ne tienne*).[33]

Reciprocal portrait of Gilles Deleuze in Jacques Lacan

A few years later, after the publication of *Anti-Oedipus*, a kind of battleground started appearing between the thought of Gilles Deleuze and that of Jacques Lacan, which progressively hardened with time thanks to their fanatical disciples. This is a small tragedy for those who want to read them with their mutual encounters in mind, be it in person or through the intermediary of their texts. It is a very comical, very farcical tragedy, as the quarrels between heirs often are, particularly when they are not at the level of what they are inheriting.[34] The reality is altogether different: on the essential points, there existed a deep agreement between the thought of Lacan and of Deleuze – nourished by different moments when the one had helped the other with the theory they wanted to develop, and vice versa. Lacan's theory of the law ultimately pertained to the same system of radical 'critique' of the general as the development of his theory proposed by Deleuze in *Presentation of Sacher-Masoch* – and it led to an identical preoccupation with the 'clinic' of the singular, constructed on the basis of the ruin of all principles.[35] Likewise, what remained of ethics in Lacan's thought (this curious injunction to orient oneself, the normative status of which was hard to formulate) turned out to be similar to what Deleuze attempted to think under the category of the 'case', namely a meticulous attention to a subject's practical construction of desire. Above all, desire in general presented the same face in the work of both thinkers: the ambiguous face of obscenity which could sometimes – once re-appropriated by subjects who had first accepted to submit to its power – and despite its emptiness, take on the role of the fulcrum inaugurating this construction. That both had to turn to the works of Sade and of Sacher-Masoch to arrive at the ruin of the law – and of everything that sustained itself through the law – to arrive at the affirmation of a desire with no other structure than that of a collapsed convention, showed to what extent

Lacan's thought shared Deleuze's taste for the 'crowned anarchy' dear to Artaud (regardless of what Lacan occasionally affirmed in regards to his 'anti-progressivism').[36] In what is undoubtedly one of the finest books on Lacan's work ever written (there are few of them), Barbara Cassin proposes that a name be given to this strange system of anarchy – a name steeped in history and misunderstanding – in keeping with Lacan's twisted rigour: the name 'sophistry'.[37] One could not put it better. Regarding law, Lacan was doubtless the greatest sophist in the history of twentieth-century thought – except that he wasn't.

Notes

1. On the history of *Tel Quel*, and this issue in particular, see Forest, Philippe, *Histoire de Tel Quel. 1960–1982* (Paris: Seuil, 1998).
2. See Klossowski, Pierre, *Sade, mon prochain* (Paris: Seuil, 1947). On Klossowski's fascination with Sade, see Arnaud, Alain, *Pierre Klossowski* (Paris: Seuil, 2000).
3. Jean-Jacques Pauvert told his version of the story in *Nouveaux (et moins nouveaux) visages de la censure*, followed by *L'affaire Sade* (Paris: Les Belles Lettres, 1994); and in *La traversée du livre. Mémoires* (Paris: Viviane Hamy, 2004).
4. See Blanchot, Maurice, *Lautréamont et Sade* (Paris: Minuit, 1949); de Beauvoir, Simone, *Faut-il brûler Sade?* (Paris: Gallimard, 1972); Bataille, Georges, *La littérature et le mal* (Paris: Gallimard, 1957); Bataille, Georges, *L'érotisme* (Paris: Minuit, 1957); Foucault, Michel, *Folie et déraison. Histoire de la folie à l'âge classique* (Paris: Plon, 1961); Foucault, Michel, *Les mots et les choses* (Paris: Gallimard, 1966).
5. Bataille, *L'érotisme*, pp. 71ff. On this concept, see de Sutter, Laurent, 'Afterword to Transgression', in de Sutter, Laurent (ed.), *Žižek and Law* (Abingdon: Routledge, 2015), pp. 191–200.
6. See Badiou, Alain, *Le siècle* (Paris: Seuil, 2005).
7. Lacan, Jacques, 'Kant avec Sade', in *Écrits II*, 2nd edn, ed. Jacques-Alain Miller (Paris: Seuil, 1999), pp. 243–69 (hereafter abbreviated as *KS*). On this text and its implications, see Alenka Zupančič's fine book, *L'éthique du réel. Kant avec Lacan* (Caen: Nous, 2009).
8. Lacan, *KS*, p. 244.
9. On this craze, read, but warily, Marty, Eric, *Pourquoi le XXe siècle a-t-il pris Sade au sérieux?* (Paris: Seuil, 2011).
10. Lacan, *KS*, p. 244.
11. Ibid. p. 259.
12. See Lacan, Jacques, *Le séminaire de Jacques Lacan, livre VII: L'éthique de la psychanalyse* (Paris: Seuil, 1986).
13. Lacan, *KS*, p. 268, n. 19.
14. See Lacan, Jacques, *Le séminaire de Jacques Lacan, livre XVII: L'envers de la psychanalyse* (Paris: Seuil, 1991), pp. 75ff. (hereafter abbreviated as *EP*).
15. Deleuze, Gilles, *Présentation de Sacher-Masoch. Le froid et le cruel* (Paris: Minuit, 1967) (hereafter abbreviated as *PSM*). See also the interview with Deleuze conducted by *La Quinzaine Littéraire* when his book was published: 'Mystique et masochisme', in *L'île déserte. Textes et entretiens 1953–1974*, Lapoujade, David (ed.) (Paris: Minuit, 2002), pp. 182ff. Deleuze returned a final time to Sacher-Masoch in 1989, with an article written for *Libération* entitled 'Re-présentation de Sacher-Masoch', then republished in *Critique et clinique* (Paris: Minuit, 1993), pp. 71–4. For a discussion of this, see

Alliez, Éric, 'Deleuze avec Masoch', *Multitudes*, 25: 2 (2006), pp. 53–68. On the exact historical context of Deleuze's interest in the figure of Sacher-Masoch (and the role played by Kostas Axelos), see Dosse, François, *Gilles Deleuze Félix Guattari. Biographie croisée* (Paris: La Découverte, 2007), pp. 149ff.

16. Deleuze, *PSM*, p. 73.
17. Deleuze, *KS*, p. 250.
18. Deleuze, *PSM*, p. 73 [Deleuze, Gilles, 'Coldness and Cruelty', in Deleuze, Gilles and Sacher-Masoch, Leopold, *Masochism: Coldness and Cruelty and Venus in Furs* (New York: Zone Books, 1991), pp. 83–4].
19. Deleuze, *PSM*, pp. 77ff. For a discussion of this, see de Sutter, Laurent, *Deleuze, la pratique du droit* (Paris: Michalon, 2009).
20. Lacan, Jacques, *Le séminaire de Jacques Lacan, livre XVI: D'un Autre à l'autre* (Paris: Seuil, 2006), pp. 257ff.
21. Ibid. pp. 257–8.
22. Lacan, *EP*, p. 75.
23. Lacan, *KS*, p. 247.
24. Lacan, *EP*, p. 75.
25. Ibid. [Lacan, Jacques, *The Seminar of Jacques Lacan, Book XVII: The Other Side of Psychoanalysis* (London and New York: W. W. Norton, 2007), p. 67].
26. Deleuze, *PSM*, pp. 75ff.
27. Lacan, *EP*, p. 75.
28. For a discussion of this, see Israël, Lucien, *La jouissance de l'hystérique. Séminaire 1974*, 2nd edn (Paris: Seuil, 1999).
29. See Deleuze, Gilles, *Différence et répétition* (Paris: Presses universitaires de France, 1968), p. 92.
30. This formula appears for the first time in Lacan, *L'éthique de la psychanalyse*, pp. 368ff. For a discussion of the formula, see Zupančič, Alenka, *Esthétique du désir, éthique de la jouissance* (Paris: Théétète, 2002).
31. On Lacan's place in the history of structuralism, see Dosse, François, *Histoire du structuralisme, vol. I: Le champ du signe, 1945–1966*, 2nd edn (Paris: La Découverte, 2012 [1992]). See also Jean-Claude Milner's major observations in *L'œuvre claire. Lacan, la science, la philosophie* (Paris: Seuil, 1998); and in *Le périple structural: figures et paradigme* (Paris: Seuil, 2002).
32. Lacan, *EP*, p. 48.
33. This is what all those who wanted to hypostasise the figure of the Law, in Lacan, failed to understand, forgetting his profound link with the permanent collapse of the Master – primarily, Pierre Legendre. See, for example, Bernet, Rudolf, 'Loi et éthique chez Kant et Lacan', *Revue philosophique de Louvain*, 4th series, 89: 83 (1991), pp. 450–68. For a counter-example, see Aristodemou, Maria, *Law, Psychoanalysis, Society: Taking the Unconscious Seriously* (Abingdon: Routledge, 2014), as well as, for a discussion, de Sutter, Laurent, 'Le côté obscur de la loi', *Droit et société* (forthcoming).
34. See Dosse, *Gilles Deleuze Félix Guattari*, pp. 221ff.
35. On this distinction, see Deleuze, *Critique et clinique*, p. 9. See also François Zourabichvili's discussion of this in 'Kant avec Masoch', *Multitudes*, 25 (2006), pp. 87–100.
36. Lacan, *EP*, p. 240; Deleuze, *Différence et répétition*, p. 55. See Montebello, Pierre, *Deleuze. La passion de la pensée* (Paris: Vrin, 2008), p. 80.
37. See Cassin, Barbara, *Jacques le sophiste* (Paris: Epel, 2012). One should pay close attention to the way in which Cassin distinguishes her reading of Lacan from how Badiou has long defined Lacan's work: as 'antiphilosophy'. See, for example, Badiou, Alain, *Le séminaire: Lacan (L'antiphilosophie 3. 1994–1995)* (Paris: Fayard, 2013). Compare with Audi, Paul, *Lacan ironiste* (Paris: Mimesis, 2015), who does not take into account the link between Lacan and sophistry, nor the distinction between irony and humour.

Chapter 3

Does the Body without Organs Have Any Sex at All? Lacan and Deleuze on Perversion and Sexual Difference

Boštjan Nedoh

According to the widespread common opinion, which is hegemonic and determines the ongoing debates about the relation between Deleuze's and Lacan's respective thoughts after a period of mutual respect and attention in the 1960s, the break between the two, and Deleuze's consequent 'revolt' against psychoanalysis, occurred in 1972 with Deleuze's publication of the book *Anti-Oedipus*, co-authored with his friend and theoretical partner from that period on, Félix Guattari. Considering contemporary debates on this topic, one of the greatest proponents of Deleuze's thought in general and of this apparent break in particular, Éric Alliez, goes even further in this schema and locates Deleuze's arrival at the unquestionable imperative to 'withdraw from psychoanalysis *completely*'[1] in the publication of *A Thousand Plateaus* (1980) and traces this back to 'a certain ambivalence maintained by the *Anti-Oedipus* with respect to Lacan'.[2]

More precisely, Alliez relocates this shift after referring (mainly) to the famous chapter in *A Thousand Plateaus* entitled 'How Do You Make Yourself a Body without Organs?', in which Deleuze and Guattari formulate their own kind of anti-psychoanalytical 'categorical imperative', which imposes the necessity to construct a 'body without organs' or the 'field of immanence'.[3] Occupying a central role in this construct is the transformation of the Lacanian notion of desire: if, according to Lacan, desire is inherently connected to the moment of negativity in the constitution of the human psyche, that is, to castration and the emergence of the object-cause of desire, then in Deleuze and Guattari's field of immanence, desire is transformed in such a way that '[it] lacks nothing and therefore cannot be linked to any external or transcendent criterion'.[4] In other words, for Deleuze and Guattari's desire, it is immanent to itself, is itself its own object and is not determined by any kind of external lack. The operation that, for Deleuze and Guattari, allows desire itself to become its own object or the field of immanence is well known: the dissolution of the pseudo link between desire and pleasure. The positivity of desire emerges precisely at the point of this dissolution insofar as the pleasure principle, from the outside, as an external or transcendent measure, interrupts or, better, represses desire as a positive entity.

Paradoxically enough, so conceived a field of immanence or body without organs does not mean simply the enclosure of the old metaphysical Self within the boundaries of the body, dismissing all of the external world and its influence upon it. Rather, the field of immanence signifies the absolute Outside, in which the very difference between inside and outside is somehow dissolved. As they put it:

> The field of immanence is not internal to the self, but neither does it come from an external self or a nonself. Rather, it is like the absolute Outside that knows no Selves because interior and exterior are equally part of the immanence in which they have fused.[5]

In this respect, it seems that we would not be going too far in claiming that the total escape from the realm of psychoanalysis is made possible by the introduction of new, often co-dependent or even synonymous, concepts, such as 'absolute Outside', 'field of immanence' and 'body without organs' (henceforward, BwO), which all appeared, at least at a terminological level, for the first time either in *A Thousand Plateaus* or in other works from that period on.

In this chapter, I will try to challenge this perspective in a threefold manner: (1) by briefly showing how these aforementioned concepts are far from being limited to Deleuze's late period and are actually present throughout all of his work, starting from the essay on Sacher-Masoch; (2) furthermore, I will show how these aforementioned concepts derive not in contrast to psychoanalysis but rather from Deleuze's explicit reference to Lacan's theory of perversion, which Deleuze nevertheless misreads by considering perversion as 'beyond [symbolic] Other' or beyond sexual difference, therefore also beyond the phallus; (3) lastly, I will conclude by highlighting the fact that Deleuze's notion of BwO, although it was meant by him to be one of the most powerful anti-Oedipal weapons against psychoanalysis, is actually just another – yet in my view wrong – way to answer the same question, the question of sexual difference, to which Lacan later answered by conceptualising 'feminine *jouissance*' as 'beyond the phallus'.[6] In this context, the apparent opposition between Lacan's (post-)structuralism and Deleuze's vitalism, far from being mere opposition or even contradiction, will prove rather to be a polemical debate concerning perhaps the most important question – that of how to say 'No!' to the Other or how to articulate the inexistence of the Other – a question which is, despite different answers, common to their respective thoughts.

Therefore, to begin with, as I already mentioned, we should first recall that the very conception of the immanence of the BwO as the 'absolute Outside' does not appear for the first time – conceptually speaking – in *A Thousand Plateaus*. In fact, albeit under different names, it is present from already many years before and, as we shall see, is not even the topic that would come to distinguish Deleuze and Guattari's philosophical project of the ontology of immanence from Deleuze's early single-authorship period of transcendental empiricism. For instance, already in the famous essay 'Coldness and Cruelty', this view presents the very core of Deleuze's interest in what he regards as Sacher-Masoch's 'invention' of masochism, namely the 'escape' from the (Oedipal) law of the father and the predominant hierarchical social order determined by it. As is already well known, according to Deleuze, in masochism the symbolic law of the father is completely devalued and suspended, all because of the transference of the symbolic authority to the mother. As he puts it: 'In the case of masochism the totality of the law is invested upon the mother, who expels the father from the symbolic realm.'[7] In this way, Deleuze insists, the masochist succeeds in escaping from or finds a way out of the Oedipal social hierarchy determined by the law of the father; he is completely deterritorialised of the geographical territory governed by Oedipal logic and the father's authority.

Similarly, Deleuze will (together with Guattari) insist years later that Kafka's literature, as a paradigmatic example of 'minor literature', is meant to 'escape' the Oedipal family triangle and the figure of the father, to find a way out from there where 'he didn't find any'. In fact, as they argue, Kafka's effort is not to establish an imaginary rivalry with the father and search for liberation, but to find an escape at the point of his deadlock, at the point of his repressed desire: 'The question of the father is not how to become free in relation to him (an Oedipal question), but how to find the path there where he didn't find any.'[8] The privileged way to do so, to escape the cage of Oedipus and free the repressed desire, is therefore not simply to refuse and resist it but rather to 'deterritorialise' it by way of enlarging the picture of the father to the point of absurdity. In other words, Kafka's work consists, by way of exaggeration and enlargement of the father as the agent of repression, in escaping the Oedipus triangle, in untying the chain that keeps the subject within it. As we can see, albeit by different terminology, the whole idea of the 'Outside' – here in terms of the 'escape' from the territory of Oedipus – is present also in Deleuze's previous works, and thus its articulation in *A Thousand Plateaus* is but a more radical way of articulating previous positions.

Here it is necessary to emphasise that Deleuze and Guattari add in *A Thousand Plateaus* to this series of examples, which are indeed all examples of perversion, the case of courtly love, especially in light of its conceptual association with Tao-masochistic (a)sexual practices of *coitus reservatus*, which founds itself exactly upon the detachment of desire from pleasure and thus constitutes it as the immanence without any lack:

> Similarly, or actually in a different way, it would be an error to interpret courtly love in terms of a law of the lack or an ideal of transcendence. The renunciation of external pleasure, or its delay, its infinite regress, testifies on the contrary to an achieved state in which desire no longer lacks anything but fills itself and constructs its own field of immanence. [. . .] Everything is allowed: all that counts is for pleasure to be the flow of desire itself, Immanence, instead of a measure that interrupts it or delivers it to the three phantoms, namely, internal lack, higher transcendence, and apparent exteriority.[9]

These last three 'phantoms' indeed pertain to (Lacanian) psychoanalysis. And yet, what is still today difficult to grasp and accept is the fact that this seemingly anti-Lacanian stance, this conviction, according to which perversions such as masochism and courtly love can avoid 'the three phantoms' – lack, transcendence and exteriority – found themselves precisely upon Deleuze's own (mis)reading of Lacan's theory of perversion in which Deleuze saw nothing but the affirmation of the argument that in perversion the imaginary relation with the other as the double prevails over the symbolic relation of the subject to the big Other as the order of differences (including that between the sexes). Namely, in his famous appendix in *The Logic of Sense*, by referring to 'Lacan and his school', Deleuze makes the following claim:

> Lacan and his school insist profoundly [. . .] on the way in which the *difference of sexes* is disavowed by the pervert, in the interest of an androgynous world of *doubles*; on the annulment of the Other inside perversion, on the position of a 'beyond the Other' (*un au-delà de l'Autre*) or of an 'otherwise Other' (*un Autre qu'autrui*).[10]

What Deleuze implicitly adopts here is the following distinction: if neurosis, on the one hand, founds itself upon the mechanism of repression of unconscious incestuous desire (Oedipus complex), then for Deleuze, the subject, by way of fetishistic disavowal, which is the main characteristic of perversion as such, on the other hand, succeeds precisely in realising this unconscious desire. If we turn back to the case of masochism, the masochist, by adopting castration, fulfils the condition for the incestuous relation with the mother. From Deleuze's point of view, perversion is therefore traversed by a paradoxical structure: he is convinced that, on the one hand, the sexual relationship is possible (by way of the transgression of paternal prohibition) in another topological realm in which, on the other hand, sexual difference is dismissed.[11]

Before coming to the very point of Deleuze's misreading of Lacan's theory of perversion, that is, to the point at which Deleuze fails to see what is at stake in it, we should stress the following: the last quote from Deleuze seems to clearly and univocally show that (1) his idea of the Outside as 'beyond the Other' originates in his early account of the clinical topic of perversion and (2) that he is, in order to develop his own position, clearly and affirmatively referring to psychoanalysis. In short, Deleuze sees the phenomenon of perversion *as* conceptualised by 'Lacan and his school' as the privileged way of the construction of the field of immanence and of reaching the (a-)topos of the Outside.

Moreover, at first sight, this statement of Deleuze's seems to fully correspond to Lacan's well-known and widespread motto that 'the Other doesn't exist'. In this respect, it would seem that we are dealing here with an inherent correlation between the position of the subject in perversion and the subject's position at the end of analysis insofar as in both cases we would be dealing with a kind of subjective destitution and with the escape from the symbolic framework of the Other.[12] Notwithstanding the fact that this conclusion may even sound catchy, it is necessary to stress that Lacan's axiom of the inexistence of the big Other does not precisely suggest its 'annulment', as Deleuze says. Differently put, from Lacan's point of view, the 'beyond the Other' of perversion does not at all mean that the Other has simply disappeared and that the subject now finds himself in an *extra-discursive* or *transcendental* position with respect to the Other. Rather, this axiom of Lacan's should be understood in the sense of the distinction within the Other between the imaginary object and the symbolic Other as inherently traversed by its own lack. It is this point, which can be associated with the moment of traversing the fantasy at the end of analysis, that, according to Lacan, differentiates psychoanalysis from psychology:

> The aim of my teaching [. . .] is to dissociate *a* and A by reducing the first to what is related to the imaginary and the other to what is related to the symbolic. It is indubitable that the symbolic is the basis of what was made into God. It is certain that the imaginary is based on the reflection of one semblable in another. And yet, *a* has lent itself to be confused with S($\cancel{A}$) [. . .]. It is here that the scission or detachment remains to be effectuated.[13]

In this context, I will focus now firstly on Lacan's consideration of perversion, and on fetishism in particular, in order to show how the latter is a symbolic structure that not only does not allow the subject to avoid or go beyond the realm of the phallus and the father, but rather, on the contrary, is essential for the emergence of the phallus supported by the repressed love toward the mother. Furthermore, if this first step could be characterised by the formula 'phallus as beyond' – we will soon see the meaning of this formulation – in the second step I will focus on the 'beyond phallus' of feminine *jouissance* in order to show how this conceptualisation of Lacan's is nothing but his answer to Deleuze's question of the 'Outside' or 'beyond' of the symbolic framework.

Let us thus begin with a very common topic in both Deleuze's and Lacan's accounts of perversion. Both authors share the conviction that fetishism is the clinical structure that represents the main and distinctive feature of perversion. It is therefore necessary to firstly give a brief insight into the structure of fetishism and the way it functions in the human psyche. According to Lacan, fetishism is inextricably connected with two mechanisms that constitute the human unconscious and operate in dream work: condensation (*Verdichtung*) and displacement (*Verscheibung*). In his 'The Instance of the Letter',[14] he further proposes two linguistic equivalents for both mechanisms of the unconscious, which are metaphor and metonymy. According to Lacan, the formula of metaphor consists in the substitution of one signifier by another signifier, so that the empty space the second takes comes about not simply from the first's leaving it, but comes about rather from the repression of the first. All of this implies the immanent distinction between signifiers and the structure, or signifying chain, that contains within it the empty spaces for the inscription of those signifiers. It is here that we are dealing with the Freudian primal repressed signifier, where, as Alenka Zupančič has pointed out, the signifier appears from the very first as already repressed,[15] so that here repression does not hit on something that has first appeared as existing and is repressed only afterwards. On the contrary, the constitutive lack of the signifier, or the signifier as lacking, is already there from the very beginning. The drive is therefore fixed to this point of the primal repressed and circulates around this constitutive void.[16] It is this metaphoric replacement where one signifier replaces the other that Lacan defines as symptomatic. More precisely, the symptom is nothing but the other signifier that takes the place of the primal repressed. Furthermore, it is here that we encounter the function of metonymy, since the primal repressed signifier remains connected with the signifying chain precisely through the metonymic sliding of the meaning or desire. Differently put, what is primal repressed appears in the form of unconscious desire as that which metonymically emerges in-between the signifiers that constitute speech.[17] This is why unconscious desire can be deciphered only between the lines, that is, at the point where speech is traversed by something heterogeneous that cannot express itself directly – the meaning is always displaced meaning. In other words, desire, insofar as it is in the fantasy attached with object *a*, operates as nothing but the metonymic displacement of a repressed element, that is, of something extra-linguistic within language itself. The meaning of the desire can be deciphered only as immanent to the manifested speech in which this extra-linguistic element continuously emerges,[18] which metonymically indicates some fundamental impasse that traverses human speech. However, the unconscious desire can be deciphered only on the condition of the *repetition* of this extra-linguistic element, that is, on the condition that the homophonic element appears in speech more than once. It is only in this case that it can be considered as associated with something repressed or something that can manifest itself only indirectly, through metonymic displacement. This is why Lacan defines the desire as always 'the *desire for something else*',[19] where this 'something else' indicates not something positive or empirically existing but rather something that appears only in the form of repression and is never given in a form of positive content that would emerge once the repression is dismissed.

According to Lacan, it is this 'perverse' fixation of desire that constitutes the very place in which the fetish arises: 'Hence its [desire's] "perverse" fixation at the very point of suspension of the signifying chain at which the screen-memory is immobilized and the fascinating image of the fetish becomes frozen.'[20] Of course, this expression of the frozen image of the fetish derives already from Freud's theory of fetishism according to which the fetish consists of the frozen image of the high heel of a woman's shoe. This is because the gaze that goes from bottom (heel) to top (woman's genitals, where man experiences his own castration anxiety) must return and be fixed to its point of departure in order to succeed in disavowing woman's castration, or her lack of penis. However, this shows that the mechanism of fetishistic disavowal is not the type of transgression of the structure of repression but is, on the contrary, inextricably connected with it. It allows the subject to make a compromise that fits the Super-ego's ambiguity insofar as the latter consists of the pressure, on the one hand, to indirectly fulfil the repressed desire and, on the other, to accept the prohibition.

It seems quite easy to argue here that this logic of repression and prohibition is the logic that governs the male side of formulae of sexuation as developed by Lacan in his Seminar XX – no wonder Lacan explicitly assigns 'polymorphous perversion' exclusively to the male position.[21] As Joan Copjec stated, Lacan, by drawing upon Kant's antinomies of pure reason, presents the male side of sexuation with two contradictory logical propositions, both of which are true:

$\exists x - \Phi x$ (there is at least one x that is not submitted to the phallic function)

$\forall x\ \Phi x$ (all x's are (every x is) submitted to the phallic function)[22]

Both formulas taken together show nothing other than the construction of universality, which founds itself upon an excluded exception: all men are submitted to the phallic function – that is, in order to symbolically exist in the realm of the Other, they must lose a part of (their own) being (the subject as a 'lack of being') – on the condition that one (the phantasmatic Primal father of the horde – *Urvater*) is not. If the figure of Primal father is associated with the realm of freedom with respect to the realm of prohibition, the reason why this is so is precisely that he has, albeit phantasmatically constructed, the access to the desire for the mother, which is precisely what must be repressed and prohibited by symbolically existing man.

At this point, fetishistic disavowal is the mechanism to indirectly satisfy – by way of displacement to a supplemental object – this repressed desire for the mother *as phallic*. More precisely, it is the construction of the fetish that constitutes the phallic or phantasmatic 'beyond' of the image of mother, which 'beyond' sustains the illusion of her phallicness. As we see, fetishistic disavowal is here far from avoiding or even dismissing repression and prohibition; rather, it is inextricably connected with and conditioned by it. However, though we might accept Deleuze's idea of perversion as the type of transgression of prohibition that allows the subject to finally achieve the prohibited object, this act does not function in Lacan's analysis of sexual difference either. Differently put, what Deleuze misreads in Lacan's theory of perversion in general and that of masochism in particular is the fact that the transgression of prohibition (also by way of adopting castration, as in the case of masochism) does not result in the realisation of the sexual relationship in the sense of the *total* satisfaction of drives (Freudian *ganze Sexualstrebung*), which would be at this point freed from the fixation on the primal repressed signifier or inexistence of the sexual relationship. In other words, man in an incestuous relation with the mother still does not reach the point of relating to her as to *The* Woman (*La femme*), that is to woman as existing symbolically in the same way man does. To explain this, it seems worthwhile to now show the logic that governs the feminine side of formulae of sexuation. As in the case of man's formulae, Lacan here, too, presents the feminine side with two logical propositions:

$-\exists x - \Phi x$ (there is not one x that is not submitted to the phallic function)

$-\forall x\ \Phi x$ (not all (not every) x is submitted to the phallic function)

Taken together, these two propositions logically reassume Lacan's clear emphasis on the problem of woman's position with respect to the phallic function: contrarily to predominant reading, which regards woman as excluded from the phallic function, Lacan insists that woman *is* submitted to the phallic function ('there is no woman (no *x*) which is not submitted to the phallic function'); the point is only that she is 'not-all' within it, that something (feminine *jouissance*) is added to her being in the phallic function.[23] In the last instance, this is the point of Lacan's expression of 'beyond the phallus'[24] of feminine *jouissance*: something more (*en plus*) is added to the phantasmatic (and therefore failed) totality of phallic *jouissance* supported by fantasy. In this respect, the *en plus* of feminine *jouissance* clearly indicates the infinity that is characteristic of the feminine position: contrary to the male side, which is based upon the exception that allows its symbolic existence in the realm of the Other, the female side is determined by the inexistent Other S(Ⱥ), that is, by the inexistence of the exception that would guarantee the symbolic existence of woman. Consequently, this is the reason why woman does not exist as universal but only ex-ists as singular and can be counted only as singular, as one-by-one. However, this counting one-by-one never achieves the totality, which would in the last instance only allow the judgement of woman's existence (in the symbolic, that is, as universal). In short, if the logic of the male side is the logic of prohibition, the logic of the female side is the logic of impossibility – it is impossible to reach the totality (universality) of Woman.

This implies above all that, as Joan Copjec stressed, in Lacan's formulae of sexuation, 'man' and 'woman' indicate two different ways, rather than one single way, of failure of the sexual relationship – and, most importantly, their sum does not form the 'totality': 'The sexual relation fails for two reasons: it is impossible and it is prohibited. Put these two failures together; you will never come up with a whole'[25] – or, as we might add – you will never come up with a univocity of being. It is precisely this point that constitutes the very core of the problem that arises in Deleuze's misreading of Lacan's theory of perversion. Namely for Lacan there is no such thing as univocity of being precisely because being, insofar as it is sexuated, implies not simply two different ontological positions but two failures of ontology. Differently put, in the (a-)topos of the 'absolute Outside' as 'beyond the Other' there does not appear a fully constituted sexual relationship in which Man would relate himself to Woman without any lack. On the contrary, the shift from the male to the female side of sexuation does not imply the abolishment of the phallic function as the common denominator that determines both sides. Rather, the 'beyond the phallus' of the feminine position implies the *non-totalisation* of *jouissance* as such, or as Lorenzo Chiesa has put it, a non-totalisation of which the condition of possibility – that is, the condition of its failure – *is* the phallic function and therefore a castration as its correlative. Furthermore, if, as we said, the male position is governed by the repressed and prohibited desire for the mother as correlative to the figure of the father, then in transgressing this prohibition the pervert does not achieve the relation to *The* Woman. Or, better yet, he relates to Woman only at the price of turning perversion into 'père-version' – literally, 'Father-version', which is in French a homophone to perversion.[26] This is the ultimate meaning of Lacan's theorem according to which Woman is one of the Names-of-the-Father, or God, which is mathematised by the sign of the signifier of the barred or inexistent Other S($\bar{A}$): the transgression of the paternal prohibition leads the subject not to the ultimate and final *jouissance* but rather to the topological position where the *jouissance* itself results as infinite or non-totalisable precisely because of the *en plus* of feminine *jouissance*.

At this point we can depict the main difference between Lacan's (post-)structuralism and Deleuze's vitalism: on the one hand, Deleuze's conviction is that perversion in general and the masochistic incestuous relation between the son and the mother in particular overcome the mechanism of repression upon which the logic of the unconscious is founded. More precisely, Deleuze seems to argue that in the transgression of the paternal prohibition we reach the position in which drives are no longer fixed to a lack and that therefore a complete satisfaction is achievable. In more linguistic terms, Deleuze's vitalism seems to insist that (1) the metonymic sliding of desire and its perverse fixation, of which the fetish is a manifested sign, is not co-dependent on the mechanism of (primal) repression; and (2) it can therefore abolish the fixation of the drive on the primal repressed signifier. The outcome of this operation is nothing but the construction of what in Deleuze's late work appears as the 'field of immanence' of the BwO where drives no longer circulate around the lack in the Other and are no longer submitted to (negative or conjunctive) synthesis.

Lacan, on the other hand, insists that the drive is in the final instance inextricably and irreducibly connected with the point of the primal repressed. If the task of psychoanalysis is, as we have already mentioned, to detach the symbolic in the form of the barred Other from the imaginary (object *a*), this act does not result in a complete abolishment of the Other or in the untying of the drive. In short, as Lorenzo Chiesa stressed, feminine *jouissance*, as additional to phallic sexual *jouissance*, is a-sexual because, insofar as it is 'beyond the phallus', it accounts for the impossibility of the phantasmatic synthesis of drives under the phallic function; yet neither is it non-sexual in the sense of being *jouissance* that goes beyond the sexual difference and remains unrelated to phallic function.

As shown, ultimately Deleuze misreads Lacanian theory of perversion at the point at which he thinks about perversion as 'beyond the Other' or as the 'absolute Outside' of the BwO, whereas a close inspection of Lacan's essay 'The Instance of the Letter' and of his formulae of sexuation show that perversion in its elementary form of fetishistic disavowal is essential for the constitution of the Other insofar as it is co-dependent on the mechanism of repression. As fetishism is essentially characteristic of the male position in formulae of sexuation, it unveils, it seems, the very reason for Deleuze's misreading of Lacan: it was Deleuze himself who disavowed the sexual difference and the peculiar *jouissance* of the woman, which does not exist.

Notes

1. Alliez, Éric, 'Deleuze with Masoch', in de Bolle, Leen (ed.), *Deleuze and Psychoanalysis: Philosophical Essays on Deleuze's Debate with Psychoanalysis* (Leuven: Leuven University Press, 2010), p. 126.
2. Ibid. p. 126.
3. Deleuze, Gilles and Guattari, Félix, *A Thousand Plateaus* (Minneapolis and London: University of Minnesota Press, 1987), p. 157.
4. Ibid. p. 157.
5. Ibid. p. 156.
6. Lacan, Jacques, *The Seminar of Jacques Lacan, Book XX: Encore* (London and New York: W. W. Norton, 1998), p. 74.
7. Deleuze, Gilles, 'Coldness and Cruelty', in Deleuze, Gilles and Sacher-Masoch, Leopold, *Masochism: Coldness and Cruelty and Venus in Furs* (New York: Zone Books, 1991), p. 90.
8. Deleuze, Gilles and Guattari, Félix, *Kafka: Toward a Minor Literature* (Minneapolis and London: University of Minnesota Press, 1986), p. 10.
9. Deleuze and Guattari, *A Thousand Plateaus*, pp. 156–7.
10. Deleuze, Gilles, *The Logic of Sense* (New York: Columbia University Press, 2004), p. 358.
11. This can be proven with two quotes from Deleuze, 'Coldness and Cruelty': 'There is a disavowal of the mother by magnifying her ("symbolically, the mother lacks nothing")' (p. 64); 'As a general rule castration acts as a threat preventing incest or a punishment that controls it; it is an obstacle to or a chastisement of incest. But when it is linked with the image of the mother, the castration of the son becomes the very condition of the success of incest; incest is assimilated by this displacement to a second birth which dispenses with the father's role' (p. 93).
12. Such a conclusion is argued for by, for instance, Dominiek Hoens in 'Toward a New Perversion: Psychoanalysis', in Clemens, Justin and Grigg, Russell (eds), *Jacques Lacan and the Other Side of Psychoanalysis: Reflections on Seminar XVII* (Durham, NC and London: Duke University Press, 2006), pp. 88–102.
13. Lacan, *Encore*, p. 83.
14. Lacan, Jacques, 'The Instance of the Letter in the Unconscious or Reason Since Freud', in *Écrits* (London and New York: W. W. Norton, 2006), pp. 412–41.
15. Zupančič, Alenka, 'Ponavljanje' [Repetition], *Filozofski vestnik* 28: 1 (2007), p. 69.
16. 'We have reason to assume that there is a primal repression, a first phase of repression, which consists in the psychical (ideational) representative of the drive [*die psychische (Vorstellungs-) Repräsentanz des Triebes*] being denied entrance into the conscious. With this a *fixation* is established; the representative in question persists unaltered from

then onwards and the drive remains attached to it' (Freud, Sigmund, 'Repression', in *The Standard Edition of the Complete Psychological Works of Sigmund Freud, Vol. XIV*, ed. and trans. James Strachey (London: Vintage, 2001), p. 148).

17. This is also a poetic aspect of the relation between metaphor and metonymy: 'Metaphor's creative spark does not spring from the juxtaposition of two images, that is, of two equally actualized signifiers. It flashes between two signifiers, one of which has replaced the other by taking the other's place in the signifying chain, the occulted signifier remaining present by virtue of its (metonymic) connection to the rest of the chain' (Lacan, 'The Instance of the Letter', p. 422).

18. The best example here, of course, is Freud's analysis of the Rat Man, where this extralinguistic element is the stem 'rat', on the basis of which is composed the homophony between *Ratte* (the rat) and *Raten* (the debt). It is this homophony that provides Freud the key with which to successfully interpret the Rat Man's symptom.

19. Ibid. p. 431.

20. Ibid. p. 431.

21. This claim is made on the basis of the connection between the 'act of love' and perversion as it appears on the male side: 'The act of love is the male's polymorphous perversion, in the case of speaking beings' (Lacan, *Encore*, p. 72).

22. Ibid. p. 78; see also Copjec, Joan, *Read My Desire: Lacan Against the Historicists*, 2nd edn (London and New York: Verso, 2015), p. 214.

23. Most explicitly: 'But, and this is the whole point, she has different ways of approaching the phallus and of keeping it for herself. It's not because she is not-wholly in the phallic function that she is not there at all. She is *not* not at all there. She is there in full (*à plein*). But there is something more (*en plus*)' (Lacan, *Encore*, p. 74). On the topic of feminine *jouissance* in Lacan's Seminar XX, see also Lorenzo Chiesa's reading, which fits that of Copjec's (Chiesa, Lorenzo, '*Jouissance* in Lacan's Seminar XX: Prolegomena to a New Reading', in de Beistegui, Miguel, Bianco, Giuseppe and Gracieuse, Marjorie (eds), *The Care of Life: Transdisciplinary Perspectives in Bioethics and Biopolitics* (London: Rowman & Littlefield International, 2014), pp. 295–308.

24. Lacan, *Encore*, p. 74.

25. Copjec, *Read My Desire*, p. 235.

26. Lacan formulates this point in a marginal remark in his 'Preface' to the French translation of Frank Wedekind's play *Spring Awakening*: 'Woman [*La femme*] as the version of the Father couldn't configure herself otherwise than as *Father-version* [*Père-version*]' (Lacan, Jacques, 'Préface à *L'éveil du printemps*', *Ornicar?*, 39 (1986), p. 7).

Chapter 4

Gnomonology: Deleuze's Phobias and the Line of Flight between Speech and the Body

Scott Wilson

> We must define a special function, which is identical to neither health nor illness: the function of the *Anomalous*. The Anomalous is always at the frontier [. . .] it traces a line-between [. . .] This is the Thing or Entity of terror.
>
> Gilles Deleuze, *Dialogues II*[1]

> Let us recognise [. . .] the subject's efficacy in the *gnomon* he erects, a *gnomon* that constantly indicates truth's site to him.
>
> Jacques Lacan, *Écrits*[2]

Φόβος

As Brian Massumi remarks in his notes to the translation of *A Thousand Plateaus*, the word 'flight' does not quite convey everything at stake in the notion of '*ligne de fuite*' that has 'a different range of meanings'.[3] For example, it has less to do with the act of flying than with that of fleeing, making an exit or vanishing. The English word flight can also mean flee, of course, as in the flight from some object of fear, or in the act of putting-to-flight. A line, meanwhile, is not just something along which one might travel, but can also function as a frontier that differentiates or separates two planes, fields or territories. Let us say between Lacan and Deleuze, for example, or even Deleuze and Guattari. No doubt we can regard these proper names as designating certain zones or discursive fields of philosophy and analysis as well as authors. At the same time there is also the question of the relation between the author and his or her work. The significant term that is highlighted by the 'line of flight', however, is neither of the proper names but the 'and' that marks the borderline between the two. As Deleuze writes, 'AND is neither one thing nor the other, it's always in-between, between two things . . . there's always a border, a line of flight or flow, only we don't see it because it's the least perceptible of things'.[4] The 'and' is imperceptible, or rather overlooked because it is there on the surface, as plain as day, the word that links and separates a couple or a concatenation of elements. Clearly, given the various meanings of the '*ligne de fuite*', 'and' does not denote a harmonious unity like *ying* and *yang*, say, but a multiplicity that may well be discordant in its conjunctive parts, a disjunctive synthesis perhaps. Such discordance might be heard in the dis-junction that grinds in the interlocking machinery of a desiring assemblage, as one part seeks to unlock and flee in order to pursue another, or in the dissonant cries of a collective enunciation where one or more voices seek solitude in an escape from the crowd. 'And' also marks the enigmatic impediment between the amorous couples of a sexual relation that Lacan describes as something that 'doesn't stop not being written'.[5] An effect and (non-)product of writing, no doubt the *hainamoration* (hat-eloving) that psychoanalysis finds in the conjunction between amorous partners necessarily also affects co-authors.[6]

In Greek myth there is a special God for this obscure object of love and hatred, desire and horror that is regarded as the cause of flight. His name is *Φόβος* (Phobos), meaning both fear and flight, born of the union between Aphrodite and Ares, Gods of love and war respectively. In battle, *Φόβος* is attendant to his father, and in Homer he is the personification of the fear that causes panic and a desire to flee the martial engagement. Phobia, for psychoanalysis, is also an attendant to the paternal principle but one that has failed in its function of providing a line of separation between mother and child. A particular phobia (arachnophobia, say) has a certain utility and value in that it crystallises in an object indefinite fears or anxieties, a crystallisation that, when it occurs very early in life, supports the process of individuation that senses mortal danger from the very universe that has given rise to it. The nascent subject who fears he or she is the object of the Other's ravenous desire, seeks to hold apart (in the absence of any paternal prop) the space of those jaws by substituting a frightening object, distracting them with the very image of their own terrifying exteriority and engulfment. As Freud suggested in his case study on Little Hans, phobia is an effect of the question that being raises for the subject 'from where he was before the subject came into the world'.[7] It is the same structure that Lacan finds in a certain tradition of Judaeo-Christianity, going back to Solomon, where the 'fear of God' crystallises all the evils that are multi-fariously present in life.[8] At the same time, the atavistic fears that this par-ticular 'name of the father' 'quilts' evokes the animalistic *jouissance* before the advent of law, the locus of exteriority beyond the signifier.[9] Indeed, it is the becoming-animal, or becoming-multiple, immanent to the fears named by the 'father' that seems, for reasons both political and clinical, to produce a multiplication of the names of the father that Lacan links to a general tendency towards psychosis.[10] In Seminar XXII, *R.S.I.*, the signifier of the master (S_1) has also multiplied into an '*essaim*' or a 'swarm', indicating a series of flights from the one to the multiple, the universal or exceptional to the indefinite or incomplete and the concept of foreclosure to the *pas tout* or not all that for Marie-Hélène Brousse delineates the path to ordinary psychosis.[11]

In *Anti-Oedipus*, Deleuze and Guattari both diagnose and embrace this simultaneously clinical and political development. The book owes its origin to Guattari's suggestion that a correlation can be made between capitalism and schizophrenia. The initial assumption of course is that capitalism cannot accommodate the schizophrenic, thereby turning him or her into an extraordinary exception. In this work, in an echo of Freud's *Civilization and Its Discontents*, capitalism is seen as the great producer of schizophrenic energies and flows, 'against which it brings all its vast powers of repression to bear'[12] producing as its limit, symptom and excess, schizophrenics. Capitalism 'continually draws near to its limit, which is a genuinely schizophrenic limit . . . schizophrenia is our characteristic malady, the malady of our era'.[13] For Deleuze and Guattari, the schizophrenic is the anomaly whose function is to trace a line of flight at the limit of capitalism. As such he or she 'is identical to neither health nor illness' but lies at the 'frontier' between one territory and another, the possible gateway to a deterritorialisation of both capitalism and schizophrenia that, for Deleuze at least, gives it the quality of a 'Thing or Entity of terror'.[14]

If there is a personification – or rather *conceptual persona* – of the relation between Deleuze and Guattari, the odd couple that was also a 'crowd',[15] then it is the schizophrenic, a point of conjunction between them that also describes a '*ligne de fuite*' that defined their writing relationship. Deleuze's fascination with and fear of schizophrenics predates his relationship with Guattari, indeed that relationship might even be regarded as an effect of the former's fascinated horror. Given Guattari's work at *La Borde*, a clinic for schizophrenics, it would not be surprising to find that Deleuze had personal contact with actual schizophrenics. But Deleuze and Guattari worked mostly by correspondence and Deleuze apparently avoided all contact with the inmates, as François Dosse recounts in an anecdote related by Jean-Pierre Muyard from his book *Intersecting Lives*. According to Muyard, Deleuze said, '"I discuss psychosis and madness, but I don't know anything about it from the inside." But he was also phobic about deranged people and couldn't have spent even an hour at La Borde.'[16] This testimony is supported by Alain Aptekman, a friend of Guattari's, who reports Deleuze saying to him "'How can you stand those schizos?' He couldn't bear the sight of crazy people.'[17]

In this chapter I am not primarily concerned with how Deleuze and Guattari both anticipated and perhaps precipitated the changes registered in the contemporary Lacanian clinic that finds a non-extraordinary, non-exceptional form of psychosis immanent to capitalism. Rather, I propose to look at the function of phobia in Deleuze that both enables his discourse and yet prevents him from becoming 'Deleuzian'. In what follows I hope to walk the line of the 'and' that articulates psychoanalysis with schizoanalysis through pursuing the path of *phobos* in the form of Deleuze's phobias for schizophrenics and milk products, as disclosed by his biographer François Dosse. I will look particularly at how Deleuze's concepts of the 'line of flight' and 'becoming' find definition in a creative rethinking of Lacan's understanding of phobia, transforming his own symptoms into a *sinthome* that links a fear of milk to the figure of the schizophrenic thereby offering a 'nonsensical' yet effective way of understanding the dynamic genesis and development of his philosophy, particularly the logic of sense. The latter, with its articulation of thought and the body, speech and eating, anticipates the *parlêtre*, the new name for the unconscious in the Lacanian clinic. Engaging the *parlêtre*, the being riven by speech, reorients interpretation away from the endless elucidation of the symptom toward an 'act of saying' 'that targets the speaking body and does so in order to produce an event', a *jouissance*-effect.[18] In so doing I posit a 'gnomonology' in which the light shed by a phobic object opens a different perspective from the real that can generate the truth of a variation in relation to a site of nonsensical *jouissance*, a block of affect or 'sinthome' that resists interpretation absolutely.

In *The Logic of Sense* Deleuze uses the figure of the schizophrenic (particularly Antonin Artaud and Louis Wolfson) to discuss the relation between sense and nonsense, the surface that separates and organises articulate speech from the corporeal sounds of the body and the schizophrenic production of a 'body without organs' that might provide the basis for the reconfiguration of that surface. I want to suggest that it is with the phobic object, here the schizophrenic, that Deleuze makes his own philosophical 'speech' out of the body, and that it is through the relation of affect to the schizophrenic that this 'speech' can be 'attributed to states of [his] life'.[19] While it would not be controversial to suggest that the figure of the schizophrenic provides a point of crystallisation for the entirety of Deleuze's *oeuvre*, my contention is twofold. On the one hand, it is through a relation of phobic affect that this *oeuvre* can be seen as the result of a becoming-schizophrenic that is precipitated along the line of flight that borders the production of phobias and (philosophical) creativity that has given rise to the proliferating discourse of the Deleuzians. On the other hand, Deleuze was the nomad who did not move, who stayed in the same place and evaded the over-codification of his cultural and academic reception.[20] There is something phobic in Deleuze that enables him to produce an object that clasps at the real that does not become and which saves him from the destiny of *les non-dupes errent*, those who imagine they have gone beyond language and have access to a truth outside discourse.[21]

The method for exploring this link between phobia and philosophical creativity follows Deleuze's own method of connecting incorporeal events of speech to bodily states of life disclosed in the correlation of selected anecdotes with various philosophical images, statements and propositions in Deleuze's own writing and with Guattari. Thus, it is not a question here of referring to specific events in the life of the author in order to tie the meaning of the work to a particular authorial intention, conscious or unconscious. Nor is it a question of effacing the author in the free play of textuality that offers numerous possibilities to mobilise the proper name in order to authorise the use of the work for one's own purposes – for example, the use of the signifier 'rhizome' in an ideology of Internet capitalism, or the characterisation of marketing strategies in terms of the communication of affective intensities, or indeed to perversely turn Deleuze into a variant of Hegel.[22] No doubt all this can be done, and textual justification found. Rather, it is a question of showing how 'event-effects [that] do not exist outside of the propositions which express them' are prolonged 'in the duality of things and propositions, of bodies and language'.[23] In their prolongation, in the non-sensical opacity that remains in the sense that flickers on the surface of nonsense, the fragments of a work can be regarded as types of 'sinthome' that pin the *jouissance* event of a *parlêtre* to a proper name, and indicate the site of its truth at the boundary between the symbolic and the real.

Zoophobia

In *A Thousand Plateaus*, Deleuze and Guattari conceive a way of thinking 'the great continuity of nature and culture' that breaks with biological and social science models.[24] Instead of defining the relationships between animals, and animals and humans, in evolutionist terms of genealogy, kinship or filiation, or of organising resemblances and differences in series and structures, Deleuze and Guattari consider relations of affect that they call 'becomings' or 'becomings-animal'. While they do not appear to endorse the term 'phobia' since it is nowhere mentioned in the chapter, it is evident that a phobic relation to an animal can provide an affect worthy of a becoming since Little Hans, who provides the primary case study in the Freudian clinic of phobia, is one of their main examples, along with Captain Ahab and Moby Dick, and Willard and his Rat from the film *Willard* (1972, Daniel Mann). However, Deleuze and Guattari reject what they see as Freud's domestication of Hans's fearful relation to horses – 'Freud sees nothing but the father in the becoming-horse of Hans' – arguing instead that the horse mediates Hans's relation to the outside, to the 'street that was forbidden to him'.[25] 'Little Hans's horse is not representative but affective' and that phobic affect is the product of the conjunction of two assemblages, one in which the horse is the main individuated figure of the assemblage 'draft horse-omnibus-street' and the other, Hans-assemblage, that includes 'his mother's bed, the paternal element, the house, the cafe, the street . . .', and so on.[26] Deleuze and Guattari recognise that this conjunction is a problem for Hans, but offer implicitly an interesting solution to the blockage conventionally understood to be represented by a phobic object. The solution would be found in the discovery, through the very relation of affect, of 'an as yet unknown assemblage that would be neither Hans's nor the horse's, but that of the becoming-horse of Hans'.[27] Such a solution would arise from an exchange of attributes and affects that might construct a different assemblage in which 'the horse would bare its teeth and Hans might show something else, his feet, his legs, his pee-pee maker, whatever?'[28] Becoming-horse therefore has nothing to do with identifying with a horse or imitating one, but with the power of its affect in producing assemblages. Similarly, as we shall see, Deleuze's phobia for schizophrenics provides the affect necessary for becoming-schizophrenic. This certainly does not imply identification and even less an imitation but the production of a schizophrenic-spider-milk-cheese-worm assemblage that is given consistency by the power of phobic affect. The other consistent aspect is of course that 'all becomings begin with and pass through becoming-woman. It is the key to all becomings.'[29] This is not the 'molar' woman, however, who is defined by her form and assigned as a subject. It is not woman as signifier. It is rather a molecularised woman whose primary affect, I will suggest following Lacan, is in the decomposed *lalangue* of her voice (and especially her tongue) out of which all forms of differentiation, all signifying and a-signifying practice derive.[30]

In his own image for conceiving of the continuity between nature and culture, Lacan lights upon a figure conventionally characterised as feminine, the spider. In the 'textual work' that emerges from her body, one can see the web-traces of a kind of writing taking form 'in which one can grasp the limits, impasses, and dead ends that show the real acceding to the symbolic'.[31] Writing for Lacan is a mode of becoming-spider – as indeed it was for Deleuze, in a slightly different way. Deleuze memorably concludes *Proust and Signs*, his book on the famously agoraphobic author, by characterising the narrator of *In Search of Lost Time* as a spider. 'The *Search*' he writes, 'is not constructed like a cathedral or like a gown, but like a web.'[32] This web is continuous with the narrator's body which we may also suggest is continuous with the author's persona who crystallises a certain block of affects and percepts – a fictional version of the person who is shaped out of various syntheses of perception, recollection and habit that ground consciousness and self-knowledge in states of fear, desire and auto-affection. Proust's spider-narrator is pre-eminently a power of sensation. It perceives through feeling, and since it is blind, sees through touch, sensing and deploying its characters and objects in its web, making 'them so many marionettes of his own delirium, so many intensive powers of his organless body, so many profiles of his own madness'.[33] While it makes sense to call the narrator of *The Search for Lost Time* a spider, the most common phobic object, it is curious to then transform that into a schizophrenic. As we know from *Anti-Oedipus*, schizophrenics have an enthusiasm for the outdoors, foregoing the couch in favour of a bracing walk in the fresh air. And yet Proust is the agoraphobic author par excellence. Yet the spider-narrator, who remained enclosed for years in his cork-lined bedroom, is called 'a universal schizophrenic' by the philosopher with a phobia for schizophrenics. Moreover, to make a universal out of a schizophrenic would run counter to schizophrenic thought, unless that is, it were to function like an object of phobia in an unsteady attempt to organise a field of multiple fears.

In *What is Philosophy?* Deleuze and Guattari invoke similar figures that are central to the powers of creation in thought and art, philosophy, film and fiction. In this book a distinction is made between the conceptual persona that crystallises the power of the concepts of a particular philosophy, and the 'one great figure' in aesthetics or literature (a kind of perceptual persona) that embodies an intensive block of affections and perceptions such that a whole system is organised around it, 'like the single sun of a constellation of a universe'.[34] Notable examples of the former are 'the Friend' (from philosophy in its Greek origin), 'the Idiot' (Descartes) and 'Dionysus' (Nietzsche). From the latter are characters like Captain Ahab and Bartleby (Melville), Homburg or Penthesilea (Kleist). The schizophrenic of Deleuze and Deleuze and Guattari operates interestingly in both registers. He is the 'great figure' that sits at the centre of Proust's universe just he is the Stoic philosopher and the excess of capitalism. The schizophrenic crystallises a particular concept that is also attributed with the power of affect like a percept that can accede to the virtual dimension of things. In their articulation of thought and affect these figures correspond to the function that Deleuze in *The Logic of Sense* gives to the anecdote. 'We must reach a secret point where the anecdote of life and the aphorism of thought amount to one and the same thing', he writes, 'it is like sense which, on one of its sides, is attributed to states of life and, on the other, inheres in propositions of thought'.[35]

Is it possible to light upon an anecdote from Deleuze's life that would provide the minimal narrative necessary to disclose the 'secret point' where life connects to thought in an example of the moment when, as Deleuze and Guattari suggest in *What is Philosophy?*, 'philosophers themselves become something unexpected and take on a tragic and comic dimension that they could not have by themselves'?[36]

Lactophobia

There is one other anecdote concerning Deleuze's phobias in Dosse's book. Perhaps significantly this anecdote locates Deleuze in an appropriately Proustian setting, in bed in his room confined by the suffocating presence of his mother. The anecdote derives from Olivier Revault d'Allones, a close student friend of Deleuze from his days at the Sorbonne:

> Deleuze was recovering from a violent asthma attack and was unable to get out of bed. 'We went to see him and as I recall, it was like visiting Marcel Proust in his bedroom with his mother, a little pink lamp, and Gilles, who was having trouble breathing.' Deleuze wanted to escape the confines of this world and passing the aggregation [. . .] made it possible for him to become financially independent. The vestiges of his conflicted family relationships manifested in a phobia of all milk products, which surprised his friends. 'We often invited Gilles to dinner. He always asked the hostess if there was any milk in the dish and if there was he couldn't eat it.'[37]

Given the significance of milk as an object of struggle in the child's anxious relationship with its mother, as a point of linkage and separation, nourishment and frustration, its emergence as an object of phobia would seem to be straightforward. As the work of Melanie Klein contends,[38] phobias are related to infant persecutory anxieties concerning the devouring, poisoning breast. At the end of the anecdote this is repeated in Deleuze marking a clear boundary between himself and the feminine hospitality he is offered when invited to dinner. The main part of the anecdote finds Deleuze confined to his bed because of asthma, and indeed Deleuze was to suffer from respiratory illnesses for the rest of his life. Here the feeling of suffocation is associated with a claustrophobic sense of confinement and, moreover, 'the confines of this world'. Escape from illness, suffocation, the pink lamp of maternal proximity, requires passing the aggregation in order to enter into another world of thought which of course means, supremely, philosophy: thought, in all its power and clarity, the creation of concepts that arises alongside the creation of phobias. As a figure for mental illness or incapacity, the schizophrenic is well suited, given this context, to be an object of fear or flight for Deleuze. This flight is enabled only in relation to the schizophrenic which is not itself at all a figure of liberation but a reminder of incapacity and confinement, the sort of confinement perhaps represented symbolically by La Borde, a place Deleuze failed to visit in spite of his close collaboration with Guattari. Indeed, lines of flight for Deleuze are established in conditions of claustrophobic confinement. As we know, 'to flee is not exactly to travel, or even to move'; nomads, as Deleuze liked to emphasise, never actually go anywhere, flight can be a paradoxical form of 'motionless travel'.[39]

To reiterate, the point here is not to suggest a clinical assessment of Deleuze on the basis of a few anecdotes, but to use the framework of phobia as part of the method Deleuze himself uses in *The Logic of Sense* of connecting, 'states of life' with 'propositions of thought'. This is the central opposition that organises Deleuze's book in its attempt to discern the logic and genesis of sense. Deleuze finds that it was the Cynics and the Stoics who first located the dimension of sense in this distinction between 'corporeal mixtures' and the 'incorporeal' events of thought that makes them the schizophrenic philosophers par excellence. Deleuze's anecdotal examples come from Diogenes Laertius and his tales of Diogenes of Sinope and Chrysippus the Stoic. Deleuze is most taken with anecdotes that for him designate the lawless (and senseless) depth of bodies in which 'everything is mixture': 'the philosopher eats with great gluttony, he stuffs himself; he masturbates in public, regretting that his hunger cannot be so easily relieved; he does not condemn incest with the mother, the sister, or the daughter; he tolerates cannibalism and anthropophagy', even though he can also be 'sober and chaste'.[40] In his selection of this and other anecdotes Deleuze brings together elements that will recur frequently in *The Logic of Sense* and elements that constitute an assemblage that is organised by a relation of affect: eating, masturbating (the production of a white substance like milk), incest – the proximity of feminine *jouissance* – cannibalism, that describes a locus of horror and fear that underlies the logic of sense as its condition, but also its redoubling into a block of nonsensical phobic excess.

It is of course in a reading of Lewis Carroll that Deleuze elaborates this logic that first has to confront the horrible dimension of corporeal mixtures characterised by eating, orality, cannibalism, incestuous combat, and indeed phobias:

> In Lewis Carroll, everything begins with a horrible combat, the combat of depths: things explode or make us explode, boxes are too small for their contents, foods are toxic and poisonous, entrails are stretched, monsters grab at us. A little brother uses his little brother as bait. Bodies intermingle with one

another, everything is mixed up in a kind of cannibalism that joins together food and excrement. Even words are eaten [. . .] Everything in depth is horrible, everything is nonsense.[41]

Claustrophobia and cibophobia (fear of food) are suggested here, constricting boxes and toxic foods marking the threshold of sense and nonsense, 'exactly [like] the boundary between propositions and things'.[42] The phobic objects do not in themselves make any sense, but are extracted from the *parlêtre*, from its body, to function like the gnomon that indicates the site of the truth of its *jouissance*. This intensive phobic boundary remained consistent and effective through Deleuze's life and *oeuvre*. Towards the end of his life in a set of interviews with Claire Parnet collected under the title *L'abécédaire*, Deleuze reflected on his conflicted relationship to food. Eating alone is an abomination, he remarks, mentioning particularly his disgust for milk products: 'The taste for cheese is a little like cannibalism, a total horror.'[43]

'The being of the *parlêtre* does not come from speech.' On the contrary, argues Jacques-Alain Miller, 'speech attributes being to this animal through a retroactive effect, and from that point on the body separates off from being in order to pass over to the register of having'.[44] The body that one *has* rather than *is* becomes hollowed out like a sack or a box too small for its contents, spilling out objects of toxic jouissance . . . spat out of the mouth, excreted out of the anus. In order for the mouth to speak, suggests Deleuze – and indeed for thought to emerge at all in the form of ideational attributes and incorporeal events – the mouth has to forgo food, the body has to stop eating, even fast. This disjunctive correlation between eating and speaking that remains consistent throughout Deleuze's *oeuvre* reaches an apparently obsessional peak in the 1970s, where it becomes the basis for his reading of Louis Wolfson, Kafka and even his tribute to the anorexic elegance of his wife in *Dialogues* with Claire Parnet:

> Rich or poor each language always implies a deterritorialization of the mouth, the tongue, and the teeth. The mouth, tongue, and teeth find their primitive territoriality in food. In giving themselves over to the articulation of sounds, the mouth, the tongue, and teeth deterritorialize. Thus there is a certain disjunction between eating and speaking, and even more, despite all appearances, between eating and writing. [. . .] To speak, and above all to write, is to fast.[45]

While there is an essential disjunction between eating and thought, eating and writing, the former is over-coded by a 'dietary regime' in which writing (in the case of Kafka) or elegance and fashion (in the case of the anorexic) attenuates eating in a strict ascetic practice of fasting.[46] This signifying regime is however predicated upon a fundamental phobia:

'(the anorexic thinks that food is full of grubs and poisons, worms and bacteria, fundamentally bad, hence the need to select and extract particles from it, or to spit it back out). "I'm starving," she says, grabbing two "slimming yoghurts".'[47] Deleuze's phobia for milk products returns here in the shape of slimming yoghurts threatened with worms and bacteria, the characterisation of alimentary depths filled with threatening microparticles. The threat is overwhelmingly characterised here and elsewhere by the figure of the worm. Fear of the worm is something the anorexic shares with schizophrenics like Wolfson, afflicting even the body without organs. 'Schizophrenic ambivalence', writes Deleuze, means that one is 'never sure that the ideal fluids of an organism without parts does not carry parasitic worms, fragments of organs, solid food, and excremental residue'.[48] Schizophrenic ambivalence brings together both the fear of and for schizophrenics themselves along an alimentary plane filled with worms, objects of toxic *jouissance*.

Vermiphobia

When Deleuze discusses schizophrenia and the fear of worms in *The Logic of Sense* his usual reference to Antonin Artaud rapidly gives way to the extraordinary schizophrenic linguist, Louis Wolfson, someone to whom he devotes a separate essay in 1970 that he later revises for inclusion in *Essays Clinical and Critical*. Wolfson was the American author of *Le Schizo et les langues* (*The Schizophrenic and Language*) for whom the sound of the English language, his 'mother tongue', caused him physical pain – especially when spoken by his mother. Wolfson spent his time in New York blocking his ears and transforming English words and phrases into phonetic combinations of new phonemes and morphemes drawn from other languages, principally French, German, Russian and Hebrew, that nevertheless resembled English in sound and sense. Here again, as with the excursions on Kafka and anorexia, Wolfson's linguistic creativity is an effect of the disjunction between eating and speaking that is mapped onto a dietary regime itself predicated on a phobia that finds food forever infested with worms: 'the morsels of food, even under the ideal conditions of the packages' sterilization, contain larva, little worms, and eggs that have been made even more harmful by air pollution, "trichinas, tapeworms, earthworms, pinworms, ankylosi, flukes, little eels." He feels as much guilt eating as he does after hearing his mother speak English.'[49] Deleuze also highlights the element of claustrophobia in Wolfson's situation, writing his book while 'living in the cramped lower-middle-class apartment of his mother and stepfather'.[50] Enclosed within the cramped apartment, Wolfson would only touch food 'enclosed in boxes, but they nonetheless contain larvae and worms, especially when Wolfson tears open the boxes with his bare teeth'.[51] Deleuze shows that Wolfson does essentially the same with language as he does with food:

> [he] translates his mother tongue *at top speed* into a mixture of other languages – this way, not of leaving his mother tongue, since he retains its sense and sound, but of putting it to flight and deterritorializing it – is intimately connected to the anorexic flux of food, to the way he snatches particles from this flux, combines them at top speed and combines them with verbal particles snatched from his mother tongue.[52]

The examples of Wolfson, Kafka, the anorexic, Fanny Deleuze, all develop in very similar ways the process described in *The Logic of Sense* where the depths of a terrifying orality (and the mother's tongue) provide the dynamic genesis for the eventual production of surfaces: speech, expression, propositions, and so on, incorporeal events that emerge from bodily states. This then provides the basic pattern for the elaboration of concepts such as form and expression generally, the molecular and the molar, assemblages and strata, even smooth and striated space in *A Thousand Plateaus*. In Deleuze's philosophical culinarism we know that it is another dairy product that provides the surface essential to the genesis of these new forms. The body without organs (BwO) is an egg, a surface traversed by intensities that have yet to become organised or take shape as organs or strata. In *The Logic of Sense*, the body without organs is introduced to 'correct' Melanie Klein's own account of the resolution of the struggle with the maternal breast and its paranoid-schizoid division into good and bad parts. Rather than the triumph of a good object over bad objects, Deleuze argues that 'what is opposed is rather an organism without parts, a body without organs, with neither mouth nor anus, having given up all introjections and projection, and being complete, at this price'.[53] In Deleuze's take on Klein, the depressive position that emerges from the splitting of the breast into good and bad objects does not result from the introjection of the good object but from the mourning for its loss in the sense of a mourning for the feeling of wholeness that has been lost in the splitting itself that becomes congealed in the BwO that is replaced by the maternal voice. This is the sound from on high that becomes the superegoic point of identification through suturing 'the entire sonorous, *prevocal* system'.[54] What we see with Louis Wolfson, however, is that the maternal voice, 'very high and piercing and perhaps equally triumphant' has the potential to disintegrate like alimentary substances into their constituent particles, 'the intolerable maternal words and the poisonous or spoiled foods . . .'.[55] 'Against the lived body, its larvae and its eggs which constitute the sufferings of life', that are defined by the maternal voice and language, the 'cry of life', 'he has to unite every atomic combination in a total formula and periodic table, as a knowledge of the body or of molecular biology'.[56] One can never be sure that voice and the organless egg do not continue to harbour 'parasitic worms, fragments of organs, solid food, and excremental residue'.[57] Clearly, the affects, the block of *jouissance* associated with the vermiphobia, refer not to language but to the 'prevocal system' of '*lalangue*'. In Seminar XX, Lacan writes:

> Llanguage [*lalangue*] serves purposes that are altogether different from that of communication. That is what the experience of the unconscious has shown us, insofar as it is made of llanguage [*lalangue*], which as you know I write with two l's to designate what each of us deals with, our so-called mother tongue (*lalangue dite maternelle*), which isn't called that by accident.[58]

Worms are the pre-linguist sounds of words that slither in and out of the *parlêtre* of Deleuze's schizos boring holes in their flesh. Worms like words devitalise and cadaverise the body turning it into cheese-flesh. Cheese is the product of the decomposition and putrefaction of milk that perhaps paradoxically has nevertheless been seen for millennia in pre- or early modern religious, philosophical and folk texts as being a substance, a bulk of generative matter, from which organic forms spontaneously emerge. Leibniz uses the example to suggest that mass is the aggregate of corporeal substances, just as cheese was sometimes believed to consist of a concourse of worms.[59] Equally interesting is the cosmology, made famous by Carlo Ginzburg's micro-history, of Menocchio the sixteenth-century miller who was tried for heresy on the basis of his belief that the universe was created out of churning chaos, just as cheese is formed out of curdled milk. And out of this cheese grew worms that became men, angels and even God himself:[60]

> I have said that in my opinion all was chaos [. . .] and out that bulk a mass formed – just as cheese is made out of milk – and worms appeared in it, and these were the angels, and there was also God, he too having been created out of that mass at the same time . . .[61]

In the strange tradition represented by Menocchio, worms emerge from the cheese that they are sometimes assumed to constitute. The word becomes flesh as the real seeks a signifier in the form of worms that consume it. Colette Soler suggests that '*lalangue*' provides the substance of the 'real unconscious' as opposed to the one structured like a language. '*Lalangue* is not Symbolic but Real. Real, because it is made of ones outside the chain and thus outside meaning (the signifier becomes real when it is outside the chain), and of ones which are enigmatically fused with *jouissance*.'[62]

Products of the real seeking a signifier, words, even the Word of God are for Deleuze's schizophrenic worms that '*essaim*', that swarm in corpses, consuming the dead flesh from which they are formed. Apparently without filiation or heredity, spreading as if through contagion, epidemic and warfare, worms are always a multiplicity and thereby exemplary of the kinds of animals that are vectors of becoming. But there is no 'becoming-worm' in Deleuze and Guattari. This is because, it seems, they lie at the other side of the boundary between fear and flight. It is from the worms that the schizo-anorexics Louis Wolfson and Fanny Deleuze have to extract the alimentary particles that no longer act as formed nutritional substances, worms that remain with them as the affect that provides consistency to the flight of language.[63] Worms are thus integral to Deleuze's culinary cibophobia as the site of its real *jouissance*, impossible objects outside of and prior to relations of becoming. They are sounds materialised as slithery worm-tongue-letters, multiple 'ones' outside the chain that are remnants of maternal voice. In their metaphorical worminess they can be seen to function in the schizophrenic, and perhaps also in Deleuze, as the *noms du père* by which one allows oneself to be duped. Single figure of a writhing multiplicity, the worm is the gnomon that points to the real that does not become, the real beyond the swarm, that arrests the slippage by which discourse is displaced by the number that in ordinary psychosis gives a real value to the semblant.[64]

Melancholia

The schizophrenic seems to disappear from Deleuze's writing after the publication of *Milles Plateaux* in 1980. Deleuze works on his cinema books and returns to his reworking of philosophical *oeuvres*, Foucault and Leibniz in this case in relation to the figure of 'the fold'. In his revision of the essay on Louis Wolfson that Deleuze produced for *Essays Clinical and Critical* in 1986, Deleuze makes the rather strange and amusing suggestion that because Wolfson used to wander around in his madness wearing a stethoscope attached to a tape recorder he anticipated the invention of the Sony Walkman. 'A makeshift schizophrenic object lies at the origin of an apparatus that is now spread over the entire universe, and that will in turn schizophrenize entire peoples and generations.'[65] Here Deleuze anticipates the generalisation of psychosis as an effect of new audio technology. Oddly enough, in an essay from 1982 on Pink Floyd's song 'Brain Damage' from *The Dark Side of the Moon*, Friedrich Kittler had already made a similar point. Advances in the technologies of sound reproduction, he suggests, culminate in the collapse of the distance necessary for aesthetic appreciation, the distance separating subject and object, listener, song and performer since everything takes place inside the listener's head: 'the explosion of acoustic media flips over into an implosion which crashes with headlong immediacy into the very centre of perception'.[66]

While Deleuze's schizophrenics may not like worms, they do indeed like machines. The schizophrenic, as Deleuze writes, 'lives in machines, alongside machines, or the machines are in him, in her'.[67] As digital machines began to reconfigure the entire field of the socius, becoming ever more ubiquitous, miniaturised and invasive, psychosis has become in this way everyone's normal state. The networked new technologies are, like a schizophrenic spider, both invasive and exteriorising. For Colette Soler, 'the symptoms that we call new, which affect orality, action and mood, are almost all symptoms outside the social bond, bearers of an autistic jouissance'.[68] This 'autistic jouissance' is partly the paradoxical effect of the networked existence produced by the twenty-first-century regime of telecommunications in which to use the title of Sherry Turkle's book, we are 'alone together'.[69]

The schizophrenic is mentioned very briefly at the end of the 1980s in *What is Philosophy?*, divided between the schizophrenic as a conceptual persona who enables thought and the schizophrenic as 'a psychosocial type who represses the living being and robs him of his thought. Sometimes the two are combined, clasped together as if an event that is too intense corresponds to a lived condition that is too hard to bear'.[70] This unbearable proximity suggests the kind of psychotic melancholia that Russell Grigg claims is increasingly found in the contemporary clinic of psychoanalysis, a melancholia that is not, as with Freud, an effect of the irreparable loss of an object, but on the contrary of a failure to separate from an object that is experienced as invasive and ravaging.[71]

Depression was something that concerned Deleuze and Guattari throughout the 1980s, up to the end of their lives in 1995 and 1992 respectively. In an essay entitled 'How to Heal a Depression', Bifo Berardi suggests that Deleuze and Guattari, while never explicitly using the word, regarded depression as 'the deactivation of desire' in the face of the chaotic, over-stimulation of the 'semiosphere'.[72] By which he means the 'acceleration of the surrounding world of signs, symbols and info-stimulation [that] is producing panic'. In his own view, Berardi argues that the 'epidemic of depression' 'has to be seen as a consequence of the new economy', that is to say, neoliberalism accelerated by new digital technology.[73]

Whatever the cause, Guattari himself became severely depressed, even 'catatonic, sitting with a pillow pressed to his stomach as if to protect himself from the outside world, watching television programmes for days on end'.[74] While they did little work together Deleuze, according to

Dosse, 'remained present' during the dark years of the late 1980s. Almost the final image of the couple in Dosse's book is of Guattari 'completely sacerdotal, sitting on the floor' watching the European Cup final on television. 'And there was Gilles sitting next to him. He would have probably given his right arm not to be at that party watching soccer on TV since, for him, two people were already a crowd.'[75] The anecdote describes two images of the line of flight that marks the point of conjunction and separation between the two men: the line of telecommunications that turns the spectacle of sport into a worldwide commodity and the line of the 'and' linking Guattari and Deleuze upon which, in spite of his apparent discomfort in his commitment to the suffering of his friend, the latter remains.[76]

Notes

1. Deleuze, Gilles and Parnet, Claire, *Dialogues II* (London: Continuum, 2002), p. 42.
2. Lacan, Jacques, *Écrits* (London and New York: W. W. Norton, 2006), p. 745.
3. Massumi, Brian, 'Notes on the Translation and Acknowledgments', in Deleuze, Gilles and Guattari, Félix, *A Thousand Plateaus* (London: The Athlone Press, 1988), p. xvi.
4. Deleuze, Gilles, *Negotiations, 1972–1990* (New York: Columbia University Press, 1995), p. 45.
5. Lacan, Jacques, *The Seminar of Jacques Lacan, Book XX: Encore* (London and New York: W. W. Norton, 1999), p. 94.
6. On Guattari's 'resentment' about being 'overcoded' by Deleuze in the writing of *Anti-Oedipus* and his 'bitterness' at being forgotten in favour of Deleuze as he was increasingly written out of the authorship of the joint works by critics who want to 'de-Guattarize' Deleuze, see Dosse, François, *Gilles Deleuze and Félix Guattari: Intersecting Lives* (New York: Columbia University Press, 2011), pp. 12, 428.
7. Lacan, *Écrits*, p. 432.
8. Lacan, Jacques, *The Seminar of Jacques Lacan, Book III: The Psychoses* (London: Routledge, 1993), p. 267.
9. Lacan, Jacques, *On the Names-of-the-Father*, trans. Bruce Fink (Cambridge: Polity Press, 2013), p. 74.
10. Lacan links the pluralisation of the names of the father to psychosis in *On-the Names-of-the-Father*, p. 56.
11. Brousse, Marie-Hélène, 'Ordinary Psychosis in the Light of Lacan's Theory of Discourse', in *Psychoanalytical Notebooks* (special issue: 'Ordinary Psychoses', Wülfing, Nathalie (ed.)), 19 (2009), pp. 7–20.
12. Deleuze, Gilles and Guattari, Félix, *Anti-Oedipus: Capitalism and Schizophrenia* (London: The Athlone Press, 1983), p. 34.
13. Ibid. p. 34.
14. Deleuze and Parnet, *Dialogues*, p. 42.
15. The first line of *A Thousand Plateaus* states: 'Two of us wrote *Anti-Oedipus* together. Since each of us was several, there was already quite a crowd' (Deleuze and Guattari, *A Thousand Plateaus*, p. 3). This is a heavily ironic opening since Deleuze had a great dislike of crowds and indeed it was one of the fundamental rules of their working relationship that Guattari respect Deleuze's 'solitude' and that he would not have any interference from Guattari's 'groups' (see Dosse, *Intersecting Lives*, p. 16).

16. Dosse, *Intersecting Lives*, p. 2. Muyard is a significant figure in the relationship between Deleuze and Guattari, having introduced them to each other and provided a point of mediation in the initial correspondence that became *Anti-Oedipus*.

17. Ibid. p. 8.

18. Miller, Jacques-Alain, 'The Unconscious and the Speaking Body', 10th Congress of the World Association of Psychoanalysis, available at <http://www.wapol.org/en/articulos/Template.asp> (last accessed 31 March 2016).

19. Deleuze, Gilles, *The Logic of Sense* (London: The Athlone Press, 1990), p. 128.

20. Deleuze, Gilles, 'Nomad Thought', in Allison, David B. (ed.), *The New Nietzsche* (Cambridge, MA: MIT Press, 1985), pp. 142–9, 149.

21. Lacan, Jacques, *Le séminaire de Jacques Lacan, livre XXI: Les non-dupes errent* (unpublished typescript, 1973–4).

22. See Žižek, Slavoj, *Organs without Bodies: On Deleuze and Consequences* (London: Routledge, 2004), pp. xii, 183. Žižek does the same thing with Lacan, of course.

23. Deleuze, *The Logic of Sense*, p. 23.

24. Deleuze and Guattari, *A Thousand Plateaus* (London: The Athlone Press, 1988), p. 234.

25. Ibid. p. 259.

26. Ibid. pp. 257–8.

27. Ibid. pp. 258.

28. It should be noted that for Lacan also, the horse is not a representation of Hans's father, but is rather an imaginary object that functions like a nonsensical signifier that signifies variously depending on the combinations (or 'assemblages') that Hans creates in his attempt to organise his symbolic reality. Far from being a negative phenomenon, for Lacan the object enables Hans (with the help of Freud) to develop 'all possible permutations of a limited number of signifiers in the form of a myth, around the signifying crystal of his phobia'. For Lacan the solution to the phobic blockage or 'problem' is to be found precisely in working-through or 'exhausting all possible forms of the impossibilities that are encountered when the solution is put into the form of a signifying equation' (Lacan, *Écrits*, p. 432).

29. Deleuze and Guattari, *A Thousand Plateaus*, p. 277.

30. Lacan, *Encore*, p. 138.

31. Ibid. p. 93.

32. Deleuze, Gilles, *Proust and Signs* (London: Continuum, 2008), p. 117.

33. Ibid. p. 182.

34. Deleuze, Gilles and Guattari, Félix, *What is Philosophy?* (London: Verso, 1994), p. 65.

35. Deleuze, *The Logic of Sense*, p. 128.

36. Deleuze and Guattari, *What is Philosophy?*, p. 73.

37. Dosse, *Intersecting Lives*, p. 98.

38. 'The attitude to food is fundamentally bound up with the relation to the mother and involves the whole of the infant's emotional life. The experience of weaning stirs up the infant's deepest emotions and anxieties, and the more integrated ego develops strong defences against them; both anxieties and defences enter into the infant's attitudes towards food [. . .] at the root of many difficulties over new food is the persecutory fear of being devoured and poisoned by the mother's bad breast, a fear which derives from the infant's phantasies of devouring and poisoning the breast' (Klein, Melanie, *Developments in Psychoanalysis* (London: Karnac Books, 2002), p. 254).

39. Deleuze and Parnet, *Dialogues II*, p. 37.

40. Deleuze, *The Logic of Sense*, p. 130.

41. Deleuze, Gilles, *Essays Critical and Clinical* (London: Verso, 1998), p. 21.

42. Ibid. p. 22.

43. Deleuze, Gilles, 'M for Malady', in Boutang, Pierre-André and Pamart, Michel (dir.), *L'abécédaire de Gilles Deleuze* (La Femis Sodaperaga Productions, 1996).

44. Miller, 'The Unconscious and the Speaking Body'.

45. Deleuze, Gilles and Guattari, Félix, *Kafka: Toward a Minor Literature* (Minneapolis and London: University of Minnesota Press, 1986), pp. 19–21.
46. Deleuze and Parnet, *Dialogues II*, p. 112.
47. Ibid. pp. 110–11.
48. Deleuze, *The Logic of Sense*, p. 42.
49. Deleuze, *Essays Critical and Clinical*, p. 13.
50. Ibid. p. 15.
51. Ibid. p. 13.
52. Ibid. p. 17.
53. Deleuze, *The Logic of Sense*, p. 188.
54. Ibid. p. 195.
55. Deleuze, *Essays Critical and Clinical*, p. 12.
56. Ibid. p. 14.
57. Deleuze, *The Logic of Sense*, p. 88
58. Lacan, *Encore*, p. 138.
59. See, for example, Seager, William, 'The Worm in the Cheese: Leibniz, Consciousness, and Matter', *Studia Leibnitiana*, 23 (1991), pp. 79–91.
60. See Ginzburg, Carlo, *The Cheese and the Worms: The Cosmos of a Sixteenth-Century Miller* (Abingdon: Routledge, 1980).
61. Ibid. p. 26.
62. Soler, Colette, *Lacan Reinvented – The Real Unconscious* (London: Karnac Books, 2014), p. 35.
63. Deleuze and Parnet, *Dialogues II*, p. 117.
64. See Brousse, 'Ordinary Psychosis', p. 15.
65. Deleuze, *Essays Clinical and Critical*, p. 13.
66. Kittler, Friedrich, 'England 1975 – Pink Floyd, Brain Damage', in Lindeman, Klaus (ed.), *Europalyrik 1775-heute. Gedichte und Interpretationen* (Paderborn: Schöningh, 1982), pp. 467–77.
67. Deleuze, Gilles, *Two Regimes of Madness: Texts and Interviews 1975–1995* (New York: Semiotext(e), 2006), p. 17.
68. Soler, *Lacan Reinvented*, p. 183.
69. Turkle, Sherry, *Alone Together* (New York: Basic Books, 2010).
70. Deleuze and Guattari, *What is Philosophy?*, p. 70.
71. Grigg, Russell, 'Why Freud's Theory of Melancholia is All Wrong', lecture delivered at Kingston University, 26 November 2014, available at <http://backdoorbroadcasting.net/2014/11/russell-grigg-why-freuds-theory-of-melancholia-is-all-wrong/> (last accessed 31 March 2016).
72. Berardi 'Bifo', Franco, 'How to Heal a Depression?', available at <http://www.16beavergroup.org/bifo/bifo-how-to-heal-a-depression.pdf> (last accessed 31 March 2016).
73. Berardi 'Bifo', Franco, *After the Future* (Edinburgh: AK Press, 2011), p. 53.
74. Dosse, *Intersecting Lives*, p. 425.
75. Ibid. p. 17.
76. No date is given for the year of this anecdote apart from the suggestion that it occurred in the late 1980s. It is possible that rather than being sunk in a catatonic stupor or desperate to get away, Deleuze and Guattari were both gripped by the remarkable European Cup final of 1989 in which the great Milan team that included Ruud Gullit and Marco van Basten beat Steaua Bucureşti 4–0, both players scoring two goals. The spectacle would have also offered a mirror to the solidarity between the two French philosophers. At the Nou Camp Stadium in Barcelona where the final was held, the Milanese supporters sang 'You'll Never Walk Alone' in the moments before the kickoff in a remarkable and moving tribute to the 96 Liverpool supporters who had been killed at Hillsborough a month before in an FA Cup semi-final in England.

Chapter 5

Lacan, Deleuze and the Politics of the Face

Andreja Zevnik

In *Cinema 1* Deleuze perhaps most poignantly writes about the face. He states that: 'There are two sorts of questions, which we can put to a face [. . .]: what are you thinking about? Or what is bothering you, what is the matter with you, what do you sense or feel?'[1] The two questions suggest a somewhat curious expectation one inherently assumes when 'faced' with the face. It implies that the face actualises or hides a particular thought or that it expresses a range of feelings, emotions and thus testifies to the general state of the person. In other words, it materialises or acknowledges the presence of something that otherwise might have remained ungraspable. Maurice Merleau-Ponty captures this peculiar face-function well when he writes: 'if we make the thought appear in the infrastructure of vision, this is only in virtue of the uncontested evidence that one must see or feel in some way in order to think'.[2] Thus the face is bursting with meaning; but as I argue elsewhere, the particular meaning or face *function* depends on the scopic field in which the face is made to appear.[3] Making sense of the face has thus become a preoccupation of modern politics and, if the face is a face of the subject, making it appear beautiful a preoccupation of the cosmetics industry. Only when the face is placed within the discourses of visibility, can the knowledge about the subject a face is to represent be revealed. In the realm of the visible a face features as an image that is unique to the subject it belongs to. It is to reveal, expose, tell something about that subject, and it is a 'turn towards' the face that will enable this knowledge transmission.

Deleuze, however, aims to disturb such a comprehension of the face and with it macro and micro practices ordering it; his philosophy strives to rescue the face from the terror of signification and subjectivisation. He allocates agency in the face when he writes:

Sometimes the face thinks about something, is fixed on to an object, and this is the sense of admiration and astonishment that the English word *wonder* has preserved. In so far as it thinks about something, the face has value above all through its surrounding outline, its reflecting unity which raises all the parts to itself. Sometimes, on the contrary, it experiences or feels something, and has value through the intensive series that its parts successively traverse as far as paroxysm, each part taking on a kind of momentary independence.[4]

Deleuze suggests that the face thinks, yet the content of the thought is not in line with meaning production (knowledge), and cannot be placed in the order of things from which knowledge can be extrapolated. In the Lacanian sense, when the face thinks, its thought is not yet part of the signifying chain or language structures. What the *face thinks* is not what a turn to the face – through modes of projection – desires to see or know. Deleuze's fixation on the face as a displaced organ can be seen in his essays on Francis Bacon, in his discussions of the cinema and 'close-ups' or in his work on faciality with Félix Guattari. 'We need to dismantle the face', he writes as a response to Bacon's paintings, 'to rediscover the head or make it emerge from beneath the face.'[5] Or as he writes with Guattari in *A Thousand Plateaus*:

> *The face, what a horror*. It is naturally a lunar landscape, with its pores, planes, matts, bright colors, whiteness, and holes: there is no need for a close-up to make it inhuman; it is naturally a close-up, and naturally inhuman, a monstrous hood.[6]

Ultimately, what is the horror of the face that Deleuze aims to escape from? The face is a metaphor for the flattening and super-linearity of time and space, and faciality a machine for the social production of the face, which facialises – symbolises and orders – the entire body.[7] With de-facialisation and deterritorialisation Deleuze sought an escape from mechanisms of signification and subjectivisation. He does not abandon the face, but the face worth looking at is one of disproportionate dimensions: eyes, mouth, scream, tongue, skin; in the end a 'face' taken over by 'organs'. The dismantling of the face does away with the symbolic order and the linguistic structures, which make the face and the subject appear as whole and invested with knowledge. Breaking the face apart is a symbolic intervention into the system of signification and orders of meaning. 'The white wall of the signifier, the black hole of subjectivity, and the facial machine are impasses, the measures of our submissions and subjections; but we are born into them, and it is there that we must stand battle.'[8] Thus, as Deleuze states, the 'face is a politics and dismantling a face is also a politics involving real becomings, an entire becoming-clandestine'.[9]

Where does my interest in the *face* lie and why does it matter in the context of the discussions presented in this volume? In this chapter I aim to discuss Lacan's and Deleuze's attempts to break away from signification or from the image the face gives to the subject in the scopic realm and in the structure of language. Perhaps countering Deleuze's attack on Lacan for his alleged 'fixation' on the gaze, I aim to show that both thinkers have a similar endeavour in mind. While Deleuze might pursue the break away from sovereign discourses of signification and subjectivation with a turn to the body, Lacan in contrast maintains the tension internally, either in the form of a returned/anxious gaze or through linguistic form, which does away with meaning. The latter, as will be discussed at the very end, speaks to Lacan's 'reinvention' of the body and its appearance in the unconscious. As this is a rather complex discussion, which in essence concerns not only how the subject is produced, the effects it has, but also the basis of both thinkers' thoughts, the chapter proceeds in two ways. First I delve deeper into Deleuze's passing critique of Lacan's gaze by focusing on Lacan's conceptualisation of the gaze and how 'the subject' (or face) emerges. The image of Lacan's subject is anything but stable or complete, as Deleuze at least implicitly made it appear. Next I turn to Deleuze to further develop his notion of the face and the processes of deterritorialisation, as a *de-facing* strategy, which can lead to the abandonment of a facialised politics. And finally, I return to Lacan and with a discussion of the unconscious highlight three moments in his thought which counter Deleuze's critique and might bring the two thinkers closer together: the politics, the body and the unconscious. In doing so, the chapter aims to put in discussion the two thinkers and show how one perhaps less significant concept mobilises almost the entirety of their respective thoughts, and how despite differences and different terminology, the two are closer than they (or their respective schools of thought) made them appear.

From Deleuze's face to Lacan's (anxious) gaze

Deleuze and Guattari distance their discussions of the face from what they call phenomenological positions, the integration of part-objects or structural and structuring systems.[10] The signifier, the language and the logic of authority produces the face as a demarcated territorialised space, which by taking over the body produces the subject. Integral to the production of the *facialised subject* is the gaze. Lacan similarly takes the gaze as central to subject formation. To grasp the point of Deleuze and Guattari's critique of Lacan, it is worth referring to their observation on the gaze at length:

> In the literature on the face [. . .] Lacan's [text] on the mirror makes the
> error of appealing to a form of subjectivity or humanity reflected in a

phenomenological field or split in the structural field. The gaze is but secondary in relation to the gazeless eyes, to the black hole of faciality. The mirror is but secondary in relation to the white wall of faciality. [. . .] Any approach based on stages in ontogenesis is arbitrary: it is thought that what is fastest is primary, or even serves as a foundation or springboard for what comes next. An approach based on part-objects is even worse; it is the approach of a demented experimenter who flays, slices, and anatomizes everything in sight, and then proceeds to sew things randomly back together again. You can make any list of part-objects you want: hand, breast, mouth, eyes . . . It's still Frankenstein. What we need to consider is not fundamentally organs without bodies, or the fragmented body; it is the body without organs, animated by various intensive movements that determine the nature and emplacement of the organs in question and make that body an organism, or even a system of strata of which the organism is only a part.[11]

Deleuze and Guattari's critique is thus one which targets the meaning and the despotic, authoritarian signifying chains – white walls – and forms of subjectivisation (recognition) – black holes. For Deleuze it is the lack of meaning a non-signified face presents that Lacan aims to 'fill', order and assign to a signifying chain, and it is the gaze whose function enables this process of stratification. When faced with the face of the other, a desire to interpret and the illusion that there is something beneath or underneath the face, hidden from the eyes of the other, persists. Merleau-Ponty, for example, wrote: 'why is it that the other appears to me as full of meaning?'[12] This is a question Lacan concerned himself with. It is through the gaze/Other that the subject is constituted and placed in relations of meaning; and it is through the recognition of the Other that the subject comes to existence, finds its place, in the Symbolic order.[13] Acknowledging the phenomenological difference of the two projects, Deleuze's and Lacan's, the question concerning the desire of subjectivation and the Other remains worth asking. How does one derive to the point where the desire of the other institutes the subject and, moreover, is something that is sought? And is Lacan's theory of the gaze really incapable of a de-subjectifying move; is it as complete as Deleuze suggests?

In his theory of the mirror stage Lacan's attention is drawn to the role the face has in the formation of a visible space and further to its particular mode of identification.[14] A child sees the face of the mother as the first point of identification, a point of reassurance as well as a point in relation to which it begins to construct the image of its own body. At first a child sees itself as part of the other (who does not yet exist as (an)other), distinguishing the face of the mother, but never missing or mistaking it for (an)other; yet the image of child's own face (and of its independent existence) is still lacking. At first, thus, 'there is no gaze of the other in relation to which the self is produced' it is only the body of the (m)other.[15]

The eye of the other (or their face) creates the awareness of one's separate existence and of a particular invocation – birth – of one's body in social reality. That is to say, the subject is instituted in the visible on the premise that, 'I am looked at and thus I am a picture' or an image.[16] It is through the gaze, as Lacan further writes, 'that I enter light and it is from the gaze that I receive its effects. Hence it comes about that the gaze is the instrument through which light is embodied and through which . . . I am *photo-graphed*.'[17] Photography as an eye constitutes the appearance of the body as an effect of the other's gaze. Yet, as Lacan continues, it is the 'gaze that circumscribes us, and which in the first instance makes us beings who are looked at, but without showing this'.[18] That is, the presence, the photographed self, the estranged image of 'myself' is a representation of 'me', which while being 'me', escapes my control and is instead placed under the government of the other (or their gaze). A way in which the subject appears in the realm of the visible suggests that the subject is governed through its image: thus, the image of the subject is a product of the other's gaze and of the predominant way of seeing. As the subject is given its image (that is particular to that subject while also universal or shared as it is moulded on the rules of scopic representation or ways of seeing), it becomes part of a symbolic order and a productive element of the world surrounding it. As a function of the Other's gaze, the subject is located in a signifying order in the form of a face, while, internally, assigned a particular identity. It is this moment that Deleuze calls the white wall of signification and the black hole of subjectivation.

Yet the face, the image one 'received' or the 'subject' one became classifies, draws lines of exclusion and determines one's social reality. The spectator – the 'self' who is constructed in a particular image of the other (and by the other) – is faced with its own image, which appears as something that is external, foreign, estranged and in need of constant negotiation. 'Is this really me?' or 'Am I really what you say I am?' The other – which as Lacan says in Seminar XI is also a point of light – works as a figure of identification and recognition of one's existence and of the difference between the self and the other, which is no less displacing for the subject as it is for the other.

Lacan explained the particularities of the face supporting the process of identification through a story about Petit-Jean. Lacan recalls a conversation he had with Petit-Jean while on a boat:

> Petit-Jean pointed out to me something floating on the surface of the waves. It was a small can, a sardine can. [. . .] It glittered in the sun. And Petit-Jean said to me – *You see that can? Do you see it? Well, it doesn't see you!*[19]

Lacan was 'disturbed' by what at a quick glance is a rather banal statement. The reason for his discomfort concerns the conditions of one's existence

which can be grasped in two different ways. On the one hand, if the existence of one always depends on the existence or the gaze of the other, the
non-existence of the sardine can in the field of the visible in turn suggests
Lacan's own lack of existence, whereas, on the other hand, the can's blindness for Lacan suggests Lacan's own displacement in the social field and in
the signifying chain of that particular situation. Indeed, what was Lacan
doing on a fishing boat and not fishing? The gaze coming from the other
is not a conscious gaze, or as Lacan himself put it: 'the gaze I encounter
is not a seen gaze, but a gaze imagined by me in the field of the Other'.[20]
Thus if it is the point of light, the other's gaze that constitutes the subject,
it makes no difference who or what is at the other end of the 'gaze' (at the
point of light). The can in Lacan's story, like everything that looks at us,
was also looking at him from the point of light placing him in a particular
subject and knowledge position. Lacan further explains:

> That which is light looks at me, and by means of that light in the depths
> of my eye, something is painted [. . .] something that is an impression, the
> shimmering of a surface that is not, in advance, situated for me in its
> distance. [. . .] If I am anything in the picture, it is always in the form of
> the screen, which I earlier called the stain, the spot. This is the relation of
> the subject with the domain of vision.[21]

The stain is precisely the point at which, as Žižek writes, 'I encounter
myself [. . .] here I am inscribed in the picture'.[22] Thus the gaze of the
other is what makes one exist as an image in the scopic regime and what
attaches one to a particular identity.

Such identification with the external or the social image of the self –
or an imaginary alignment with the screen – is crucial for the subject's
participation in the everyday life. One needs to become an engaged actor
reproducing the fantasmatic social reality not for reasons of compliance
or resignation to the Other's image of the subject, but from the need to
understand the thresholds of social and cognitive fields, with a view to
manipulating and pushing their limits. When those limits of existence
and a place within the socio-political order are recognised, the subject,
to turn to Foucault's *oeuvre*, can test these limits, engage with and learn
about what one can do, and how one can transgress. In other words, one
has to 'see' what the other has made visible; one has to participate in
the gaze of the other to gain access to the despotic regimes of signification and subjectivation. Or as Silverman writes: 'The spectator constituted
through such an alignment seemingly looks from a vantage outside spectacle. Primary identification also implies a vision which is exterior to time
and the body, and which yields an immediate epistemological mastery.'[23]
Silverman points to the existence of the invisible, disembodied, timeless

and all-knowing vision, which governs the socio-political world creating the impression that there is only one way of seeing and representing. For as long as one does not lose sight of what one is for the other (a point of identification and a reference to knowledge), a certain epistemological mastery of the subject over the gaze and the image imposed on the subject can be maintained. Perhaps, to put it differently, the subject plays a game of (visual) frames which are on the one hand exposed but which, on the other hand, remain in place maintaining the existing regimes of visibility. The subject is thus always already a spectator and a witness, looking at and testifying to that which is taking place. The spectator is, as Hitchcock would say, a made-to-order witness whose gaze governs the gaze itself while it also always escapes from what Lacan would call 'a grasp of vision that is satisfied with itself in imagining itself as consciousness'.[24]

Thus the face of the other is both a producer and a product of someone else's gaze and of social ordering. The face creates, places and orders bodies and unconsciously recreates these scopic frames for the function of identification. There is no doubt that this at first appears as a stable relation between the self and the other, one Deleuze had in mind when critiquing the signifying orders of the face, and in particular pointing to Lacan's gaze facilitating the emplacement of these very orders. However, as already noted, the gaze does not institute a stable subject; quite the contrary, the subject is radically displaced, and if taken further, its existence only functions with the support of fantasies. This radical displacement introduces a moment of anxiety in the act of gazing.

What is a returned gaze that initiates anxiety? Anxiety evokes a feeling of unease where its object (or a referent) is left unclear. That is not to say that it does not exist, it does – as Lacan in *On Anxiety* emphasises – only that its form remains unknown. The object of anxiety is *objet petit a*, which disturbs the subject's social field. The anxious gaze, in turn, appears at the vanishing point of one's existence. But in contrast to the gaze discussed earlier, the anxious gaze is not someone else's gaze, it is not a gaze of the other or of someone looking at you like a sardine can in Lacan's example. Instead it is a gaze of the spectator, of the one looking: you, me, her. The spectator expects to recognise that which appears at the other end of the gaze, to place it within the existing known narratives and in doing so to satisfy the desire for self-affirmation. In knowing what the receiving end of the gaze represents (an image), the spectator reaffirms its subject position, its identity, and receives an answer to the core question of identification, that is: 'Who am I?' But when the word is about 'a returned gaze' or 'anxious gaze', the 'exchange' of a gaze is disturbed. The gaze is returned in its unchanged form. The spectator is thus faced with a moment of anxiety to which no meaning can be attached. 'Who am I?' is met with no answer.

This moment reveals what Lacan in his discussion of the graph of desire named as a moment of 'Che vuoi?' or 'What does the Other want?'[25] Yet the other here is not an imaginary substance or a reference point, but the subject's own internalised 'structure'. This is the subject's relation to desire, which appears as the desire of the other. 'What do they want from me?', 'How do they see me?', is only a sample of questions the subject asks in the illusion that he will penetrate or crack the Other's desire.[26] The authority, the father, the despotic regime that the subject believes has authority are reaffirmed in their positions of authority precisely by these questions and in those moments of anxiety.

The anxious gaze pushes the subject to actually *see*: to either traverse the fantasy or to seek out other fantasies. Yet, a gaze that is returned does not support the subject's fantasies, it only acknowledges the presence/existence of something. In an anxious gaze what 'returns' is the question of 'Who am I?' or 'What do you want from me?' in its perverted form. Similar to a photographic negative, instead of a response to 'Is this who I am?', an anxious gaze states, 'I know something is there, but what is that?' An anxious gaze counters the blindness of the spectator who gazes at the other to seek recognition, yet with their own eyes they cannot see. The subjects '*have eyes that they might not see*', as the Gospel goes. 'That they might not see what?', Lacan asks: 'Precisely, that things are looking at them.'[27]

Perhaps such an anxious gaze is similar to the stain Didi-Huberman speaks about: while aware of its presence, the ambiguity of representation begs the question: 'but what is this?'[28] The stain fixates the spectator's gaze and sets in motion their imagination. An anxious gaze thus leads to the collapse of fantasies and asks the subject to re-engage and reassess his own engagement with the structure/way in which the signifier is inscribed on his body. In this move, the anxious gaze puts one's identity and one's place in the social fantasy under question. That latter move, the re-questioning of the self and a search for a new bond of 'belonging', is a key moment of the anxious gaze, and a key disturbing feature that any subject when met with 'the face of the other' is bound to face.

What then is at stake when one's face is met with an anxious gaze? At the point of encounter, the mask of the face falls. The subject has to revisit and renegotiate its relation to the unconscious. It faces its own black hole, that is, it faces a realisation that the structure of language, the form, is tangible and that the signifier (to which I shall return later on) can be (re)inscribed on its body differently. The dismantlement of the illusion or the 'mask' the face wears is precisely what the anxious gaze brings to light. Or as Deleuze and Guattari write, 'subjectification is never without a black hole in which it lodges its consciousness, passion, and redundancies'.[29] The contingency and the instability of the subject is what is at the heart of every being – thus the mastery of that instability, the predictability of where and how it is to manifest, and in what it is to evolve obsesses the face as politics. Not the management and the governing of the 'black hole', but rather the management of how the 'black hole' is expressed; what symptoms sur-face and further how to identify, group and combine them in milieus of meaning.

What an anxious gaze exposes is that a being is different from a face – a face is a mask beings wear. A face is a particular embodiment of being. The face can be seen as that which creates the subject and expresses how the sign is inscribed on the body of the being. Further, it exposes that the subject is different from the gaze; the former stands for a symbolic order, language and identity, whereas the latter, the gaze, is an attempt to represent all of that. Yet as anxiety intervenes, the ordered image of the face falls and exposes the trauma of that which is held as truth. The moments when identity and discursive formations are disturbed are moments when the face crumbles and governing mechanisms fall. As Lacan famously said, 'a signifier is what represent the subject to another signifier'; in the order of the visible, the face is this 'signifier'.[30] Thus faces are given to beings, objects, ideas, material and immaterial forms and placed in a world of social fantasies. Inanimate objects or use-objects, as Deleuze and Guattari point out, are given faces and carefully placed in a matrix of political power relations and reasoning.[31] Lacan's reading of the gaze showed how the subject emerges as an effect of the structure in the spectre of the visible; and further how its structure is contingent on the effects of the structure of language, in other words, on how the subject sees itself, responds to the gaze of the other. Gaze displaces, opens and exposes the fact that fantasies, identities and subjectivations are only to mask what in effect is a primary lack.

Unconscious – politics – body: the limits of 'deterritorialisation' in Lacan

How to make sense of Deleuze's and Lacan's projects about 'the face'? Deleuze states that the 'face is a politics'[32] and further, that the 'face is a landscape'.[33] This suggests that the face is a product of the various power relations, signifying structures which compete for meaning, representations with an aim to appropriate and make something – the face – count. Deleuze's – at least implicit – critique of Lacan's gaze as a constitutive form of subjectivation and an act of faciality[34] targets the function of the gaze. That is, the gaze makes the subject appear in the realm of vision and the visible. That concerns not only the appearance but also the subject's

emergence in the signifying chain. Deleuze's own attempts to de-facial-
ise the face, deterritorialise or make the face turn clandestine target these
representational structures. The idea of the face is in line with Deleuze's
early pre-1968 philosophy where he more directly addresses the question of
structuralism and positions himself in relation to it. He redefines it rather
than dismisses it. Even in his work with Guattari, Deleuze's discussion
of the face as a subjectivising and signifying frame is in line with his earlier
endeavours. If Deleuze's immanent ontology (or his reinterpretation of
structuralism) is seen in light of his endeavours with Guattari on faciality,
then Deleuze's move away from the face suggests a break in the structure.
Deterritorialisation stands for an element that is immanent and excluded
from the structure. It is also one that needs to be singular and non-personal.
Heads, giant heads, close-ups, mouths and deformations of the face are
thus material disfigurations of the otherwise assumed neat ordering of the
face. Deleuze's fascination with the work of Francis Bacon is thus anything
but surprising. Bacon's dismantlement of the face speaks to the horror of
signification and to 'becoming' which deterritorialises the face, but also to
the structures that inevitably uphold thought. Deleuze writes:

> The body is the figure not the structure. Conversely, the Figure, being a body,
> is not the face, and does not even have a face. It does not have a head, because
> the head is an integral part of the body. It can even be reduced to the head.
> As a portraitist, Bacon is a painter of heads, not faces, and there is a great dif-
> ference between the two. For a face is a structured, spatial organization that
> conceals the head, whereas the head is dependent on the body, even if it is the
> point of the body, its culmination. It is not that the head lacks spirit; but it
> is a spirit in bodily form, a corporeal and virtual breath, an animal spirit. It is
> the animal spirit of man: a pig-spirit, a dog-spirit, a bat-spirit . . . Bacon thus
> pursues a very peculiar project as a portrait painter: to dismantle the face, to
> rediscover the head or make it emerge from beneath the face.[35]

There is nothing 'behind the face',[36] as Deleuze and Guattari state, the face
is only an appearance, to displace it means to turn it into something else
either through practices of becoming or through deterritorialisation.

> [S]tarting from the forms one has, the subject one is, the organs one has
> [. . .] becoming is to extract particles between which one establishes the rela-
> tions of movement and rest [. . .] that are closest to what one is becoming,
> and through which one becomes.[37]

Becoming is a constant practice of transformation that is taking place
on the planes between the molar and the molecular. Becoming means
breaking away from the signifying structures and turning oneself into that
which is minor. In more psychoanalytic language, as Slavoj Žižek explains,
the becoming can acknowledge the realisation that the Other does not

know.[38] A fantasy serves as a support for our 'reality': 'an "illusion" which structures our effective, real social relations and thereby masks some insupportable, real, impossible kernel'.[39] The fantasy, as Lacan describes it, structures political space. The Deleuzian idea of 'becoming' refers directly to such fantasmatic constructions and challenges their supremacy, not by directly opposing them, but by creating another being, an appearance in the world, a form of existence that is no longer a subject frozen in a particular moment with all its stable characteristics, but rather a being that is in a constant process of becoming, for example, becoming-minor, becoming-child, becoming-woman, becoming-animal, and so on. As Paul Patton in his thought on becoming-animal writes: 'it follows that becoming-animal, becoming-child, becoming-woman and becoming-coloured are potential paths of deterritorialization of the "majority" in this non-quantitative sense of the term'.[40]

Dismantling the face and giving primacy to the body and its sensations is a move away from the politics of the face, that is, a politics whose primary concern is the allocation of identity and meaning. Not de-politicised, the body for Deleuze simply constitutes a different kind of politics, perhaps one, to refer to Lacan, which is liberated from the terror of the despotic father. Deleuze gives primacy to the body and seeks to break with signification by resorting to the senses and sensations of the body. If Deleuze's attempt to 'escape' the totality of structures rests on sensations rather than logics or structures, Lacan's own endeavour is somewhat different. Looking at how Lacan locates the body within the unconscious, the two thinkers might not be as far apart as they might have presented themselves as being. If Deleuze states that the 'face is a politics', Lacan's own mantra is that the 'unconscious is politics'.[41] Politics, which seems to unite these two statements, is of supreme significance. Deleuze states that the face is a territory of politics, which needs to be taken apart and de-faced. Moreover, it is also for the face that the body is ordered as a machine for meaning production rather than a landscape of sensations. In contrast, Lacan's notion of the face is tied to the gaze and the primary separation from the mother, which comes on the back of the intervention of the master signifier (father) onto the body. It is through the body that a being is subjectivised. A close reading of the relationship between politics, the unconscious and the body in Lacan's thought offers an interesting insight into the signification of the body, the politics that is at stake, and what might escape these signifying processes. The relationship between these three elements might suggest that Lacan is not all that distant from Deleuze's process of deterritorialisation. I am by no means suggesting that the two thinkers have similar accounts of the 'face' (or the subject/being which appears in the world) or the body, or that the aims of their respective thoughts correspond, but merely that there is a moment, an opening in Lacan's thought, which Deleuze in his critique of psychoanalysis fails (or is unwilling) to recognise and that has the possibility of bringing closer the aims of the two separate bodies of thoughts. In what is to follow I focus on the politics, the unconscious and the body, and on the back of what Lacan and Deleuze implied in the two statements, place the two thinkers in a relationship that might well be one of disjunctive synthesis.

In the not yet published Seminar XIV on *The Logic of Phantasy*, Lacan makes an observation about the status of the unconscious, which indicates a rather radical departure from how he conceived of it in his prior work. The 'unconscious ex-sists, [it] is motivated by the structure, that is, by language',[42] Lacan states in *Television*. In other words, it is not only that the unconscious makes the subject dependent on the language; but also that the unconscious is dependent on the structure of language.[43] Lacan's statement that 'the unconscious is structured like a language',[44] is curiously only a more refined statement of the aforementioned 'unconscious is politics'. How to read the two together?

The unconscious is politics can be translated into a political space, which determines the topological intersection between the inside and the outside. Further, it suggests that the political space is decentred in the same way as the subject.[45] Put differently, as argued by Tomšič and Zevnik:

> What is most political in the discovery of the unconscious is the logic of its mechanisms and the impossibility of reducing the subject to unconscious rationality, on which philosophy, and legal and political-economic theories grounded their respective representations and idealizations of subjectivity.[46]

Thus if there is politics in the unconscious, this politics can only be understood in strictly Freudian terms. That is, politics in psychoanalysis cannot refer to the difference, possibilities and negotiations of the subject in the political space; instead it is only a politics insofar as it is 'hinging on the father'.[47] Unconscious is politics only in the Freudian sense, when it is in pursuit of the father. Its starting point is not from the father, but in the unconscious as that which needs to be defined.[48] The striving for the father, or the structure, is what determines the subject and is also where the negotiation of the form is to take place. Politics in the Lacanian sense constitutes the unconscious negotiations, which when translated into signifying chains and forms of subjectivation position themselves in relation to the father. Politics is not emancipatory – it is precisely the opposite, it is how one becomes the subject of the despotic regime of the father (master signifier). It is a negotiation in which the subject is put in relation to the primary repressed signifier, in which the subject seeks that which could come into place instead of the primary repressed. Deleuze's politics of the face is similar insofar as the face stands for a *sur-face* upon which identities, knowledge and meaning are produced. It is a politics that aims to leave its mark or make itself visible precisely by ordering the face, by making it visible in a despotic order in a particular way.

Intriguingly, from Lacan's remark about the nature of the relationship between politics and the unconscious emerges a redefinition of the unconscious, which importantly becomes anchored in the body. In a lecture in May 1967 Lacan suggests that the Other is the body, and not the mind, thought, signifier or soul. Lacan writes:

> The Other, when all is said and done, and if you have not already guessed it, the Other here, as it is written, is the body! [. . .] The fact that the body is made to inscribe something that is called the mark would avoid a lot of worries for everyone and the resifting of a lot of stupidities. The body is made to be marked. It has always been done.[49]

Why this interesting turn to the body in Lacan's thought? With Seminar XIV Lacan opened the door to what was to come later on – namely a new term for the unconscious. In 'Joyce the Symptom' Lacan begins to speak about the *parlêtre* or the speaking being.[50] With *parlêtre* the phrase 'the unconscious is politics' invoked language's inscription on the body or what Lacan in *Television* called the bodily event.[51] This move, which interlinks the body and the unconscious, is paramount for a full grasp of the relationship between Lacan and Deleuze.

Jacques-Alain Miller offers reflections that can help us to understand Lacan's rationale for his move towards the *parlêtre*. In his text 'The Unconscious and the Speaking Being' Miller reminds us of Lacan's dissatisfaction with the term unconscious. Unconscious, what a strange term, yet there is no better one, as Miller reports.[52] In *Television*, Lacan speaks of the centrality of the unconscious for his theory, of his ambivalence towards the term, and of the move towards the body. It would indeed be impossible to speak of inhibitions, repressions and anxieties, if there were no unconscious.[53] But what matters more is the relation between the unconscious and the speaking being. 'There is no unconscious except of the speaking being', Lacan states.[54] 'It speaks, does the unconscious, so that it depends on language, about which we know so little.'[55] The unconscious is a thought that cannot be thought, but whose presence determines or has effects on the subject. It affects the subject as a form through structure/language (which is reduced to non-sense)[56] and as a structure inscribed on the body.

Lacan succinctly explains the task of the unconscious. He writes:

> Whence the unconscious, namely the insistence through which desire manifests itself, in other words, the repetition of the demand working through it

> [. . .] whence the unconscious, if it is true that the structure – recognized as producing, as I say, language out of *lalangue* does indeed order it, reminds us that to the side of meaning that fascinates us in speech – in exchange for which being [. . .] acts as speech's screen – reminds us, I conclude, that to the side of meaning the study of language opposes the side of the sign.[57]

The relationship between language and *lalangue* that Lacan invokes in the above exegesis depicts what is going on in the unconscious and how unconscious itself is politics. *Lalangue* is a form of language that does not reduce itself to the production of meaning or to linguistics. It is different from language inasmuch as it can be reduced to a 'sign'. Word-formations, word-plays in no particular order determine *lalangue*. It is in Joyce that Lacan theorised this different form of *lalangue*, which while maintaining some structure does not give in entirely into the master signifier. In his study of Joyce Lacan famously said that one can do without the master signifier (or without the father) for as long as one knows what to do with it.[58] This, again, identifies two important moments in Lacan's discussion of the unconscious. It demonstrates how unconscious is politics with a reference to *lalangue*. As a chain of signs – which are not yet subdued to the master signifier – *lalangue* is the prime place of politics, and the political itself emerges in the moment when *lalangue* is transformed into language. In this translation from *lalangue* to language – and this is the second moment – the subject emerged but not as a lost/emptied substance, but rather as the embodiment of the structure:

> To embody what the structure entails, namely allowing [. . .] the subject of the unconscious, to take him as the cause of the subject's own desire. In fact it is through the abjection of this cause that the subject in question has a chance to be aware of his position, at least within the structure.[59]

Taking this further, Lacan's new word for the unconscious – *parlêtre* or the speaking being – highlights the status of the subject in the unconscious. It is *it* who speaks and it is *it* that needs to be listened to. Not the subject but the *speaking being*. While Deleuze problematises the entire concept of the unconscious, the discussed structure nevertheless speaks to the pre-symbolised moment which is not something outside the structure but, similar to Deleuze's immanence, is internally excluded. In other words, the transformation from *lalangue* and language is never complete or appears in totality, there is always, and Joyce is a testimony to that, something that comes in addition to the structure and that repeatedly (in an almost pulsating way) intervenes in the structure.

The subject of the unconscious is a structure of language conducive to the order of signifiers. However, as Lacan's *parlêtre* suggests, the structure is not foreign to the body. Just like the law, language also makes a mark on the body of the subject and introduces it into the symbolic order – makes the world comprehensible to the subject.[60] In *Autres écrits* Lacan makes the connection between the body, the unconscious and the structure of the language very clear when he states:

> In fact the subject of the unconscious touches the soul only through the body, by introducing thought into it. [. . .] He thinks because a structure, that of language – the word implies it – a structure that has nothing to do with anatomy cuts up his body. Witness the hysteric. This shearing happens to the soul in the obsessional symptom: a thought that perplexes the soul, and with which the soul knows not what to do. Thought is in disharmony with the soul. [. . .] whereas this world is merely a fantasy through which thought sustains itself, 'reality' no doubt, but to be understood as a grimace of the real.[61]

This introduction of the body into the structure of the unconscious, which in a way makes for a primary condition of the subject's experience, opens a whole new theoretical plane. While the body with all its bodily functions is an effect of the structure, its experiences, affects and senses do not remain unrecognised by Lacan. In the first instance the signifier's intervention onto the body institutes different structures of enjoyment. Lacan acknowledges this when he says that 'what Freud articulates as the primary process in the unconscious [. . . has] to be deciphered [*se déchiffre*]. I mean *jouissance* itself.'[62] That is *jouissance* as the effect of language. In Seminar XX when discussing the 'materiality' of the body Lacan clearly defines the relation between the signifier, *jouissance* and the body:

> The signifier is the cause of jouissance. Without the signifier, how could we even approach that part of the body? [. . .] How could we center that something that is the material cause of jouissance? However fuzzy or confused it may be, it is a part of the body that is signified in this contribution.[63]

However, even more paramount for this discussion of the relationship between Lacan and Deleuze than the effect the signifier has on the body, and its institution of *jouissance*, is how such a theorisation of the unconscious makes room for affect. Deleuze in his own philosophy abandoned the structure of language and instead speaks of senses and sensations. While affect might not come as far as sensation, its intervention on the body opens some doors in the direction of the experienced. In *Television* Lacan is particularly angry with those who seemed to have accused him of neglecting affects. He states: 'To accuse me of neglecting affect, so as to puff oneself up as the one who stresses it – could you make the claim unless you'd forgotten that I'd devoted one year, the last year of my commitment at Sainte-Anne, to dealing with anxiety.'[64] Lacan then continues with perhaps two of the most brilliant observations about affect and why in particular it can (indeed must) emerge in relation to the structure of the unconscious. He writes:

> Does what I say about the unconscious go further than expecting affect to fall, adequately, into your lap? This *adequatio*, being even more grotesque by coming on top of yet another one [. . .] this time conjoining *ret* – of the thing – with *affectus* – the affect whereby it will get repigeonholed. [. . .] The mere subsectioning of the passions of the soul, as Saint Thomas more accurately names these affects, the subsectioning since Plato of these passions on the model of the body: head, heart, even, as he says επιθυμία, or over-heart, doesn't this already testify to the need to approach them via the body, a body which is, I say, affected only by the structure?[65]

Moreover, Lacan's observation about the speaking being – one which in turn needs to be listened to – complements the structure of the unconscious whereby the body emerges as its affect, and as affected by the signifier. Bodily symptoms, bodily events are grounded precisely in this structure: in the negotiation between the sign, the repressed and the master signifier. They emerge on the back of the unconscious as politics; a politics which strives for an inscription or to be put in relation with the father. The affect, for Lacan, is thus not an intervention from the outside of the structure or from the repressed; instead, affect is itself a product of the structure. As he states, affects can only be 'repigeonholed'.

Whilst Deleuze's philosophy of the sense or sensation focuses on the affects, its first step is a destruction of the body as an abstract machine. For Deleuze what needs to be considered first is not organs without bodies, or the fragmented body but 'body without organs, head rather than the face, animated by various intensive movements that determine the nature and emplacement of the organs in question and make that body an organism'.[66] Deleuze wishes to think 'the body' prior to the intervention of the signifier, in the space, to use Lacan's language, where *lalangue* does not strive for becoming language. Two observations come to mind while discussing Lacan and the unconscious: can Joyce be Lacan's response to Deleuze's search for deterritorialisation or is the condition of deterritorialisation a complete 'wash away' of the space of 'politics'?

Acknowledging the different conceptualisation of the body the two thinkers have, Lacan's position of politics in relation to the unconscious is intriguing for two reasons: first, politics comes only when in the unconscious the signifier is struggling to put itself in relation to the father. It is a 'willing struggle', where a signifier is looking to be subdued; second, the body is marked by politics, it is not the face, or the gaze. The primary institution comes at the level of the unconscious and its intervention onto the body. The *body speaks*, as we heard Lacan say. And yet, at this very level, it is precisely the body, which cannot be signified fully, which exceeds, over-boils or comes in excess of the signifier. Thus the body always remains at least to an extent deterritorialised. And the gaze? Does not the anxious gaze stand for the moment in which the meaning, the social fantasy the subject has constructed fails? It might well be a momentary act, but it is one that leaves affects; and it leaves them precisely on the signifier and on the body. An anxious gaze is also a prime moment of politics. 'Che vuoi?' is invoked from the supreme point of authority: in the face of the Other (the father) in relation to which the signifier in the unconscious aims to position itself. It is a moment that displaces the father as a figure from whom the subject seeks its affirmation, but it is also a figure against whom the subject (as we have seen in anxiety) persistently loses that very affirmation. Can we then say and with it also conclude: the politics of the face is a politics of the body and a politics that always and already fails but in its failure it dialogues with desire?

Notes

1. Deleuze, Gilles, *Cinema 1: The Movement-Image* (London: Continuum, 2009), p. 91.
2. Merleau-Ponty, Maurice, *The Visible and the Invisible* (Chicago: Northwestern University Press, 1968), p. 146.
3. Zevnik, Andreja, 'The Politics of the Face: The *Scopic Regime* and the (Un-)masking of the Political Subject', *Journal for Cultural Research*, online first (November, 2015).
4. Deleuze, *Cinema 1*, p. 91.
5. Deleuze, Gilles, *Francis Bacon: The Logic of Sensation* (Minneapolis: University of Minnesota Press, 2003), p. 19.
6. Deleuze, Gilles and Guattari, Félix, *A Thousand Plateaus* (London and New York: Continuum, 2008), p. 190.
7. Ibid. p. 181.
8. Ibid. p. 189.
9. Ibid. p. 188.
10. Ibid. p. 171.
11. Ibid. pp. 171–2.
12. Merleau-Ponty, *The Visible*, p. 187.
13. Lacan, Jacques, *The Seminar of Jacques Lacan, Book XI: The Four Fundamental Concepts of Psychoanalysis* (London: Karnac, 1977).
14. Lacan, Jacques, 'The Mirror Stage as Formative of the I Function as Revealed in Psychoanalytic Experience', in *Écrits* (London and New York: W. W. Norton, 2006), pp. 75–81.
15. Van Alpen, Ernst, *Francis Bacon and the Loss of the Self* (London: Reaktion Books, 1992), p. 115.
16. Lacan, *Four Fundamental Concepts*, p. 106.
17. Ibid. p. 106.
18. Ibid. p. 75.
19. Ibid. p. 95.
20. Ibid. p. 84.
21. Ibid. pp. 96–7.

22. Žižek, Slavoj, *Enjoy Your Symptom!: Jacques Lacan in Hollywood and Out* (London: Verso, 2008), p. 19.
23. Silverman, Kaja, 'What is a Camera? or: History in the Field of Vision', *Discourse*, 15: 3 (1993), pp. 3–4.
24. Lacan, *Four Fundamental Concepts*, p. 74.
25. Lacan, Jacques, 'The Subversion of the Subject and the Dialectics of Desire', in *Écrits* (London and New York: W. W. Norton, 2006), pp. 671–702.
26. Ibid.
27. Lacan, *Four Fundamental Concepts*, p. 109.
28. Didi-Huberman, Georges, 'The Index of the Absent Wound (Monograph on a Stain)', *October*, 29 (1983), pp. 63–81.
29. Deleuze and Guattari, *A Thousand Plateaus*, p. 186.
30. Lacan, *Écrits*, p. 694.
31. Deleuze and Guattari, *A Thousand Plateaus*, p. 194.
32. Ibid. p. 181.
33. Ibid. p. 172.
34. In this context *faciality* should be understood as an act or a movement in which through the recognition in the Other the face is either given or it emerges out of the signifying chain.
35. Deleuze, *Francis Bacon*, p. 19.
36. Deleuze and Guattari, *A Thousand Plateaus*, p. 189.
37. Ibid. pp. 300–1.
38. Žižek, Slavoj, *Sublime Object of Ideology* (London: Verso, 1992), pp. 128, 132.
39. Ibid. p. 45.
40. Patton, Paul, 'Becoming-Animal and Pure Life in Coetzee's *Disgrace*', available at <http://ariel.ucalgary.ca/ariel/index.php/ariel/article/viewFile/3891/3828> (last accessed 31 March 2016), p. 103.
41. Lacan, Jacques, *Seminar XIV: The Logic of Phantasy* (unpublished seminar), Lecture on 10 May 1967, trans. Cormac Gallagher from unedited French manuscripts, available at <http://www.lacaninireland.com/web/wp-content/uploads/2010/06/14-Logic-of-Phantasy-Complete.pdf> (last accessed 24 March 2016).
42. Lacan, Jacques, *Television: A Challenge to the Psychoanalytic Establishment* (New York and London: W. W. Norton, 1990), p. 28.
43. Ibid. p. 28.
44. Lacan, Jacques, *The Seminar of Jacques Lacan, Book XI: The Four Fundamental Concepts of Psychoanalysis* (London and New York: W. W. Norton, 1998), p. 20.
45. Tomšič, Samo and Zevnik, Andreja, 'Introduction', in Tomšič, Samo and Zevnik, Andreja (eds), *Jacques Lacan Between Psychoanalysis and Politics* (London: Routledge, 2015), pp. 5–6.
46. Ibid. p. 6.
47. Laurent, Éric, '"The Unconscious is Politics," Today', *Lacan.com*, available at <http://www.lacan.com/actuality/2015/06/eric-laurent-the-unconscious-is-politics-today/> (last accessed 31 March 2016).
48. Lacan, *The Logic of Phantasy*, 10 May 1967.
49. Ibid.
50. Lacan, Jacques, 'Joyce le Symptôme', in *Le séminaire de Jacques Lacan, livre XXIII: Le sinthome* (Paris: Seuil, 2005), pp. 161–70.
51. Laurent, '"The Unconscious is Politics," Today'.
52. Miller, Jacques-Alain, 'The Unconscious and the Speaking Being', presentation of the theme for the 10th congress of the WAP in Rio de Janeiro in 2016, available at <http://www.wapol.org/en/articulos/Template.asp?intTipoPagina=4&intPublicacion=13&intEdicion=9&intIdiomaPublicacion=2&intArticulo=2742&intIdiomaArticulo=2> (last accessed 31 March 2016).
53. Lacan, *Television*, pp. 5–8.

54. Ibid. p. 5.
55. Ibid. p. 5.
56. Ibid. p. 8.
57. Ibid. p. 8.
58. Lacan, *Le sinthome.*
59. Lacan, *Television*, p. 15.
60. Lacan, Jacques, *On the Names-of-the-Father*, trans. Bruce Fink (Cambridge: Polity Press, 2013), p. 74.
61. Lacan, Jacques, *Autres écrits* (Paris: Seuil, 2001), p. 512.
62. Lacan, *Television*, pp. 18–19.
63. Lacan, Jacques, *The Seminar of Jacques Lacan, Book XX: Encore* (London and New York: W. W. Norton, 1998), p. 24.
64. Lacan, *Television*, p. 21.
65. Ibid. pp. 20–1.
66. Deleuze and Guattari, *A Thousand Plateaus*, pp. 171–2.

Chapter 6

Denkwunderkeiten: On Deleuze, Schreber and Freud

Tadej Troha

For Deleuze, language has two opposing tendencies: 'it is the task of language [. . .] to establish limits', while being the one 'to go beyond them'.[1] The first tendency is articulated by words that consolidate identities, that indicate qualities, that '*denote* the state of affairs', that is, nouns and adjectives, while the second tendency corresponds to verbs, which '*express* events or logical attributes':[2]

> On one hand, there are singular proper names, substantives and general adjectives denoting limits, pauses, rests and presences; on the other, there are verbs carrying off with them becoming and its train of reversible events and infinitely dividing their present into past and future.[3]

In the first step, the verb is put into opposition with two other categories, while both sides of the opposition are at the same level as parts of speech. Later, Deleuze develops another opposition, which initially only seems to be a repetition of the first. Yet here opposites are no longer at the same level. When he tries to think of how an event exists within a proposition, he argues: 'not at all as a name of bodies or qualities, and not at all as a subject or predicate. It exists rather only as that which is expressible or expressed by the propositions enveloped in a *verb*.'[4] Changing the first element of the opposition, replacing the noun and adjective with the subject and predicate also in some respects transforms the status of the verb. If we limit ourselves to the first opposition, this could lead to the conclusion that the close link between verb and event is only a result of the fact that a verb expresses an event. Shifting the opposites creates a much more delicate situation, as the verb is one of the components of the predicate, so in some respects it is presented at both opposing poles. The verb is an inherent part of the first element, while being a singular element on the opposite side, thereby demonstrating the inner surplus of the proposition and the inability to be fully subsumed under the category 'part of speech'. The verb is both a type of word and *the* 'word' (*le verbe, das Zeitwort*[5]), at the same time it *exists* and *insists*.

This inner antagonism leads Deleuze to determine two poles of the verb, the present and the infinitive. The former 'indicates its relation to a denotable state of affairs in view of a physical time', while the latter 'indicates its relation to sense or the event in view of the internal time which it envelops':[6]

> The pure infinitive is the Aion, the straight line, the empty form and the distance; it permits no distinction of moments, but goes on being divided formally in the double and simultaneous direction of the past and the future. [. . .] It connects the interiority of language to the exteriority of being. It inherits, therefore, the communication of events among themselves. As for univocity, it is transmitted from Being to language, from the exteriority of Being to the interiority of language. Equivocity is always the equivocity of nouns. The verb is the univocity of language, in the form of an undetermined infinitive, without person, without present, without any diversity of voice.[7]

Insofar as the infinite verb is the univocity of language and univocity is ultimately that with which we can singularly think both sense and nonsense, a certain change in strategy in relation to the image of nonsense can be observed, referred to by Deleuze as the paradoxical element, the *differenciator*.[8] Whereas in the first, 'structuralist' strategy, nonsense is regarded as the object of sense, the sense as an object that is being presented as a noun (*the letter* with Poe, *debt* with the Rat Man), in the strategy of univocity it is the verb that summarises sense and nonsense into one. We are interested in the following question: can both strategies be combined? Is a progression to the verb necessarily progression to univocity? Or can a verb be thought of as an object *within a single series*? We attempt to answer this question by reading *Memoirs of My Nervous Illness* by Daniel Paul Schreber.

Our reading, however, is not extensive, but instead focuses on an intense moment, the moment of formation. Indeed, Schreber's *Memoirs* includes an infinite number of intriguing details and very rich content, providing so many points of departure that in principle there is room for everyone: theoreticians of power can focus on parallels with the sadist father, on the violence inherent in any power; feminist theory examines Schreber's desire to become a woman; gay and lesbian studies address the homosexual aspect of paranoia; psychoanalysis examines the problem of psychosis, and anti-psychiatry the problem of repression in asylums; while legal theory examines Schreber's question as to the *circumstances in which a person considered insane can be detained in an asylum against his declared will.*[9] The problem, however, is not that focusing on individual topics cannot lead to relevant findings, but that without an intense moment, Schreber's *Memoirs* would not exist in the primary sense of the word, it would never have been written – as strictly speaking, the tangible materiality of individual topics is the result of the paradoxical materiality of a singular verb, *wundern*. The whole material of his *Denkwürdigkeiten*, all the miracles, all the wonders experienced by Schreber and subsequently taken as points of departure of every single theoretical take on Schreber, are nothing but actualisations of a peculiar absolutisation of *wundern*. It is in this sense that his *Denkwürdigkeiten* should be regarded as 'Denkwunderkeiten', as a result of a strictly 'verbal' mental production of wondering.

***

Delegating the crucial role in the interpretation of Schreber to the verb, as the foremost feature of his language, may seem surprising; what most strikes the eye is rather the opposite. Instead of its privileged position, we first may recognise the neutralisation of the verb, as crucial verbs are turned into nouns. This tendency is presented in two modifications. First, the verb is merged with a noun to form a compound noun, such as, for example, the verb *aufschreiben*, 'to write down', which is turned into *Aufschreibesystem*, 'the writing-down system'. Second, the verb itself assumes the form of a noun and begins to function as a noun. Such is the example of the verb *anbinden*, 'to tie', which is transformed into *Anbinden* and then used in the phrases *Anbinden an Strahlen*, tying-to-rays, and *Anbinden an Erden*, tying-to-celestial bodies.

In her semiotic analysis of *Memoirs*, Janet Lucas links this tendency to the process of literalisation. In a psychotic universe, speech is always marked by a tendency to reify words, connotation turns into denotation, and denotation turns into concretisation.[10] In Schreber, literalisation is the very mechanism that enables the establishment of the nerves–rays–voices series, and is what makes the words not merely become but literally *be* flesh.[11] As such, it is impossible to discuss creation in the standard meaning of the word with Schreber, because everything that he denotes as creation is essentially only 'a *transformation of that which already exists*'.[12]

In this respect, the only creativity left to Schreber would be the strategy of collage. According to Lucas, reconstructing the Order of the World is nothing more than an assemblage of signifying elements: 'Because Schreber exists in a closed imaginary circuit, nothing new can be introduced, i.e., by definition, he cannot "*create*." Rather, Schreber rebuilds his signifying structure by *manipulating existing elements*; in particular by *juxtaposing existing* though *disconnected* signifying elements.'[13] This tendency is best seen in the substantivisation of verbs, 'verbs are transformed (or concretized) into nouns (and nouns with only a single denotation)'.[14] In this way, we are faced with a radical triumph of actuality and territorialisation: a closed imaginary circle in which there is no creation, a world where we can hardly speak of becoming, a language that is only 'pauses, rests, and presences'.[15] In other words, if this presentation of Schreber is suitable, any analogy with Deleuze is excluded in advance.

Disregarding the disjunction of creation and transformation mentioned above, which is problematic in itself,[16] another, in some respects no less obvious reading of Schreber's language should be suggested. Insofar as the former strategy is abridged to a thesis of the substantivisation of the verb, the transformation of the verb into a noun, that is, the suspension of the creative potential of a language, in the latter strategy, transformation takes place within the verb: it also affects the verb, but the product is not a noun; rather, a verb is transformed into a verb.

It should be stressed immediately that this tendency is not radically opposed to the first one insofar as both procedures include the word becoming independent in some respect. While the argument that the product of Schreber's substantivisation of verbs is a word with a single denotation may at first seem appropriate, it is rather problematic in that it misses the strictly conceptual nature of these substantives. Even a superficial reading of *Memoirs* clearly shows that these are not terms that should first be deciphered, thereby producing a conceptual charge. On the contrary, their *Eindeutigkeit* is in itself conceptual. For Schreber, the substantivised verbs are concepts that evolve and transform in the course of his illness and in the process of writing his *Memoirs*.

Although the second strategy therefore is not to be regarded as a radical opposition to the former, it is nevertheless specific, and, as it will be argued, the fact that it is not pure opposition puts their linguistic relationship in the wider context of Schreber's universe; more exactly, it demonstrates that the whole 'wider context' is already contained in the relationship.

***

Freud was the first to have detected that the core of Schreber's gesture can be captured precisely at the level of the form of language. In short: insofar as, for Freud, the core of any paranoia in men is the existence – or, better yet, *insistence* – of a homosexual fantasy, then all types of paranoid delusion are a way of reacting to the *proposition* – and not the *thought* – '*I (a man) love him (a man).*' According to Freud, this proposition can be objected to in three ways.

The *delusion of jealousy*, which objects to the proposition at the level of the subject – 'It is not *I* who love the man – *she* loves him' – is in a certain sense a borderline form of paranoid delusion; it subsists without projective distortion, 'since, with the change of the subject who loves, the whole process is in any case thrown outside the self. The fact that the woman loves the man is a matter of external perception to him.'[17] Put differently, in this type of objection, the projection in which 'internal perceptions – feelings – shall be replaced by external perceptions'[18] does not assume the proper form insofar as one internal perception is transformed into the perception of *another* internal perception (this is no longer my internal perception but hers). Strictly speaking, the subjective feeling is not objectivised but merely transferred to another subject.

In view of this complexity, the delusion of jealousy is followed by *erotomania*, which is characterised by objecting to the object of the original proposition: 'I do not love *him* – I love *her*.' It is immediately evident that, contrary to the delusion of jealousy, here the subjective feeling is not directly transferred to another person, which is why projection is the necessary third step: 'In obedience to the same need for projection, the proposition is transformed into: "I observe that *she* loves me."'[19]

> 'I do not love him – I love her, because *she loves me*.' Many cases of erotomania might give an impression that they could be satisfactorily explained as being exaggerated or distorted heterosexual fixations, if our attention were not attracted by the circumstance that these infatuations invariably begin, not with any internal perception of loving, but with an external perception of being loved.[20]

In this case, too, it is not yet possible to talk about objectivation proper: ultimately, the product of the transformation is again an external perception of an *internal perception*, a perception of the subjective feeling of another subject. If, in the case of the delusion of jealousy, the objection to the homosexual fantasy and projective distortion of the latter coincided, if objection fully took on the role of projection, then with erotomania we get the situation in which projection functions as the argument of the proposition objecting to the original one: *Because she loves me, I love her and not him.*

For Freud, objection at the level of the object is not exclusive ('It is, after all, possible to love her as well as him'[21]), which is why in erotomania the intermediary proposition can also become conscious. Because the coexistence of the first and the second proposition is not contradictory, the third, projective proposition can, according to Freud, be omitted. As we can see, the projection here plays an auxiliary role. It supports the concessionary coexistence of a non-exclusive opposition, it strengthens the weaker element, and at the same time it does not oppose the original unconscious tendency. If, in the first case, the projection merged with the second proposition, it has no autonomous existence here either, but is reduced to an argument; it has no actual causal power.

The purest type of projection can thus be found in the third type, where the objection is aimed at the predicate. The *delusion of persecution* is the one in which both elements of the love–hate ambivalence, which was so crucial for Freud, open up already in the first step by way of the proposition 'I do not *love* him', turning into the proposition 'I *hate* him':

> This objection (*Widerspruch*), which must have run thus in the unconscious, cannot, however, become conscious to a paranoiac in this form. The mechanism of symptom-formation in paranoia requires that internal perceptions – feelings – shall be replaced by external perceptions. Consequently the proposition 'I hate him' becomes transformed by *projection* into another one: 'He *hates* (persecutes) me, which will justify me in hating him.' And thus the impelling unconscious feeling makes its appearance as though it were the consequence of an external perception: 'I do not love him – I hate him, because *he persecutes me*.'[22]

We can immediately see the difference in comparison with erotomania. The intermediary sentence, which could there become conscious because the opposition was not exclusive (it is not contradictory to love a man and a woman at the same time), here remains unconscious, whereby the function of the projective proposition also changes. If, in the case of erotomania, it functioned as an argument of a subjective feeling, it here figures as its *objective cause*. Although the structure of the three propositions is identical in both cases, as in both cases the projective proposition contains the conjunction 'because', it is nevertheless possible to point out two indications justifying this differentiation.

First, in Freud in general, the him–her pair has a different status than the love–hate pair. In the analysis of the Rat Man, for example, he stresses that the first of both conflicts corresponds 'to the normal vacillation between male and female which characterises every one's choice of a love-object'.[23] It is a conflict that accompanies one throughout one's life,

> but normally this opposition soon loses the character of a hard-and-fast contradiction, of an inexorable 'either–or'. Room is found for satisfying the unequal demands of both sides, although even in a normal person the higher estimation of one sex is always thrown into relief by a depreciation of the other.[24]

The second conflict, for which Freud later adopts the term *ambivalence*, coined by Bleuler, is much more complex already in compulsive neurosis, insofar as it is unappeasable. At the conscious level, the love–hate conflict is, as a rule, manifested as *overly intense love*, which thereby is nothing other than the symptom of ambivalence:

> We should have expected that the passionate love would long ago have conquered the hatred or been devoured by it. And in fact such a protracted survival of two opposites is only possible under quite peculiar psychological conditions and with the co-operation of the state of affairs in the unconscious. The love has not succeeded in extinguishing the hatred but only in driving it down into the unconscious; and in the unconscious the hatred, safe from the danger of being destroyed by the operations of consciousness, is able to persist and even to grow. In such circumstances the conscious love attains as a rule, by way of reaction, an especially high degree of intensity, so as to be strong enough for the perpetual task of keeping its opponent under repression. The necessary condition for the occurrence of such a strange state of affairs in a person's erotic life appears to be that at a very early age, somewhere in the prehistoric period of his infancy, the two opposites should have been split apart and one of them, usually the hatred, have been repressed.[25]

Put differently, ambivalence is to be considered an *objective contradiction* that cannot be fully resolved by way of a consecutive alternation of one and the other; rather, it is the selection of one element that generates the other, the excessive intensity of one that increases the intensity of the other. And since the contradiction is objective, it is no longer certain that ambivalence consists of the conflict of two autonomous subjective feelings, love and hate; rather, it is ambivalence that is original, while love and hate are merely actualised manifestations of this contradiction. Freud himself hints at this in his analysis of the Wolf Man when he deviates from the established use of the concept and relates it to the coexistence of passive and active-sadistic trends; more precisely, this coexistence counts as one of the manifestations of ambivalence.[26]

Again, Freud's formula of the delusion of persecution is as follows: 'I do not love him – I hate him, because *he persecutes me*.' If we have shown that the first two propositions reflect objective ambivalence, this objectivity can also be ascribed to the third, projective proposition as evidenced by the last transformation of the predicate, the third verb. In Freud's definition of the mechanism of persecutory delusion cited above, there is an intermediary step. When it already seems that the projective proposition will be: *he is the one who hates me*, Freud immediately, as if he changed his mind at that very moment, adds in brackets: *persecutes*. The projection is thus not satisfied merely with transference to another subject, but demands another transformation. What is essential here is that the subjective feeling, the internal perception of another subject, is replaced by an 'objective' verb, a verb that can no longer be ascribed to merely one or the other subject, but denotes the independent materiality of the delusion itself.

The result is thus as follows: on the one hand, there is the pair *I (do not) love – I hate*, but precisely insofar as this negation does not work out, the ambivalence is preserved. On the other hand, it is precisely this unresolvable contradiction – and not only its second element – that is transformed into the third verb, *to persecute*. The projection resolves the original contradiction with the second, internal contradiction of the verb itself, from which it is not possible to infer with certainty the subjective intentions of the other subject in delusion. As we know, *Verfolgung*, persecution, pursuing, stalking, can be a consequence of love, as well as of hate; or, better yet, it can be ascribed this or that subjective feeling. Ambivalence is in the air – and what seemed a subjective vacillation between love and hate turns out to be a consequence of external ambivalence and is thus necessarily itself objectivised and gains autonomy.

***

Let us now return to Schreber, to the very material that triggered Freud's proto-Lacanian metapsychological construction. Whereas in Freud the projective objectivation takes place with the replacement of the verb in the position of the predicate, in Schreber the difference between the two levels of language is blurred, so that the transformation of the predicate takes place within one and the same verb. Thereby, the objectivity of the projection entails the objectivation of the verb in which the level of the subject and the level of the Other merge, that is, the verb that joins the subjective feeling of wondering and the wonder giving itself to this wondering – the verb *(sich) wundern*.

To illustrate this, let us take a look at a few examples from Schreber's *Memoirs*. In addition to the basic *wundern* ('sobald man ein Geräusch in meiner Nähe wundert'[27]), we also come across derivative verbs with a prefix added to the base: *hereinwundern* ('indem man mir die geschwärzten Nerven [. . .] in den Körper hereinwunderte'[28]), *verwundern* ('wenn nur meine Kniescheibe nicht verwundert würde'[29]), *anwundern* ('so war mir [. . .] ein . . . sog. "Judenmagen" angewundert worden'[30]), *herumwundern* ('an allen meinen Muskeln wurde [. . .] herumgewundert'[31]). An exception in this series is the verb *verwundern*, which keeps to its standard use in two cases – in one case it coincides with the transformed form ('war ich [. . .] auf Höchste verwundert'[32]) and is formally indistinguishable from it, while, in the second case, *verwundern* addresses the reader ('es ist daher nicht zu verwundern'[33]) who, contrary to Schreber, still wonders subjectively.

The above examples already show that much more is at stake than a simple turn from the first, passive agent of wondering, to the second, active agent, which generally constitutes the basis of a conspiracy theory. The transformed verb itself appears in both the passive and the active voice, and it is clear that this secondary transformation in itself says nothing of Schreber's transformational procedure. Put differently, the condition of its possibility has to be sought at the point where the original meaning tipped over into another meaning, that is, in the formal procedure, which is also the reason that the original and the transformed verb do not stand in pure opposition.

If nothing else, the opposition between the active and the passive would imply a relation between Schreber and God that is completely incompatible with the key axiom of Schreber's universe: that both man and God are part of one nerve substance. It follows from this that every division of the active and the passive subjective positions is a matter of derivation, and if there is someone in this relationship who is losing their nerves it is precisely God, who in the struggle for his own existence invents numerous reactionary mechanisms.[34] To put it more graphically, it is not only Schreber that is God's bitch, he is not the only one of whom the voices babble: 'Fancy a person who was a *Senatspräsident* allowing himself to be f . . . . d';[35] rather, there are numerous rumours about God, too: 'O damn, it is extremely hard to say that God allows himself to be f . . . . . .'[36]

In order, then, to capture the sense of Schreber's transformation, we suggest a three-stage construction that can be read as a repetition of Freud with other, more limited means, with three steps of one verb.

The point of departure: 'I wonder.' Since wondering does not have its direct antipode – by negating the verb we would only get an absurd repetition of 'I do not wonder, I wonder not' – the first step involves a formal negation of reflexivity and subjective feeling, the negation of the subject as the agent of the wondering. I do not wonder, *ich wundere mich nicht*, it is 'Not-I' that wonder(s), *nicht-ich wundere mich* – therefore: *Es wundert mich*, 'It wonders me.' This stage, which remains in the field of standard use, thus denies that the wondering is Schreber's subjective impression; on the contrary, it claims that the agent of the wondering is an impersonal *Es*.

In view of its sense, the first transformation coincides with Freud's love–hate pair as understood above in relation to the concept of ambivalence. But if Freud still insisted on a pair of two internal perceptions that together constitute the contradiction of ambivalence, here the situation is put in another perspective. Because this is a transformation within a verb and not a replacement of one verb with another, the contradiction is ascribed a primary status. Even more, since both elements of the contradiction have the same meaning, being merely two formulations of one and the same content, we are here faced with an entirely formal contradiction where, in view of the content, neither the first nor the second element can be pushed into the unconscious. As we have seen, in the love–hate pair, there is still the temptation to characterise only one of the elements as unconscious. By contrast, the formal transformation shows us that the unconscious itself is a contradiction, that the incapacity to isolate the elements from one another is as such already a feature of the unconscious.

This seems to be the way to understand Freud's words that also takes us to the next transformation: 'This objection, which must have run thus in the unconscious, cannot, however, become conscious to a paranoiac in this form.' Freud is clear on this point – it is not only the other element, that is, *I hate*, that is unconscious, but also the very objection that includes the negation of the verb to love. The reason that this objection is unconscious is precisely in the substitutional proposition (*I hate*) not coinciding with the negation of the first. In view of its meaning, the opposition in content does not coincide with formal negation and is in relation to it merely a secondary substitute.

Furthermore, it is precisely the transformation of one and the same verb with no objection at the level of content – *ich wundere mich* and *es wundert mich* are synonyms – that shows this formal paradox in its pure form. In Schreber, it is not the opposition of meaning that triggers the need for projection; quite the contrary, the non-contradictory meaning of the two variants established in everyday language is precisely what enables his projective invention, which is actually the only thing that exists for Schreber – projection grabs onto a pre-existent possibility in language and develops it regardless of the content. This is precisely why Schreber's unconscious can only be a product of construction and is in a certain sense merely formal – which does not mean, of course, that it does not *affect* the content.

We have already pointed out that, in the third step of the formula, Freud introduces the verb *persecute*, from which it is impossible to derive the subjective impulse and with which the paranoiac materialises the objectivity of the love–hate contradiction. But, here, the third stage is still bound to a certain agent: 'He' is the one persecuting 'me'. The content of the verb is 'objective', but this is still not the objectivity manifested in Schreber's projection – which has to do precisely with the formal objectivity of the verb when the verb starts functioning as an object.

In Schreber, the third, projective stage, therefore, does not simply transform the impersonal, grammatical 'it' into *him* (God or Flechsig, his former psychiatrist); its final scope is not the proposition that he wonders (something to) me, *Er wundert mich/mir*. The reactionary nature of projection, that is, a domestication of the two-way nature of the reflexive verb, the determination of its agent, at the same time emerges as its own negation. The externality in projection should not be understood as an externality proceeding from another subject, rather it is an externality that has *no agent*; in the end, the emphasis is transferred to the autonomous verb *wundern*. The formula of Schreber's delusion is thus as follows: *Ich wundere mich – Es wundert mich – wundern*, 'I wonder' – 'it wonders me' – 'to wonder(ise)'.

And, which is crucial, the last infinitive should by no means be capitalised. What is at stake is not *das Wundern*, wondering as a transcendental principle of Schreber's universe, but an infinitive as the name of the affirmation of the verb in purely formal terms independent of any established content. In Schreber, pure form as such already figures as materiality; all the wonders that Schreber perceives on his body and in his environment day after day are consequences of the materiality within language, the consequences of the objectivation of the verb. It is precisely this objectivised wonder that will produce the Order of the World, finally free of every presupposition of a conspiracy theory – which means: of every hope and reliance on the already existing other system.

Notes

1. Deleuze, Gilles, *The Logic of Sense* (London: The Athlone Press, 1990), p. 8.
2. Ibid. p. 24.
3. Ibid. p. 24.
4. Ibid. p. 182.
5. 'The verb is not an image of external action, but a process of reaction internal to language. This is why, in its most general notion, it envelops the internal temporality of language' (ibid. p. 186).
6. Ibid. p. 184.
7. Ibid. pp. 184–5.
8. Briefly: 'The paradoxical element [. . .] is nonsense' (ibid. p. 78).
9. The essay with this title was written to show that it is wrongful to assume that a patient with a mental illness has a priori legal incapacity. See Schreber, Daniel Paul, *Memoirs of My Nervous Illness* (New York: New York Review of Books, 2000), pp. 313–24 [363–76]. Square brackets indicate the original pagination in *Denkwürdigkeiten eines Nervenkranken*, which is also used in Freud's analysis.
10. See Lucas, Janet, 'The Semiotics of Schreber's Memoirs: Sign, Sinthome and Play', *The Symptom 4*, available at < http://www.lacan.com/semofmem.htm> (last accessed 1 April 2016).
11. In Schreber's universe, the concepts of nerves, rays and voices function as synonyms, or mutually bestow features; the nerves speak, and the voices are loud in a very material and nervous way.
12. Lucas, 'The Semiotics'; original emphasis.
13. Ibid.; original emphasis.
14. Ibid.
15. See Deleuze, *The Logic of Sense*, p. 8.
16. The vital dilemma in the analysis of Schreber is the status of the Order of the World (*Weltordnung*). While Schreber clearly distinguishes between the 'Order of the World' and 'circumstances contrary to the Order of the World', it can be shown that both

types of order share the fundamental axiom of a single materiality of nerves: everything that exists derives from the nerves. Therefore, the Order of the World itself is a secondary deduction, which is no less natural than its opposite. Therefore, the dilemma is as follows: is the Order of the World sought by Schreber a reconstruction or rather a construction *affirming its conditions*? Here, it seems, Janet Lucas implicitly opts for the first.

17. Freud, Sigmund, 'Psychoanalytic Notes on an Autobiographical Account of a Case of Paranoia', in *Case Histories II* (Harmondsworth: Penguin, 1988), p. 202.
18. Ibid. p. 201.
19. Ibid. p. 201.
20. Ibid. p. 201.
21. Ibid. p. 201.
22. Ibid. p. 201; translation modified.
23. Freud, Sigmund, 'Notes Upon a Case of Obsessional Neurosis', in *Case Histories II*, p. 118.
24. Ibid. p. 118.
25. Ibid. pp. 118–19.
26. 'No doubt was left in the analysis that these passive trends had made their appearance at the same time as the active-sadistic ones, or very soon after them. This is in accordance with the unusually clear, intense, and constant ambivalence of the patient, which was shown here for the first time in the even development of both members of the pairs of contrary component instincts. Such behaviour was also characteristic of his later life, and so was this further trait: no position of the libido which had once been established was ever completely replaced by a later one. It was rather left in existence side by side with all the others, and this allowed him to maintain an incessant vacillation which proved to be incompatible with the acquisition of a stable character' (Freud, Sigmund, 'From the History of an Infantile Neurosis', in *Case Histories II*, p. 256).
27. 'every noise created by miracle around me' (Schreber, *Memoirs*, p. 135 [142]).
28. 'by miraculously placing the blackened nerves [. . .] into my body' (ibid. p. 97 [95]).
29. 'if only miracles would not affect my knee-cap' (ibid. p. 126 [130]).
30. 'miraculously produced [. . .] a very inferior so-called "Jew's stomach"' (ibid. p. 144 [151]).
31. 'all my muscles were (and still are) the object of miracles' (ibid. p. 148 [156]).
32. 'I was extremely surprised' (ibid. p. 93 [90]).
33. 'it is therefore hardly surprising' (ibid. p. 247 [279]).
34. The example of this struggle is given in the substantivised infinite *Anbinden an Erden*: 'As the expression denotes, a tying to some distant stars occurred which from then on excluded the possibility of a complete dissolution in my body in consequence of my power of attraction; on the contrary withdrawal was safeguarded through the mechanical fastening so established' (ibid. p. 122 [125]).
35. Ibid. p. 164 [177].
36. Ibid. p. 179 [194].

Chapter 7

Snark, Jabberwock, Poord'jeli: Deleuze and the Lacanian School on the Names-of-the-Father

Guillaume Collett

Introduction[1]

From 'From Sacher-Masoch to Masochism' (1961) to *Anti-Oedipus* (1972), Deleuze's primary target when writing about psychoanalysis has been what he calls in 1961 Freudian psychoanalysis's 'inflation of the importance of the father'.[2] By 1967's *Coldness and Cruelty* he was training his sights on the Lacanian 'Name-of-the-Father', remarking critically that 'Lacan appears to look upon this as a primary and irreducible operation which is independent of all maternal influence.'[3] In *Anti-Oedipus*, Deleuze pulls no punches, explicitly associating the Lacanian Name-of-the-Father with the despot in 'barbarian' societies, who phonetically re-'codes' and ultimately represses the primarily visual graphic inscription of desire on the body in 'primitive' societies (as carved out of 'mother' nature).[4] Yet, as can be inferred from the above, while being critical of certain aspects, Deleuze also took psychoanalysis seriously enough during this decade of work to develop in painstaking technical detail an internal reconstruction of psychoanalysis's conception of, amongst others, infantile development, language acquisition and Oedipus.

Of these texts, *Anti-Oedipus* with its combative historicisation of the ontogenetic necessity and universality of the Oedipus complex has undoubtedly received the most attention. Yet a quieter, 'structuralist', critique of Oedipus already appeared in the pre-Guattari *The Logic of Sense* from 1969,[5] and it is this critique that is arguably more interesting from a psychoanalytic and Lacanian perspective.[6] *Anti-Oedipus*, with its nascent post-humanism, would pave the way for the cosmic theory of machines completed in *A Thousand Plateaus*, but *The Logic of Sense* remained embedded in a framework which, while philosophically antithetical to Lacanian concerns,[7] was close enough theoretically to structuralism-influenced psychoanalysis to offer partial and productive bridges.[8]

A reason for this, not least, is the historical coincidence of Deleuze's work in *The Logic of Sense* with parallel developments occurring at the time within the Lacanian school. Lacan famously elaborated a structural theory of Oedipus in the 1950s, reducing the father to the prohibitive 'No!/ Name' (*Non/Nom*, the two are homophonous) which metaphorises the infant's libidinal attachments to the mother (the 'Desire-of-the-Mother') such that, as signifiers, they are collected and repressed as the unconscious signified of the Name-of-the-Father (as signifier of symbolic Otherness and castration).[9] Yet, already in the early 1960s, for instance at the end of the tenth seminar (on anxiety) and in the unrealised seminar that would have come after it (entitled *The Names-of-the-Father*),[10] Lacan was beginning to counterbalance – or, seen most sympathetically, to correct misunderstandings surrounding – the perceived unilateralism with which the Desire-of-the-Mother is subjected to the Name-of-the-Father during ontogenesis.[11] This pluralised figure (Name*s*) indicates also singularisation, that is, a move away from the universality of the process, or, from the subtraction of the body's singular materiality by the universality of structuralist form.

Nonetheless, Lacan did not really fully broach this topic until the 1970s.[12] Between the early 1960s and 1970s, the critique of the Lacanian Name-of-the-Father of the 1950s was carried out, it seems, primarily by Lacan's disciples and interlocutors. In what follows I will focus on two of these – Serge Leclaire and Deleuze – before returning to Lacan's 1970s work.

Leclaire and the body of the letter: Poord'jeli as *repère*

Serge Leclaire was a core member of Lacan's school from the first seminar, later joining Lacan's École Freudienne de Paris in 1964 while also attempting during the mid-1960s to reconcile the tensions which had formed between Lacan's school and the Freudian International Psychoanalytic Association.

Leclaire's position can be characterised as an attempt at arriving closer to an immanent psychoanalytic structuralism.[13] As he puts it in his 1968 book *Psychoanalysing*:

> the term *structure*, in its common use, is not altogether correct to describe what surfaces of the unconscious in the singularity of the cases with which the analyst is confronted [. . .] [W]hat is important for him or her [the psychoanalyst], above all, is the renewal of this structure in every singular adventure [. . .] [A] correctly conceived structural approach intrinsically includes the study of this moment of engendering of *an* unconscious.[14]

It is helpful to contextualise this passage and the book it comes from within the second half of the 1960s, during which time Lacan was exerting influence on, and being influenced in turn by, the contemporary Parisian philosophical scene. If we look for instance at the now famous journal *Cahiers pour l'analyse*,[15] to which Leclaire was a regular contributor, we can identify amongst others a tension between the contributions of Jacques-Alain Miller, and then Badiou, on the one hand, who were mobilising during this time Lacan's thought against phenomenology and appeals to embodied experience, and on the other hand, Leclaire's warnings against such an abstraction from the bodily and lived, all the while maintaining the need to conceive of the body structurally.[16]

For Leclaire, a singular unconscious emerges each time an infant progresses through the stages of psycho-sexual development, because the unconscious can to an extent be conflated, for Leclaire, with the body. Here we find arguably Leclaire's chief contribution to psychoanalytic thought, which is that the unconscious is composed of signifiers, or letters, inscribed on and subsequently inseparable from erogenous zones, and that the structural fabric of the unconscious can be unearthed by mapping out the differential play of the letter, which is to say the set of differential relations between erogenous zones – as necessarily mediated by letters – composing a body. For instance, in Leclaire's reopening of Freud's case study of the Wolf Man, the letter 'V' comes to be fundamentally inscribed on the anal zone, but insofar as the V is a letter it is inseparable from the differential relations it forms with other letters, and through them, with other zones.[17]

Such a conception of the unconscious allows Leclaire to anchor structure to the singular development of an erogenous body, without ever going as far as grounding structure in some savage pre-linguistic experience. If the body is to be viewed as a set of erogenous zones, which is to say a set of letters as well as the system of differential relations pertaining between these letters, the body's self-relationality as integrated libidinal economy is not pre-given in corporeality but fully mediated by the letters that crisscross it. Nonetheless, this system of letters emerges from singular sensations experienced by and constituting each zone, which while always inseparable from a literal inscription accompanying such erogenous experiences provides the letters inscribed there with a singular foundation rooted in bodily intensity.[18]

Furthermore, this leads Leclaire to posit a theory of fantasy and of psychic agency which again brings these letters, in their singular irreducibility, to the fore. Insofar as letters, for Leclaire, are inscribed on the body according to the dynamics of the pleasure principle, they form a layer of nonsense which continues to jar with referential statements produced in conscious discourse, as submitted to the reality principle and according with everyday conceptions of common sense. For Leclaire, it is this resonance of sense and nonsense, of generality or universality and singularity, that drives fantasy and psychic life.[19]

Now, while Leclaire's overarching attempt, at the level of his contribution to Lacanian theory, to inject singularity and immanence into psychoanalytic structuralism was influenced by numerous factors, I think it is also clear that such a project lent itself to and would later converge with anti-Oedipal elements of the Lacanian school detectable during the late 1960s and 1970s. In this regard it is interesting to examine Leclaire's 1969 seminar given at the University of Vincennes, published as *Oedipe à Vincennes*.[20] If this text could be said to attest to the anti-Oedipal climate of Vincennes in the early 1970s (*Anti-Oedipus* would soon emerge from its philosophy department),[21] it also demonstrates how such a position could have been arrived at endogenously from within Lacan's school.

In the first two sessions or chapters, Leclaire argues that the 'paternal function' is to 'articulate the singularity of the erogenous [body]' (the 'maternal function'[22]), as set of letters, with the 'universality of discourse', so as to form a 'singular fantasy presiding over the libidinal organisation of the individual' and not an 'originary and universal fantasy'.[23] Advancing upon the Name-of-the-Father of the 1950s, the paternal function is now to knot universality and singularity equally, rather than to submit the one to the other. Although the anti-Oedipal dimension of this argument fully appears in this lecture course, it nonetheless directly builds on Leclaire's work from the preceding years, and particularly, I would suggest, from his case study of the dream with the unicorn.

In this case study, Leclaire reconstructs the unconscious literal organisation of one of his analysands, Philippe Georges Elhyani, convincingly arguing that the kernel of Philippe's unconscious is the nonsensical word 'Poord'jeli'. Leclaire calls this nonsensical combination of letters the 'secret replica of the proper name, cipher of the unconscious',[24] and of all its associations and connections with the subject's erogenous zones,[25] the most immediately visible structure of Poord'jeli lies in its doubling of the proper name (*Phili**ppe** **G**eorges **El**hyani*). Leclaire claims here that in the absence of a symbolically efficacious Name-of-the-Father or paternal 'No!/Name', the young Philippe had to create his own name – his Symbolic bearings (*repère*) as a repeat (*re-*) father (*père*)[26] – from the letters or fragments of his interactions with his mother and maternal kin (particularly his mother's cousin Liliane). Indeed, it is the middle name ((G)eorges) in its differential *opposition* to the subject's Symbolically given forename (the internal syncope of *ppe'(G)eorges*) and paternal surname – Leclaire also writes it Poor(d)j'e-li, signalling the disjunction-conjunction between (G)eorges and the paternal surname (Elh/i),[27] which is now conflated with the first syllable of Liliane – which constitutes Poord'jeli.

This self-naming (or self-castration) again attests to a knotting of the body's singularity with the universal and general forms of fantasy (above all castration) communicated to the infant in his interactions with others within the Symbolic domain. Leclaire's argument is not that a Name-of-the-Father was completely absent, but that it had to be progressively built by the infant from the normative and phallic fantasmatic forms (above all the Lacanian 'symbolic phallus' which points beyond the imaginary dyad of early Oedipus) extracted from the speech of his mother and Liliane, and inscribed as letters on the infant's erogenous zones. By building it in this way, the Name-of-the-Father is knotted together with the Desire-of-the-Mother (signifiers inscribed on the infant's body), and does not simply repress it.

Leclaire only hints at the anti-Oedipal implications of this argument in his most sophisticated treatment of the case, given in 1968's *Psychoanalysing*, and it is interesting to see how from 1968 to 1969–70, perhaps indeed in the wake of May 1968 and with his arrival at Vincennes, his argument had taken such a directed and focused turn.

Deleuze's theory of events: Poord'jeli as esoteric word

Rather than turning now to *Anti-Oedipus*, I would like to extend further my claim above that elements of an anti-Oedipal position emerged from within Lacan's school, by showing how one finds such a position being developed within Deleuze's *The Logic of Sense* (1969). While not typically considered a Lacanian text, and while very distant from Lacan's ontology and theory of the subject, *The Logic of Sense* is a text in tune with the spirit of the time and even with the developments occurring during these years within the Lacanian school,[28] incorporating as it does singularity, singular 'events', into any definition of linguistic structure. Moreover, although not immediately noticeable, *The Logic of Sense* hinges on a theory of incarnated structure, which Deleuze explicitly borrows from Leclaire, and, I will show, which underlies his theory of 'events' (as propositional 'sense-events'). In short, it is because the proposition and more deeply linguistic structure are anchored to the erogenous body that, for Deleuze, structure is populated by singular events. Lastly, I will show that this already implies a critique of the Lacanian conception of the Name-of-the-Father.

While the psychoanalytic portion of *The Logic of Sense*, the 'dynamic genesis', draws heavily on the work of Melanie Klein, and spends its first three chapters discussing her reading of infantile development (through the 'schizoid', 'depressive' and Oedipal positions), it is a mistake to attribute too much importance to this reference. Rather, we need to investigate, contextualise and understand this reference in terms of its overall function in the text. At the start of the dynamic genesis, Deleuze makes it clear that Klein's importance derives from her having staked out the 'orientations' or 'dimensions' proper to infantile development[29] – what Deleuze calls the schizoid material 'depths' of the drive, the ideal depressive 'heights' of identification with linguistic form and the Oedipal 'surface' where the two are knotted – and this can be read partly as a criticism of Lacan, particularly the Lacan of the 1950s and early 1960s. Lacan builds his structural reading of Oedipus in Seminars IV–VI partly through a critique of Klein's work, arguing that her work only accounts for the infant's imaginary ties to the mother, and not for the symbolic intervention of a third term (the symbolic phallus, a demand addressed to the Other), without which, for Lacan, there is no way that the infant can pass from even the first, oral, stage to the second, anal, stage.[30]

Deleuze seems to use Klein primarily to loosen the earliest stages of infantile development, along with the corporeal processes or drives underpinning them, from their almost immediate subsumption, in the early Lacan, under linguistic form (as a demand directed at the Other), so as to better appreciate both the contribution made by each dimension to structure and the heterogeneity of these dimensions. This does not mean that the dynamic genesis should be read as a valorisation of the generative matter of the body to the detriment of linguistic form,[31] and I will show below that such a reading flies in the face of the most basic tenets of Deleuze's ontology.

He makes this point unambiguously explicit on a number of occasions in the text. For instance, Deleuze writes that:

> Structuralism is right to raise the point that form and matter have a scope only in the original and irreducible structures in which they are organised. [. . .] For life, and even sexuality, lies within the organisation and orientation of these dimensions, before being found in generative matter or engendered form.[32]

This is indeed Deleuze's own immanent vision of structuralism rather than the hyper-formalism of someone like Lévi-Strauss; but it is also the vision of structuralism one finds in Leclaire and in parts of the Lacanian school in the late 1960s. Structure, as Deleuze puts it in the celebrated essay from 1967 'How Do We Recognize Structuralism?',[33] is the third term which bypasses the opposition imaginary/real, and ideal/material.[34] It is the dimension proper to the third developmental position (Oedipus followed by castration), not as a third triangulating term which finally

subsumes matter under form or body under language, but as the immanent effect of their equal articulation.

Furthermore, this immanent vision of structure weaves itself into a tacit
critique and reworking of Lacan's Name-of-the-Father. While Deleuze is
ultimately indebted to Lacan's concept in *The Logic of Sense*, as he considers infant development to be inseparable from language acquisition
(Oedipus as structural), the text can be read as an attempt to temper the
inflation of the father's importance in (the early) Lacan's concept by aligning the Lacanian Name-of-the-Father with Klein's 'good object', which is
initially both mother and father.[35] (In this way Deleuze builds on *Coldness
and Cruelty* but does not go as far as *Anti-Oedipus*, which condemns the
very concept.) We see this early on in the dynamic genesis when Deleuze
defines the good object of the depressive position – the mythical idea
of bodily unity, and of parental reconciliation and unification – as the
'Voice'. Deleuze states that the Voice 'awaits the *event*' – namely the event
of castration – 'that will make it a language',[36] which the *infant* furnishes,
such that the Voice as prohibitive 'No!'/Name-of-the-Father is incapable
of linguistically carrying out its function, or rather the infant is retroactively castrated by the very element with which it provides the Voice.
Hence the Voice figures as an impotent castrating agent, withdrawn into
its own dimension of ideality and incapable of having direct effects on the
physicality of the infant body.

The allusions to the Name-of-the-Father come out more clearly if the
original French text is examined. Deleuze writes that not only does the
Voice 'conve[y] tradition' (the paternal surname), it requires that the infant
be viewed from, and inserted into, the viewpoint of its proper name, even
before it can understand what it means.[37] This is what Bruce Fink refers to
as the suturing function of the proper name in Lacan, which names something which does not exist (namely a subject of language) prior to this very
naming.[38] Now, Deleuze writes that the Voice fails on both counts to carry
out the function of the Lacanian 'No!/Name'. As 'no!', it 'forbids without
our knowing what is forbidden, since we will learn it only through the sanction [castration]',[39] a sanction the Voice cannot itself directly impose; as
'name', it is surpassed by the infant's singular *self-nomination/self-castration* –
which occurs when the infant constructs for itself a new name using an
'esoteric word'. To explain the latter, Deleuze turns to Leclaire's 'extremely
interesting thesis'[40] that the erogenous zones during ontogenesis are literally
inscribed and coordinated as a global erogenous body or 'physical surface'
by the construction of a nonsense word, giving 'Poord'jeli' as a prime
example of the 'the secret name [. . .] that a child creates'.[41]

The Voice first appears as a 'familial hum of voices which already speaks
of [the infant]'[42] before the infant has acquired the organising principle

which makes of the Voice in its own dimension (that inhabited by the parents and care-givers) a language capable of conveying sense and referring outside itself to states of affairs. Nonetheless, its importance lies in its ability to communicate something of the 'heights' of language still foreign to the infant, yet through which the infant will gradually bridge the distance separating itself (as physical 'surface' of the body) from it (as language of the 'heights'). What the Voice communicates is above all the phonemic differences spoken by the primary care-givers, prior to their being packaged into larger signifying or morphological units, and within still larger semantemes and denoting propositions.

Deleuze notes the infant's 'extreme sensitivity to phonemic distinctions of the mother tongue',[43] while being 'indifferent' to morphemes and semantemes. Although the infant does not have access to what the Voice *signifies* ('all the concepts and classes which structure the domain of preexistence'[44] inhabited by the care-givers, and which structure the phonemes, morphemes and semantemes composing their speech); and, although the infant can only grasp what the Voice *denotes* at the level of the good object itself (or on the other hand the introjected and projected bad partial objects which the good object serves to mythically unify), the Voice nonetheless 'manifests' – through 'intonation'[45] or 'tonality'[46] – the 'emotional variations of the whole person (the voice that loves and reassures, the voice that attacks and scolds, that itself complains about being wounded, or withdraws and keeps quiet)'.[47] By bringing together Klein and Leclaire, Deleuze suggests that these (pre-'linguistic') phonemic differences are inscribed on the infant's zones, to the extent that the infant's erogenous centring on the Voice as good object is entirely mediated by the Voice's 'manifestations' in intonation.

While during the Kleinian depressive position the infant's drive initially patterns itself after the Voice as good object because of its apparent greater self-unity, the Voice is nothing but an ideal and mythical unity lacking any internal principle of auto-synthesis and more importantly remaining absent from the infant's body and libidinal intentionality, forever withdrawn into its own transcendent dimension. At the cusp of the Oedipal position,[48] it becomes the role of the infant to reconstitute the good object as synthesised unity on the 'surface' of its own body. The infant does this by cutting 'pre-linguistic' phonemic elements out of the Voice, inscribing them on its erogenous zones, and by agglomerating these inscribed phonemes within the construction of a singular esoteric word. The esoteric word is both the nonsensical surface-effect, and the running total as outer form, of the differential relations of phonemic elements progressively inscribed on zones during the Oedipal position and simultaneously amassing in the esoteric word, as form of the body and conjunction of letters. The esoteric word operates outside the propositional orders of sig-nification, denotation, manifestation and meaning (sense), functioning to redouble a body's zones – operating initially as 'partial surfaces' – as a global 'physical surface' identical to the nonsense produced by differential relations of erogenous phonemes or letters.

By referring to Poord'jeli as an 'esoteric word' and thereby drawing Leclaire's case study into his own framework, Deleuze, I would suggest, is adapting Leclaire's thesis concerning his analysand Philippe and in a way generalising this process of self-naming or self-construction for all (non-psychotic) subjects. We all lack a Symbolically efficacious or inscrip-tive Name-of-the-Father because the ideal Voice cannot by itself bridge the distance separating it from bodies, requiring the infant to literally incarnate the Voice and in a way which orients the infant in relation to language and sexuality in a singular manner. This hinges on a theory of the 'event' inseparable from Deleuze's understanding of esoteric words, which we must now examine further.

Deleuze's theory of esoteric words derives from his reading of Lewis Carroll. In Carroll, Deleuze identifies the articulation and poetic bypass-ing (if not overcoming) of a fundamental ontological and psychoanalytic dualism (or better quasi-dualism) underlying his entire logic of sense, that of 'to eat or to speak'.[49] Psychoanalytically, eating/speaking concentrates the dualities of the oral zone: both site of the oral drive, organ of speech, and fed by the sublimation of corporeal drive (the body's affects) into the incorporeal sense expressed by propositions attempting to make 'sense' of these affects through the construction of concepts. The mouth is indeed locus of the disjunctive synthesis of bodies/language as such ('The univoc-ity of Being signifies that Being is Voice, that it is said'[50]).

Ontologically, eating/speaking or bodies/language is the manner in which Deleuze's overarching ontology manifests itself in *The Logic of Sense*. From his very first writings on Spinoza and Bergson to his late *What is Philosophy?*, Deleuze's ontology (or better onto/logic) has functioned to bypass the opposition between dualism and monism through a violent confrontation outside of any dialectical mediation. What he terms the 'plane of immanence' in the 1990s, or 'sense' in the 1960s, is the disjunc-tive monism or better monism-effect produced by the non-relation (as a relation of a 'deeper sort')[51] or the radical disjunction between being and thinking, ontology and epistemology. There being no common measure or medium of communication between being/thinking (or bodies/lan-guage), they can only communicate by means of their very in/ability to communicate, which produces from this dualism an incorporeal monism (qua pure difference), which while solely thinkable is entirely real and not merely ideal.

As he puts it in *The Logic of Sense*:

> Things and propositions are less in a situation of radical duality and more on the two sides of a frontier represented by sense. This frontier does not mingle or reunite them (for there is no more monism here than dualism); it is rather something along the line of an articulation of their difference: body/language.[52]

Esoteric words function in *The Logic of Sense* as the mechanism by which such a quasi-dualism of bodies/language or eating/thinking can be disjunctively synthesised. As such they are vehicles for the generation of events: events are forged within and emerge from esoteric words. I must now answer these three questions: Firstly, what is an event? Secondly, how and why are they produced within esoteric words? Thirdly, how does this relate to the dynamic genesis?

An event, in Deleuze's ontology, is this monism-effect I have referred to. An event is incorporeal yet it is the surface effect of bodies, of their intensive relations as relations of force (stemming initially from the 'depths'). It emerges at the point where a concept *fails* to account for, to re-present, its corporeal cause. The propositional function of denotation serves to point 'outside' language to a spatio-temporal state of affairs which conditions the truth-value of a proposition (as intentionally 'filled' or unfilled).[53] But denotation reduces bodies to language, to a reflection of the image the denotative intention expects to find in a particular state of affairs and on the basis of which the proposition determines its truth or falseness.[54] Deleuze thereby opposes denotation to 'expression', which is the dimension of language's immanence to bodies. Propositions 'express' sense, and they express sense as an event (or 'sense-event'), when they fail to convey within their own medium (language) what caused them at the level of corporeality. This failure converts itself into the production of being – or more precisely of thought/being, pure difference (/), the plane of immanence – because it expresses their fundamental non/relation. Events are produced by propositions at the level of this gap (bodies/language).

Language is hence composed of two heterogeneous base series, denotation/expression, which redouble *within language* the very dualism bodies/language, and on account of which language can entertain a kind of relation with bodies.[55] Drawing on Stoic ontology and logic, Deleuze shows how the event expressed by the verb 'to green' cannot be viewed as a predicate referred back to a propositional subject (for instance a green *tree*), but is rather a 'logical attribute' that whisks its would-be subject away with it within a becoming-incorporeal of the tree, which 'greens' not at the level of materiality, nor at the level of conceptuality, but in the disjoint between the two.[56] As David Lapoujade helpfully phrases it, the event is always said *of* things and of what happens to them (the intermingling of intensive forces), this is its immanence; but it is never said of *things*.[57] Language oscillates between its two poles, denotation/expression, using the failure of denotation to 'feed' expression and thus requiring them both in their oscillation (expression is *the failure* of reference and not the failure *of reference*).

Now, Deleuze identifies in Carroll's work three 'types' of esoteric word: connective, conjunctive and disjunctive.[58] Events are forged within esoteric words in their internal evolution through these three types, which function to connect bodies, and to conjoin and then disjoin bodies and language. Taking the nonsense word 'snark' from Carroll's *The Hunting of the Snark* as an example of the second, conjunctive, type, Deleuze shows how the word is a noun denoting more than one body, and which through this denotational blurring manages to connect a series of bodies and to conjoin bodies with language: 'snark', much like the word 'it', entails a denotational slippage – the word combines the names 'shark' and 'snake', but reveals itself at the end of the tale to denote the 'boojum', the sense and reference of which are not any clearer than those of 'snark'.[59] However, by failing to denote a body and express its corresponding sense, the 'snark' conjoins or synthesises a series of heterogeneous bodies, as well as the founding heterogeneity on which language is built, that of bodies/language: The bodies the word 'snark' conjoins are synthesised nowhere else than within the esoteric word itself, within which bodies and language become inseparable.

The conjunctive esoteric word, however, only *conjoins* bodies and language and does so by using only *denotation*, sidestepping language's founding dualism of expression/denotation, and avoiding the disjunction this dualism entails at the level of the larger dualism of bodies/language. The third, disjunctive, type of esoteric word, brings both series of language into play, and entails a disjunctive synthesis of bodies and language. The classic Carrollian example here is the word 'Jabberwock', which compounds the (*expressive*) verb 'jabber' (to speak volubly) and the (*denoting*) noun '*wocer*', a nonsense word for fruit; 'snark' on the contrary compounds only nouns (shark + snake). 'Jabberwock' is a disjunctive synthesis of eating (fruit) and speaking (volubly), but since it is also a word (albeit a nonsensical one) it provides a shared form or medium within which heterogeneous series can affirm their difference.[60] The key point, however, is that the disjunctive esoteric word can only do this because it is the result of the internal development of the esoteric word, which must pass through all three types.[61]

We see this when Deleuze applies his theory of esoteric words to the dynamic genesis. This occurs the moment he refers to Poord'jeli as an esoteric word. Shortly after, Deleuze explains that Poord'jeli begins as a conjunctive esoteric word, and we can see that it slides over the bodies (erogenous zones) which it synthesises through this slippage (differential relations of letters or phonemes).[62] Poord'jeli as conjunctive esoteric word is both word and body: it is only within this word that Philippe's global erogenous body is synthesised. Poord'jeli then develops into a disjunctive esoteric word with the evolution of Oedipus, according to Deleuze, and with the infant's progressive acquisition of language. This is because the nonsense phonemes inscribed on the body's zones inevitably come into contact with, or resonate with, the infant's eventual propositional structuring of phonemes into referential statements expressive of sense – and we have seen that the disjunctive esoteric word essentially resonates nonsense (*wocer*) with sense (jabber), denotation with expression.

Leclaire gives as an example of this his analysand's description as an adult of his mother's cousin Liliane lying on a beach, whom Leclaire surmises had a pivotal role in the infant Philippe's passage through the Oedipus complex. If the adult Philippe is capable of producing the meaningful and referential statement 'Joli corps de Lili' ('Lili's beautiful body'), he cannot do so without causing such conscious representations to resonate with the unconscious ones subtending and ultimately supporting conscious discourse, namely with the erogenous letter 'li' and more completely with the esoteric word 'Poord'jeli' which covers the subject's erogenous body.[63] If Poord'jeli is a conjunctive esoteric word synthesising bodies/zones within it, Poord'jeli as disjunctive esoteric word (i.e. resonating with *Joli corps de Lili*) serves as the fundamental meeting point in a structure between the order of bodies and the order of language, the erogenous letter and conscious discourse, and functions as the im/possible site of their articulation.

Philippe's fundamental fantasy, his psychic agency, is concentrated in the difference Poord'jeli/*Joli corps de Lili*. *Joli corps de Lili* is a sign or proposition referring to a state of affairs – and not a sequence of signifiers or letters – as long as the 'li' breaks off its links to corporeality and erogeneity (i.e. to 'Poord'jeli'); 'li' exists as a pure signifier or letter within any resulting friction between 'li' as signifier and 'li' as component of a sign. For Deleuze too, this resonance underlies fantasy. Deleuze considers fantasy precisely as an event because of its inability to conceptually account for its corporeal cause. He implicitly alludes to Freud's Wolf Man case as a prime example of this.[64] While the Wolf Man may or may not have witnessed the parental *coitus a tergo* which Freud unearths beneath the famous anxiety dream of wolves, Freud suggests towards the end of his case study that the traumatic 'cause' of the subject's symptoms and fantasies is located in the past only retroactively, by the supposed cause's verbal re-presentation within the fantasmatic scene.[65] Likewise, the conscious and referential statement 'Lili's beautiful body' makes 'sense' to Philippe because it fails to denote or account for its corporeal cause, the unconscious erogenous letter as medium of bodily affect, and in this failure (repression of the letter) establishes the very opposition (word/thing) presupposed by the propositional dimension of denotation, though now as an opposition *within* language (as conscious discourse).

To sum up, by incarnating the Voice through the construction of an esoteric word, the infant self-nominates/self-castrates, expressing the event which will finally make of the Voice a language – and belatedly or retroactively a paternal 'No!/Name', within an immanent and singular horizon. In short, the transcendent and ideal Voice's inability to directly castrate the infant is mitigated by this incarnating self-nomination which defines the esoteric terms of its own castration as event. The event is hence ultimately the event of castration, a singular 'castration "effect"'[66] produced in and by fantasy through the resonance within the disjunctive esoteric word.

Through the theory of esoteric words, Deleuze accounts for the difference in kind between bodies and language within a theory of nonsense which shows how the two orders can also be disjunctively synthesised. The relation between letter and conscious re-presentation (Poord'jeli/*Joli corps de Lili*) is radically barred by secondary repression (castration), but it is precisely through the non/relation framed and made possible by the disjunctive esoteric word in its entirety that this barrier becomes the site of its own evental self-bypassing, making language as such possible.

In his most directed critique of Leclaire, Deleuze questions the linguistic status of the letter in Leclaire, particularly the influence grammar and syntax have on it, stressing that it can never be anything but nonsense, even while endorsing the overall theory of erogenous inscription.[67] Ultimately, Deleuze's aim seems to be to push Leclaire's work further by further equalising the relative contribution body and language, singularity and universal form, 'mother' and 'father', make to the genesis of a structure. Resultantly, in problematising the extent to which language can write itself on bodies in the thought of the Lacanian school, and through the innovation of his theory of esoteric words, Deleuze's work gives rise to the possibility that from this impossibility of inscription emerges the 'event' of the body.[68]

Conclusion: Lacan and the Names-of-the-Father

In 1973–4, Lacan would finally give his seminar on the pluralised/singularised Names-of-the-Father, with the homophonous Seminar XXI *Les non-dupes errent*, signalling the beginning of the final phase of his teaching. While *Anti-Oedipus* (1972) is often given as an (albeit, I would add, primarily combative) influencing factor behind the appearance of this seminar in 1973, I have shown how such an anti-Oedipal position was already being arrived at from within more internal and/or sympathetic quarters, and traces of this more constructive influence can indeed be found in the text.

In his earlier *Coldness and Cruelty* from 1967, in a crucial passage, Deleuze writes:

> The masochist experiences the symbolic order as an intermaternal order in which the mother represents the law under certain prescribed conditions; she generates the symbolism *through which the masochist expresses himself*. It is not a case of identification with the mother [. . .] [who] literally expels the father from the masochistic universe. [. . .] [The father] is deprived of all symbolic function.[69]

Deleuze makes it clear in the same passage that Lacan's Name-of-the-Father is what is at issue here, which makes no room for a maternal contribution to this symbolic and superegoic function. This masochistic 'self-expression' in the absence of the father directly extends itself into *The Logic of Sense*, with 'the secret name "Poord'jeli", that a child creates'.[70]

In Seminar XXI, session of 12 February 1974,[71] Lacan alludes to *Coldness and Cruelty*, and in relation to this says approvingly that the masochist 'invents himself'. This is not wholly specific to masochism, however, and points to a larger reconfiguration of Lacan's teaching in this seminar, whereby the imaginary, the symbolic and the real (or the body, language and *jouissance*) are now to be seen as 'knotted' together in what Lacan stipulates is a 'singular' manner. Instead of being over-structured by the symbolic (and paternal), as we find in the Lacan of the 1950s, the imaginary, and the mother–infant dyad along with it, is now given a more dynamic role, to the relative detriment of the importance of the symbolic, and with the real figuring as that which is in part *produced by* this new arrangement. Furthermore, throughout the session of 18 December 1973, he will refer to this knotting as an 'event' – and for both Frenchmen, speech speaks the event.[72] Indeed, for Lacan it is the event which *does the knotting*,[73] bringing him in close proximity with Deleuze's emphasis on the event's function of disjunctively synthesising bodies-language.

Hence we come full circle, since I have shown that Deleuze's event was itself an attempt to singularise Lacan's Name-of-the-Father.

Notes

1. This chapter draws on, and provides a condensed overview of aspects of, my *The Psychoanalysis of Sense: Deleuze and the Lacanian School* (Edinburgh: Edinburgh University Press, forthcoming).
2. Deleuze, Gilles, 'From Sacher-Masoch to Masochism', *Angelaki*, 9: 1 (2004), pp. 125–33, p. 128.
3. Deleuze, Gilles, *Masochism* (New York: Zone Books, 2006), p. 137, n. 18.
4. Deleuze, Gilles and Guattari, Félix *Anti-Oedipus: Capitalism and Schizophrenia* (London: Continuum, 2004), pp. 155–8, 201–2, 227–8.
5. Deleuze, Gilles, *The Logic of Sense* (London: Continuum, 2013).
6. *The Logic of Sense* is now beginning to receive significant attention in anglophone secondary literature for its psychoanalytic portion. See particularly chapter 5 of Bowden, Sean, *The Priority of Events: Deleuze's Logic of Sense* (Edinburgh: Edinburgh University Press, 2011), and Świątkowski, Piotrek, *Deleuze and Desire: Analysis of The Logic of Sense* (Leuven: Leuven University Press, 2015).
7. The most obvious of these is the Descartes/Spinoza impasse.
8. This revolves around the location and definition of the phallus in both texts, as Guattari makes clear in his essay 'Machine and Structure', in Guattari, Félix, *Molecular Revolution: Psychiatry and Politics* (London: Penguin, 1984), pp. 111–19. *The Logic of Sense* perceives the phallus as part of structure (it is its third 'minimal condition' (p. 60)), *Anti-Oedipus* views the phallus as a detachable machine which when constrained and contained by structure becomes phallic and Oedipal.
9. On this see particularly Lacan's Seminar V, *The Formations of the Unconscious* (1957–8) (unpublished).
10. Only two sessions of this aborted seminar exist. They have recently been translated by Bruce Fink and published as *On the Names-of-the-Father* (Cambridge: Polity Press, 2015).
11. For Lorenzo Chiesa, this shift in the conception of the Name-of-the-Father, in short from transcendence to immanence, occurs around the time of 'Subversion of the Subject'. The Name-of-the-Father becomes folded into the very processes it previously looked over as external guarantor. See Chiesa, Lorenzo, *Subjectivity and Otherness: A Philosophical Reading of Lacan* (Cambridge, MA: MIT Press, 2007).
12. It seems that he had to traverse feminine sexuality (Seminars XIX–XX) in order to arrive at a more singular conception of structure and Oedipus, positing women precisely as the irreducible 'not-all' which escapes the totalising and universalising ambitions of the phallus and male fantasy.
13. On this point see also Eyers, Tom, *Post-Rationalism: Psychoanalysis, Epistemology, and Marxism in Post-War France* (London: Bloomsbury, 2013), pp. 18–23.
14. Leclaire, Serge, *Psychoanalysing: On the Order of the Unconscious and the Practice of the Letter* (Stanford: Stanford University Press, 1998), pp. 124–5; original emphasis.
15. Available at <http://cahiers.kingston.ac.uk/> (last accessed 1 April 2016).
16. As Adrian Johnston puts it, Leclaire's work functions as a 'balance between phenomenological and structuralist approaches to psychoanalytic theory' (Johnston, Adrian, *Time Driven: Metapsychology and the Splitting of the Drive* (Evanston: Northwestern University Press, 2005), p. 352).
17. The 'V' on its side appears as the grapheme '<' (or '>'), connoting the jaws of the wolves from the famous dream and connecting with the subject's oral zone, as well as the wolves' open eyes connecting with the scopic drive. The V when inverted (∧) connotes the open ears of the wolves and the subject's invocatory drive, as well as the protruding posterior of the female figure when on all fours (connecting with both the scopic and anal drives). Leclaire defines this as the letter's two-sidedness (*biface*) – each letter is at once (1) *binarité*, an element inseparable from the binary or differential

relations it forms with other letters; and (2) *bi-polarité*, an element which vacillates between its two poles – its status as letter and a libidinal movement of the body insepa-rable from a corresponding partial object. See Leclaire, Serge, 'Compter avec la psy-chanalyse (Séminaire de l'ENS, 1966–67)', *Cahiers pour l'analyse*, 8 (October 1967), pp. 91–119, available at <http://cahiers.kingston.ac.uk/pdf/cpa8.6.leclaire.pdf> (last accessed 28 August 2015).

18. See Leclaire, *Psychoanalysing*, ch. 3.

19. See Leclaire, Serge, '*Duroc, ou le point de vue économique en psychanalyse*', in *Démasquer le réel. Un essai sur l'objet en psychanalyse* (Paris: Seuil, 1971), pp. 168–88, especially p. 181, and in relation to Poord'jeli, *A Child is Being Killed: On Primary Narcissism and the Death Drive* (Stanford: Stanford University Press, 1998 [1975]), p. 39.

20. Leclaire, Serge, *Oedipe à Vincennes. Séminaire 69* (Paris: Fayard, 1999).

21. Indeed, Leclaire's lecture course is referred to positively in the final chapter of Deleuze and Guattari's *Anti-Oedipus*, particularly Leclaire's definition of the body in its rela-tion to the maternal and paternal functions.

22. The maternal function for Leclaire is the mechanism which distinguishes between the bio-physiological body (in short, need), and the erogenous body, by marking organs of consumptive and excremental need (the mouth, anus, and so on) with maternal desire thereby establishing demanding zones (as repetitive circuits which seek to bring this founding mark, the partial object, back to the zone). The mother thereby distinguishes erogenous demand from biological need, whereas the paternal function disjunctively articulates the singular erogenous body with universal desire and castration.

23. Leclaire, *Oedipe à Vincennes*, pp. 27–8; my translation.

24. Leclaire, *Psychoanalysing*, p. 81.

25. The two most important of these are (1) '*corne*' (a fragment of which is found in Poord'jeli), meaning horn and callus, in French, with ties to the infant's callused feet, to the infant's forehead (both privileged erogenous zones), and to the mythical 'horn' of the unicorn (*licorne*); and (2) 'li', with ties to 'Liliane' (or 'Lili') (appearing at the end of Poord'jeli), Philippe's mother's cousin, with whom Philippe iden-tified when relations with his mother led to a developmental impasse during the Oedipal stage, and again which figures as one half of the '*li-corne*'. See Leclaire, *Psychoanalysing*, ch. 5. On this see also Lacan, Jacques, *The Seminar of Jacques Lacan, Book XI: The Four Fundamental Concepts of Psychoanalysis* (London: W. W. Norton, 1998), p. 250.

26. See Peggy Kamuf's translator's note to Leclaire, Serge, *Psychoanalysing*, pp. 150–1, n. 15.

27. We can also note that Poord'jeli replicates the three syllables of the surname.

28. For instance, Deleuze was clearly aware of the debates occurring within the *Cahiers pour l'analyse*.

29. Deleuze, *Logic of Sense*, p. 216.

30. See Lacan, *Four Fundamental Concepts*, pp. 180–9.

31. This line of argumentation underpins Świątkowski's book *Deleuze and Desire*, which develops a Kleinian and anti-Lacanian reading of the dynamic genesis. One also finds this mistaken anti-Lacanian reading in Widder, Nathan, 'From Negation to Disjunction in a World of Simulacra: Deleuze and Melanie Klein', *Deleuze Studies*, 3: 2 (December 2009), pp. 207–30.

32. Deleuze, *The Logic of Sense*, p. 105.

33. Deleuze, Gilles, 'How Do We Recognize Structuralism?', in *Desert Islands and Other Texts 1953–1974* (Los Angeles: Semiotext(e), 2004), pp. 170–92.

34. See, for instance, 'heights [*ciels*] of imagination' (ibid. p. 172), the 'heights' being associated with Platonic ideality in Deleuze (see *The Logic of Sense*, pp. 145, 219).

35. See, for instance, Kristeva, Julia, *Melanie Klein* (New York: Columbia University Press, 2001), pp. 129, 172–4. As Deleuze puts it, the Oedipal good object is mother with a penis, father with a breast (*The Logic of Sense*, p. 234).

36. Deleuze, *The Logic of Sense*, p. 221; original emphasis.
37. Compare Deleuze, *The Logic of Sense*, p. 221 with p. 225 of the French (Paris: Minuit, 1969). See also *Anti-Oedipus*, which refers to the despot – the 'veritable origin' (p. 227) of Lacan's 'Name-of-the-Father' – as the 'voice from on high' (p. 224).
38. See Fink, Bruce, *The Lacanian Subject: Between Language and Jouissance* (Princeton: Princeton University Press, 1996).
39. Deleuze, *The Logic of Sense*, p. 221.
40. Ibid. p. 264.
41. Ibid. p. 265. As we saw in Leclaire, this means both that the erogenous zone is fundamentally marked by a letter, and that each letter is defined both by the phonemic differential relations it forms with other letters and by an intensive quantity determined in part by a zone's drive and corresponding partial object. See ibid. pp. 259, 264.
42. Ibid. p. 263.
43. Ibid. p. 263.
44. Ibid. p. 221.
45. Ibid. p. 269, n. 8.
46. Ibid. p. 279.
47. Ibid. p. 221.
48. This argument is developed throughout the second part of the twenty-seventh series. The unity of the good object lies solely in the pure, unliveable, past, as a creation of remembrance, and is lived in the ('physical') present as fragmented phonemes tied to zones. Transcending lived experience, it is the Voice's topological location in the ideal 'heights' of memory alone which unifies it from the infant's viewpoint.
49. Deleuze, *The Logic of Sense*, p. 29.
50. Ibid. p. 205.
51. See Deleuze, Gilles, *Foucault* (Continuum: London, 2006 [1986]), p. 53.
52. Deleuze, *The Logic of Sense*, p. 30.
53. Ibid. p. 17.
54. Ibid. p. 17.
55. Ibid. p. 45.
56. Ibid. p. 25.
57. See Lapoujade, David, *Deleuze, les mouvements aberrants* (Paris: Minuit, 2014), p. 115.
58. Deleuze, *The Logic of Sense*, pp. 56, 270.
59. See ibid. pp. 52–3. See Carroll, Lewis, *The Hunting of the Snark: An Agony, in Eight Fits* (Oxford: Oxford University Press, 2007 [1876]).
60. Deleuze, *Logic of Sense,* pp. 53–4.
61. We actually see this in 'Jabberwock', which is the addition of an everyday verb (to jabber) to an esoteric word (*wocer*) which as a noun points to the remnants within the disjunctive esoteric word of the conjunctive type.
62. Ibid. p. 265.
63. See Leclaire, *Psychoanalysing*, pp. 112–13.
64. See Deleuze, *The Logic of Sense*, pp. 241–2. Note the reference to 'parental coitus', and the fact that Deleuze's model of fantasy is strongly Laplanchian, the Wolf Man case also featuring heavily in Laplanche and Pontalis's 'Fantasy and the Origins of Sexuality', a major influence on Deleuze. See Laplanche, Jean and Pontalis, Jean-Bertrand, 'Fantasy and the Origins of Sexuality', in Burgin, Victor, Donald, James and Kaplan, Cora (eds), *Formations of Fantasy* (London: Methuen, 1986), pp. 5–34.
65. See Freud, Sigmund, 'From the History of an Infantile Neurosis [The "Wolfman"]', in *Sigmund Freud: The 'Wolfman' and Other Cases* (London: Penguin Books, 2002 [1918]), chs VII–IX.
66. Deleuze, *The Logic of Sense*, p. 241.
67. See ibid. p. 264.

68. Leclaire does not confront this difficulty in his work and, likening this aspect of his concept to the Derridean notion of *différance*, considers the letter to *precede* and unstably found the classical philosophical distinction between the sensible and the intelligible. See Leclaire, *Psychoanalysing*, pp. 147–8, n. 18. It is hence not problematic, for Leclaire, for the letter to inscribe itself on bodies and bridge the dualism of mind and body. Éric Laurent has recently suggested, however, that Lacan's usage of topology in his conception of the relation between body and language avoids what Laurent calls the 'flattening' of the two dimensions in Leclaire's work, which suggests that Deleuze's critique could be more applicable to Leclaire than to Lacan himself. See the first three of Laurent's podcasts on the site *Radio Lacan*, available at <http://www.radiolacan.com/en/topic/583> (last accessed 1 April 2016).

69. Deleuze, *Masochism*, pp. 63–4; my emphasis.

70. Deleuze, *The Logic of Sense,* p. 265.

71. Available in unedited form at <http://staferla.free.fr/S21/S21%20NON-DUPES. . ..pdf> (last accessed 28 August 2015).

72. Lacan, however, will associate the event with the real and sense with the imaginary, whereas for Deleuze the sense-event is univocal being.

73. In Seminar XXIII, *The Sinthome*, this event becomes a 'fourth' ring, in addition to the imaginary, symbolic and real, which binds these other three. In the session of 18 November 1975 he describes this fourth ring as the father, available at <http://staferla.free.fr/S23/S23%20LE%20SINTHOME.pdf> (last accessed 1 April 2016).

Chapter 8

Baroque Structuralism: Deleuze, Lacan and the Critique of Linguistics

Samo Tomšič

Nowadays it is still common to see Deleuze and Lacan as two rivals standing on entirely opposite shores. The legitimation of this opposition is sought in Deleuze and Guattari's notorious *Anti-Oedipus* project, whose very name attacks one of the cornerstones of Freudian psychoanalysis, the Oedipal drama of castration and the corresponding notion of negativity. On the other side, Lacan's teaching is said to have pushed structuralism to the extreme, privileging lack and negativity, while also promoting an overall pessimistic vision of politics. However, this perspective could also be inverted. Deleuze and Guattari's project contains a peculiar radicalisation of psychoanalysis, a consequent substitution of the psychological with the schizological: schizo-analysis took a step further in the depsychologisation and deindividualisation of the mental apparatus, or if one prefers, of thinking. *Anti-Oedipus* pursued the anti-humanist orientation of their 'arch-rivals', structuralism and psychoanalysis, whereby it went beyond the boundaries of concepts such as structure and analysis. With Freud, psychoanalysis took the first step by abolishing the metaphysical hypothesis of the soul. The etymology of 'psychoanalysis' already contains this point: *analysis* (decomposition, dissolution, deconstruction) of *psyché*. Freud's discipline is anti-psychology, which still remains *logos* of *psyche*, the science of the soul. With the discovery of the unconscious no soul-hypothesis could be sustained any longer, and in this respect Freud indeed produced a ground-breaking epistemological, philosophical and political rupture. From here on the subject could finally be envisaged beyond its anthropomorphic mask: the subject of the unconscious has no human face; it is a decentralised, constitutively alienated and split entity. Yet, Freud did not go beyond the split that the abolition of the soul revealed in the psychic reality. Consequently, psychoanalysis never made the effort to become more than a royal road to negativity, while other attempts to step out of Freud's shadow only amounted to worse. Jung's mysticism brought about the obscurantist regression, while the Anglo-Saxon development continues to represent a conformist regression in accordance with the demands of the free market ideology. Then there is Wilhelm Reich, the bastard psychoanalyst, who in an exaggerated and somewhat delusional way demonstrated that there is something beyond the schism of the mental apparatus discovered by Freud.

The predominantly vitalist and vehemently critical orientation of *Anti-Oedipus* suggested that Freud failed to envisage the positive, productive and nomadic function of desire. He may have decentralised the mental apparatus by pushing forward the triad composed of negativity, lack and metonymy, yet this was only the appearance of unconscious desire, which was thereafter re-centralised, normalised, domesticated by means of the Oedipal family triangle: Father, Mother, Child. Positivity, productivity and nomadism got overshadowed and the subject's polymorph character was reintegrated into what Freud called *Familienroman des Neurotikers*, the neurotic's family novel, and what Lévi-Strauss described as Freud's greatest myth. Lacan is said to have pursued this original Freudian sin under the guise of its rationalisation by means of the linguistic notions such as metaphor, metonymy and structure, to which Deleuze and Guattari immediately opposed metamorphosis, nomadism and rhizome. Within these oppositions the main task of schizo-analysis would consist of moving beyond the hypothesis of *Spaltung*, the negative structure that became the privileged departure for the entire structuralist movement. Schizo-analysis would then stand for psychoanalysis without negativity, dissolution of the split. It would think the main Freudian achievement, the decentralisation of thinking, beyond the conceptual triangle composed by the phallus, castration and loss. We can remark here that Lacan remained sceptical toward such dichotomies, which always seem to sound too good to be true. The question, however, remains whether this was what Deleuze and Guattari actually intended and whether the later developments in Lacan's teaching could not offer a slightly different view of the problem.

In the following I would like to examine some of the intersections between structural psychoanalysis and schizo-analysis. These points of encounter will be addressed through their common critique of linguistics, the confrontation with what could be described as the persistence of Aristotelian philosophy of language in modern linguistics. In the second part, the critical perspectives of Lacan and Deleuze will be linked to their efforts to construct a new topology, which both thinkers claimed to have found in the baroque.

The sins and blind spots of linguistics

As already indicated above, Deleuze and Guattari's opposition targeted the affinities of psychoanalysis and structuralism, and more broadly the epistemic foundations of structural linguistics, for which neither of them cultivated much sympathy. In *A Thousand Plateaus* they attack what they call the 'postulates of linguistics', and one can hardly overlook that their critique targets both Saussure and Chomsky, whose generative linguistics by then had won the battle against continental structuralism and reintroduced positivist epistemology into the science of language. The postulates of linguistics propose a negative summary of the modern science of language in the following four theses:

1. 'Language is informational and communicational.'
2. 'There is an abstract machine of language that does not appeal to any "extrinsic" factor.'
3. 'There are constants or universals of language that permit us to define it as a homogenous system.'
4. 'Language can be scientifically studied only under the conditions of a standard or major language.'[1]

Beyond the specific developments provided for each point, the common feature that traverses this critical summary of linguistics' scientific tendencies can hardly be overlooked: normalisation and domestication of language accompanied by the presence of mastery. Saussure, too, persisted in the frames of the master's discourse (the general structure that grounds the relations of domination and subjection; it was none other than Lacan who identified Saussure with this structural framework). Instead of bringing about an 'emancipation of language' – something that Deleuze and Guattari appreciated in literature, this counterpart of linguistics, or at least in certain writers, such as Kafka and Beckett – structural linguistics ended up renewing its servitude, under the banner of the four postulates. Structuralism would thus stand for the scientific taming of language. Still the overall situation is more complex, and structuralism does not entirely match this critique either – not even for Deleuze, who wrote a famous text not simply *on* but moreover *for* structuralism.

By prioritising information and communication, linguistics remained within the old Aristotelian frames: it treated language as *organon* (instrument and organ) serving pragmatic purposes such as transmission of information, adequate representation of reality, constitution and regulation of stable social relations, and so on. Thereby, language remained centred by an ideal and normative communicational model. This is one crucial aspect of Deleuze and Guattari's notion of abstract machine, the other one being that language is envisaged in its absolute detachment from other registers of reality, be they human or inhuman. Once transformed into a scientific object, in other words, extracted and isolated from its concrete manifestations (recall that for Saussure linguistics is grounded on the differentiation of language from speech), language is turned into an ideality, which, as such, does not exist. The object of linguistics is inexistent but it nevertheless serves well for regulating the practice and the experience of language. In the very same way the psychoanalytic language of Oedipus domesticates the subjective dialects of unconscious desire: Oedipus does not exist, yet it is imposed onto the subject as the regulative frame, which teaches him or her how to desire 'correctly'.

Constructing the constants and the universals that are supposed to be common to all languages enables the isolation of the scientific object. This isolation is inevitably accompanied by the homogenisation of language – in fact, it is the same process. Language is cleansed of surpluses, deviations and movements that accompany concrete speech situations. Deleuze and Guattari's last point, the study of language under the paradigm of a major or standard language, most explicitly questions the presupposed ideological neutrality of linguistic treatment of language. The very expression 'major language' indicates the persistence of a power relation within the science of language and should be evidently correlated to the opposite idea of a minor language,[2] which can, within the abstract linguistic regime, only appear as particular subjective dialect, actualisation of the universal features of any language. For the science of language, and this is again a moment that could be qualified as Aristotelian, living language is subordinated to language as such, the scientific object that linguistics supposedly extracts from the Babylon of natural languages.

Here we can hardly avoid evoking Deleuze's controversial statement in his posthumously released *Abécédaire*, where he remarks that linguistics has caused a lot of harm (*mal*: damage, evil). Linguistics is a negative science, which needs to be contrasted to the lessons of literature, where 'minor language' is practised beyond the abstract linguistic machine and against the idea of universal grammar. Literature – critique of linguistics and clinics of language. No surprise that the *Abécédaire* closes with very brief and hostile remarks on Wittgenstein and the analytic philosophy. Wittgenstein and his followers are accused of 'assassination of philosophy' – they constructed a 'system of terror' and presented poverty as greatness ('pauvreté installée en grandeur', says Deleuze in his video interview). All this could be associated to the various stages of Wittgenstein's philosophy, whose guideline remained the attempt to conceive first logic and then grammar as therapy of philosophy and more broadly therapy of language, which abolishes the false problems and shifting meanings of concepts and words. These linguistic and philosophical evildoers are then the main enemies of any attempt to overcome the abstract linguistic hegemony with the concrete experience of language in literature, in childhood and finally in the unconscious. From this perspective we can hardly overlook that Deleuze already in the 1960s replaced the notion of 'structure' with a more flexible 'becoming', which he associated with Nietzsche.[3] Language, too, was approached from this perspective, thereby exposing an aspect of symbolic systems that the classical structuralist programme supposedly neglected. Here, a topological lesson is at stake, which will be more directly addressed further below, a lesson that brings Deleuze closer to Lacan.

So, linguistics did a lot of harm. This claim is made in Deleuze's response to the letter S, which stands for style. Linguistics is equally avoided under the letter L, which stands for literature as an *experience* of the *life* of language, its becoming, metamorphosis and autonomy. Opposite to this stands the structuralist obsession with mathematical formalisation, its scientism, which strives to establish linguistics as a positive science, whose object (*la langue*) is obtained through an act of abstraction and subtraction: *la langue* is *le langage* (language) minus *la parole* (speech), as Saussure has already formulated. Language is thus language without speech, numb language. Linguistics treats language as if no living being would speak it, as *no-body*'s language, language without body. Could we not see here another critical axis of Deleuze's concept of the body without organs? Linked to the linguistic problematic such an organless body would stand for a language, which is – against Aristotle and the pragmatic, analytic and positivist philosophy of language – *not* an *organon*, but which remains a body. A materialist science of language, what structuralism strived to become, would need to think language beyond the four postulates of linguistics.

Deleuze's condemnation of linguistics is formulated in the following context:

> In order to understand style, you must know nothing about linguistics. Linguistics has done a lot of harm. Why is this the case? Because there is an opposition between linguistics and literature, which do not go well together. According to linguistics, *langue* is a system in a state of equilibrium, which can thus be an object of science. All the rest, all the variations are set aside as belonging not to *langue* but to *parole*. But a writer knows well that a language is a system that is by nature far from equilibrium, a system in a perpetual state of imbalance, so that there is no difference between a level of *langue* and a level of *parole*. Language is made up of all sorts of heterogeneous currents, in a state of multiple disequilibrium.[4]

For linguistics language is autonomous, homogeneous and constituted on an underlying *relation*. For Deleuze – and this is where the opposition between him and Lacan begins to weaken – language is essentially *non-relation*, which immediately problematises its presumed isolation and homogeneity. However, the question is whether structuralism can be entirely subsumed to this denouncement and categorised exclusively as a normalising tendency in the science of language. Deleuze had the intuition that structure is not merely a normative system that the scientific apparatus imposes to the free, vital and raw linguistic materiality. On the contrary, structure is indeed the privileged name for the *disequilibrium of language*, and Lacan is *the* structuralist, who thought this discovery in the most rigorous way, without amounting to the dichotomies such as structure and life, mathematics and poetry or linguistics and literature.

Deleuze, too, does not simply choose speech against language, denouncing the systematicity and opting for linguistic spontaneity. Rather, he rejects the very pertinence of the dichotomy language/speech, and consequently that between abstract structure and living experience. As Lecercle writes:

> Deleuze does not deny the possibility of a system, of thinking in terms of *langue*. What he denies is the ontological hierarchy, and separation from *parole*. A system there may be, yet it is a strange one, which a systematic linguist would fail to recognize.[5]

To speak of structure is not false. What is false is that linguistics recurred to ontological hierarchisation, and we know that for Lacan ontology is *the* discipline grounded on the master's discourse; and even here, Lacan does not target just any ontology but the closed ontological system par excellence, that of Aristotle. Deleuze, too, opts for linguistics without the spectre of Aristotle. His condemnation of linguistics should therefore be additionally specified. What did a lot of harm in linguistics is grammar, which tames the dynamic of language, and rejects its immanent becoming, which strives to no external and normative end. Grammar does this in order to present language as a fixed and stable constellation, which is supposed to represent the real of language. This grammatical normalisation and its ontological aspirations are not at all characteristic for structuralism, which explains linguistic stability from the perspective of instabilities such as the unconscious, aphasia or child language (Jakobson being the most evident example of this orientation). The centrality of grammar is what the materialist core of structuralism openly strived to leave behind by pursuing a consequent decentralisation in the field of language.

Incidentally, Lacan denounced the same restriction of linguistics, when he openly thematised the insufficiencies of the structuralist 'opinion movement'.[6] The media image of structuralism, which involved severe imprecisions, neutralised the epistemic dilemmas as well as the dialectical and materialist core of the structuralist research programme. Lacan addressed this problem in an interview from 1966: 'Structuralism will last for as long as the roses, symbolisms and Parnassus: one literary season. [. . .] The structure, however, will not go away any time soon, because it is inscribed into the real.'[7] Lacan envisaged an intensified understanding of structuralism throughout his teaching. The structural realism, expressed in the formulation 'the inscription of the structure into the real', affirms the rational character of the real, without thereby concluding that the notion of structure should be thought exclusively through the linguistic paradigm (this would equate the real with the symbolic and entirely overlap reality and the real, something that Lacan rigorously distinguished). The point here is rather in affirming that, while reality is linguistic and discursive, there is also something like a *real of language*, which can become the object of a science of structures, which found its first and hitherto most accomplished exemplification in structural linguistics. The end of structuralism as an opinion movement thus *does not imply* the end of structuralism as a movement of episteme.

The quarrel of Deleuze and Guattari with Lacanian psychoanalysis turned around this major point, as Lecercle has already noted:

> The center of Deleuze's hostility to linguistics [. . .] can best be expressed as a rejection of Milner's central tenet in his philosophical reconstruction of the science of language: that there is a Real of *langue*, and that this Real is the object of a calculus.[8]

Still, Lacan and Deleuze share a common denominator: there is a real of language. This linguistic real is irreducible to grammatical structure and – this is where Milner might be corrected – is formalisable without therefore being reducible to the calculus (abstract quantification). The question remains: can the structural instability, dynamic, non-relation be more than experience of literature? Can it become a scientific object? A positive answer to this question conditions the possibility for a materialist science of language. Lacan, who was vehemently opposed to every reduction of linguistics to grammar, proposed several names for the real of language: unconscious, *lalangue, jouissance*, which all come down to the conception of structure as a feature of the real. His later seminars, where the real is defined with three negative features, address this problem most directly: absence of the law, foreclosure of sense and fragmentation (non-all). None of these features suggests that the real is not structured – they merely postulate that it does not contain a stable law, which would make the real entirely predictable and invariable; nor does it contain sense, which would support its univocity and consistency; and finally, the pieces of the real do not form a closed totality. However, this non-all is already the privileged

Lacanian name for the structure of the real, for the real as structured – not structured like a language (that axiom applies only to the unconscious, the real of language), but simply structured without being necessary, univocal or totalised. In order to come closer to Deleuze one could say: the structure of the real manifests as becoming, and the features of this becoming-structure, this structure-as-becoming are grasped with *topology* rather than with classical linguistics – and the same holds for the linguistic structure: 'Topology is not "made to guide us in structure". Topology is this structure – as retroaction of the chain order of which language consists.'[9]

One could remark something similar about rhizome, which is Deleuze and Guattari's attempt not simply to reject the concept of structure but to name a dynamic structure, which has nothing in common with the transcendentalism of structure. This, of course, does not mean that rhizome overlaps with the Lacanian non-all, but it does represent an effort to preserve a systematic approach. As Lecercle insists, Deleuze was not blindly opposed to the system, nor was he a non-systematic thinker. He merely strived for a decentralised and dehierarchised system, hence the choice of literature against linguistics, Anti-Oedipus against Oedipus or becoming against structure.

For Lacan, too, linguistics has done a lot of harm, but unlike Deleuze, he strived 'to construct a linguistics, which would take language more "seriously"'.[10] The given linguistics then does not take language seriously enough. It either reduces it to *langue* (Saussure) by separating structure from becoming, excluding temporality from structure and evacuating speech from language; or it renews the organonic conception of language (Chomsky). To this development a Deleuzian-sounding problematic would need to be added: 'But is language branched to something that could be admitted in terms of some life, that is a question, which would not be bad to be awaken in linguists.'[11] We seem to be back at the dichotomy 'abstract structure versus living experience'. But is this truly the case? Could we not think the introduction of language in the sense suggested by Deleuze, namely as the name for the instability and disequilibrium of language – something that Lacan addressed through his concept of the barred Other? His stubborn repeating that the Other does not exist points to a paradox in the structure, namely that it is not as transcendent and detached from the body and the real as the simplified readings of structuralism suggest.

In order to pinpoint the insufficiencies of Saussurean structuralism, Lacan similarly resorts to literature. Joyce, for instance, turns out to be anti-Saussure par excellence, a move beyond the horizon of popularised structuralism, since the main value of his literature consists in the fact that it involves something like martyrdom of the subject and of language. Joyce's literature exposes the actual meaning of the 'life of language': language as a factory of *jouissance*, a torture-house rather than a 'house of being'.[12] In this way a critical aspect of the bar that Saussure placed between the signifier and the signified can be thematised:

> What happens in Joyce's work? The signifier stuffs the signified. It is because the signifiers fit together, combine, and concertina [. . .] that something is produced as signified that may seem enigmatic, but is clearly what is closest to what we analysts, thanks to analytic discourse, have to read – lapsus.[13]

The stuffing of the signified goes further than Saussure's notion of arbitrariness, which remains a form of *relation*. It fully acknowledges that something between both poles of the linguistic signs does not work, a *non-relation*, which results from the insight that the dynamic between the signifiers involves a *double* production, of which the effect of the signified is merely one side. What makes Joyce unreadable is the other aspect of production, which concerns *jouissance*, something which not only 'serves no purpose',[14] but which is entirely meaningless and non-referential. *Poiesis* is thus internally doubled on the production of reality (in this respect performativity is the main feature of language) and the production of *jouissance* (which is precisely *not* performative but real discursive consequence). Saussure was not entirely unaware of this critical dimension, given his preoccupation with anagrams. But as he was searching for codified messages, enigmatic, hidden or repressed meaning, which needed to be brought back to the surface, he remained within the effects of the signified.

The minimal materialist thesis concerning language would then be the following Lacanian axiom: the signifier is the material cause of *jouissance*. Thereby we enter yet another polemic with Aristotle, whose theory of causality is here openly overthrown. Not only does Lacan subvert the notion of matter by detaching it from its immediate, sensual, qualitative context, but he includes among causes something no consequent Aristotelian would ever agree to: the signifier. For this reason, Lacan could claim that the Saussurean bar is both a bearer of epistemic revolution and an obstacle to be overcome in the passage from language as scientific object to language as experience of structural instability. Here, literature and speech revolve around the same problem: linguistic non-relation, or multiple disequilibrium. Language is thus not simply grounded on the bar between the signifier and the signified. Language itself *is* a bar. Again, this is the critical point of Lacan's barred Other, the disclosed and dynamic system of differences, deprived of a stable mode of existence. This means then that the autonomy of the signifier should not be understood in terms of the transcendentalism of the symbolic order either. Its autonomy grounds on an immanent short-circuit between linguistic communication and production – and this interruption, this non-relation, should become the object of a materialist science of language.

The Saussurean signifier is clearly not conceptualised as a material cause. This is not the case in psychoanalysis, for which the signifier produces two essential effects, the subject and *jouissance*, which violate the regime of signification and are not included in the regime of the signified. The organonic notion of language and the foreclosure of speech from the science of language both repress the subject. Due to this incapacity of linguistics to think the subject of the unconscious, Lacan introduced the term *linguisterie*, the main task of which is to account for the real of language: 'Structure is real. In general this is determined by the convergence toward impossibility. Precisely through this it is real.'[15] The equation 'structure = real' makes little sense for the structuralist doxa, where structure simply describes the system of differences and the abstract character of the symbolic. The structuralist research programme can only become materialist under the condition that it abolishes this transcendental perspective. We are dealing with 'hyper-structuralism' (Milner), which is already beyond classical structuralism but not beyond its revolutionary kernel, its detachment of language from the communicative model. Structuralism conditioned the first thoroughly non-Aristotelian philosophy of language. Deleuze's philosophy and Lacan's teaching represent two ways of traversing structuralism in order to overcome its restrictions, by placing the accent on becoming (Deleuze) and on the impossible (Lacan).

The topological turn of the structuralist screw

Lacan and Deleuze thus share a common *philosophical* displacement, not *against* structuralism, but *within* structuralism. This shift is, among others, expressed by the effort to think the structural paradoxes by means of topological models: Borromean knots in Lacan, and the fold in Deleuze. These tools enable one to think structure as a peculiar synthesis of negativity and becoming. Deleuze and Lacan meet in the observation that topology directs philosophy toward a materialist theory of the subject and of language. This is where for both contexts the topological lessons of the baroque become crucial.

The baroque reference has been associated with Lacan's impenetrable and equivocal style from very early on. Indeed, this feature seems to bring him furthest from the structuralist formalism. The baroque style plays with the breakdown of the presupposed linguistic equilibrium. In this respect style raises the same structural problems as speech. In the light of Lacan's remark that his axiom 'the unconscious is structured as a language does not belong to the field of linguistics',[16] style obtains an additional weight, as far as it directs psychoanalysis away from science towards literature. Freud acknowledged this tendency early on, when complaining that his case studies read more as novels rather than rigorous scientific treaties. In the end the psychoanalytic and the linguistic object seem to address two different aspects of the real of language and consequently two different notions of structure. The definition of the signifier requires a topological turn: 'the signifier is first of all that which has an effect of the signified, and it is important not to elide the fact that between them there is something barred that must be crossed over'.[17] Literature and speech introduce a corporeal dimension, which complicates the topology of the symbolic. The space of linguistic production is curved, decentralised, the structure is disclosed – or to paraphrase Koyré, the notion of structure initiated the passage from the closed world of Aristotelian linguistics into the infinite universe of the materialist science of language.

As a point of curiosity we can remark that the critical stance, according to which classical linguistics elaborates an abstract geometry of perfect shapes, was adopted by the least likely person: Joseph Stalin. His late intervention in the Soviet linguistic debates contains the following remark:

> Abstracting itself from anything that is particular and concrete in words and sentences, grammar treats only the general patterns, underlying the word changes and the combination of words into sentences, and builds in such a way grammatical rules and laws. In this respect grammar bears a resemblance to geometry, which, when giving its laws, abstracts itself from concrete objects, treats objects as bodies deprived of concreteness and defines their mutual relations not as concrete relations of certain concrete objects but as relations of bodies in general, namely, relations deprived of any concreteness.[18]

Though Stalin missed one crucial thing: the main problem is not in the opposition abstract–concrete, universal–particular but in the fact that the geometrisation of linguistic space through grammar leaves linguistic production out of the picture and thereby overlooks the real of language. Grammar is equivalent to Euclidean geometry, which deals exclusively with idealisations and homogenous space, leaving the linguistic space abstract and immaterial. Only angels could potentially speak such 'Euclidean' language, where nothing except representation and communication takes place. Aspheric topology, knots and folds, in contrast, take a step further.

Let us at this point continue with Lacan's topological definition of the signifier:

> The effects of the signified seem to have nothing to do with what causes them. This means that the references or things the signifier serves to approach remain approximate – macroscopic, for example. What is important is not that it's imaginary [. . .] At the level of the signifier/signified distinction, what characterizes the relation of the signified and what serves as the indispensable third party, namely the referent, is precisely that the signified misses the referent. The jointer doesn't work.[19]

What is problematised as imaginary are the relationality in language, the stable linkage between words and things, and, again, the Aristotelianism in linguistics. Lacan's conclusion points in a different direction: 'the signifier is stupid',[20] it does not ground any positive knowledge, which would support and guarantee the stability and regularity of language; and further, the Other does not exist, which again means that language is not a frozen grammatical constellation but a disequilibrium in permanent movement. Together, the stupidity of the signifier and the inexistence of the Other form the truth that linguistic Aristotelianism always systematically rejected. An alternative to linguistics that Lacan baptises *linguisterie* is required: 'under the term [. . .] I group whatever claims [. . .] to intervene in men's affairs in the name of linguistics'.[21] This *linguisterie* inevitably proposes a different geometrisation of the linguistic real by rejecting the grammatical geometrisation of language. But what is *linguisterie* other than a materialist science of language, 'the science that concerns itself with *lalangue*, which I write as one word, so as to specify its object, as is done in every other science'?[22] Lacan never simply gave up on linguistics. Instead, he intended to determine its epistemic object more rigorously.

Let us now turn to Deleuze's discussion of structuralism, for there we find the best possible accentuation of its materialist potentials. The first criterion of structuralism is the differentiation between the symbolic, the imaginary and the real, and the isolation of the epistemic object, which is the autonomy of the symbolic. As Deleuze writes, 'the symbolic must be understood as the production of the original and specific theoretical object',[23] meaning that it distinguishes the science of language from other sciences, while also placing it within the same epistemic paradigm as physics, biology, psychoanalysis, and so on. Deleuze also detected well the specificities of this autonomous symbolic order, on the one hand its topological features, and on the other hand its internal multiplicity: 'Space is what is structural, but an unextended, pre-extensive space [. . .] The scientific ambition of structuralism is not quantitative, but topological and relational' and further 'every structure is a multiplicity'.[24] The notion of structure is equated with a 'transcendental topology',[25] which is '*real without being actual, ideal without being abstract*.[26] This is precisely the materialist quarrel: how to think real effects beyond the dualism of potentiality and actuality, and how to think an idea beyond the metaphysical dualism of abstract and concrete. It is also clear that a rejection of another major feature of Aristotelianism, pragmatism and positivism is at stake here, an aspect that concerns the ontological status of mathematical, geometrical and topological objects. For Aristotle, and this was the main point of his refutation of Plato, these objects are mere idealities, in the pejorative sense of abstractions, which have hardly anything in common with the empirical objects of science. They are, in the best case, potentialities, which nevertheless lack every actualisation. However, for scientific modernity, at least according to Koyré's critical epistemology, mathematics becomes the privileged tool for exploring the real beyond the restrictive frames of human cognition and consciousness. Mathematics and topology are two materialist weapons against the shadow of Aristotle, which remains to exercise its formal influence in the hegemony of analytic epistemology and empiricist materialism.

To the autonomy of the symbolic professed by structuralism a specific subjectivity should be correlated, a subjectivity that becomes visible only after science erases the figure of man. This erasure should be correlated to the abolition of the soul, yet another metaphysical hypothesis, the rejection of which inaugurated scientific modernity and undermined the foundation of Aristotelian epistemology. In his *Order of Things*, Foucault wrote the famous lines that later inspired Deleuze:

> It is no longer possible to think in our day than in the void left by man's disappearance. For this void does not create a deficiency; it does not constitute a lacuna that must be filled. It is nothing more, and nothing less, than the unfolding of a space in which it is once more possible to think.[27]

The abolition of man indicates that an emancipation of science and a decentralisation of knowledge took place. They are no longer correlated to the figure of a neutral human observer or subject of cognition, which both imply a centralised topology of thinking and language. Consequently, the subject that can finally be grasped in the void, unveiled by the foreclosure of man from scientific knowledge, appears as a fold in space. How to approach this fold? It is not a simple rupture but a discontinuous continuity, a disturbance or torsion. It breaks space without making a crack. Curiously enough, Deleuze saw in structuralism a science, which is grounded on a rigorous theory of the subject, a non-psychological, non-individual and non-anthropomorphic subject:

> Structuralism is not at all a form of thought that suppresses the subject, but one that breaks it up and distributes it systematically, that contests the

identity of the subject, that dissipates it and makes it shift from place to place, an always nomad subject, made of individuations, but impersonal ones, or of singularities, but pre-individual ones.[28]

The critical value of the baroque points in the same direction. Lacan, for instance, reverts to the baroque through yet another rejection of Aristotelian ontology: 'the unconscious is not the fact that being thinks [. . .] the unconscious is the fact that being, by speaking, enjoys, and [. . .] wants to know nothing more'.[29] Bernini's sculpture of Saint Teresa, a baroque masterpiece from the church Santa Maria della Vittoria in Rome, exemplifies the lessons Lacan intended to draw for the notion of structure. The question concerns the bodily experience of *jouissance* that the subject does not know anything about. There is no knowledge, which means that there is no science of *jouissance*. The baroque style already contains a significant break with representational art. Artistic production is no longer subjected to the narrow frameworks of the utilitarian function or a representational model (a move that became radicalised in modernist art such as suprematism).[30] The critical value of the baroque is that it points out something that concerns the very essence of Christianity, an unintended scandal that only a true materialist can appreciate and that concerns the resurrection not of the soul, but of the flesh. While for Aristotle, man thinks with his soul, for Christianity, one could argue, man thinks with his body. Baroque art most openly displays the materiality of thought. But it also displays that thinking always comes in a pair with *jouissance*:

> Nowhere, in any cultural milieu, has this exclusion been admitted to more nakedly. I will even go a bit further [. . .] nowhere more blatantly than in Christianity does the work of art as such show itself as what it has always been in all places – obscenity. The dit-mension of obscenity is that by which Christianity revives the religion of men.[31]

Dit-mension, another famous Lacanian neologism, is loaded with epistemological value. It situates the connection between speech and space, saying and extension. So the dimension of obscenity, the causing of enjoyment in the speaking body demands an entire topological, geometrical and artistic apparatus. The baroque provides this in an unusual way, with the function of the fold, which abolishes the topological divide on the inside and the outside: 'The baroque is the regulating of the soul by corporal radioscopy.'[32] Another aspect concerns the breakdown of adequate representation of reality. The excess of *jouissance* and the real of discourse are visualised through exaggeration, but what gets represented is a kind of inadequacy, imbalance or non-relation. That is why it makes sense to claim:

> those representations are themselves martyrs. You know that 'martyr' means witness – of a more or less pure suffering. That was what our painting was

about, until the slate was wiped clean when people began to seriously concern themselves with little squares.[33]

Not the images of torture but tortured images. The same point can be
extended to literature. Style does not stand for the language of torture
but for the tortured language. The baroque would then indeed lead to an
encounter with structuralism, since it no less approaches structure from
the viewpoint of instability and breakdown. It is here that structure is
most real.

These lessons are to some extent contained in the very terminology. The
expression 'baroque' originates from the Italian *barocco*, used by scholastic
philosophers for describing an obstacle in propositional logic. The first
point would then address a linguistic hindrance or irregularity, a particularly complex and sophisticated syllogism. In later periods the meaning of
'baroque' was extended to designate 'any contorted idea or involuted process of thought' (which remains in line with linguistic deviation). Another
potential source is the Portuguese *barroco* 'used to describe an irregular or
imperfectly shaped pearl; this usage still exists in the jeweler's term baroque
pearl'.[34] In this second meaning another feature is added: the incorrect or
deformed shape is the opposite to the ancient ideal of the sphere, which
obtained its scientific expression in cosmology and premodern astronomy.
Deleuze pointed out precisely this epistemic dimension in relation to the
fold in baroque sculpture and architecture:

> What is Baroque is this distinction and division into two levels or floors. The
> distinction of two worlds is common to Platonic tradition. The world was
> thought to have an infinite number of floors, with a stairway that descends
> and ascends, with each step being lost in the upper order of the One and
> disintegrated in the ocean of the multiple. The universe as a stairwell marks
> the Neoplatonic tradition. But the Baroque contribution par excellence is
> a world with only two floors separated by a fold that echoes itself, arching
> from the two sides according to a different order. It expresses, as we shall see,
> the transformation of the cosmos into a 'mundus'.[35]

The deformed or irregular shape, the distortion of presumably perfect forms
and the possibility of a topology and geometry, which is no longer rooted
in the divide between the inside and the outside, between empty space and
full space – this is what accompanies the replacement of the old *cosmos* (the
closed world) with the modern *mundus* (the infinite universe). The two
features of the baroque would thus be irregularity and decentralisation, to
which a third should be added, and that is exaggeration. Still according
to the etymological analysis, the word 'baroque' subsequently began to
describe 'anything irregular, bizarre, or otherwise departing from established rules and proportions',[36] the overblown and over-decorated bodies

and buildings, which seem to leave no place for the void. This is where the unconscious subject enters the picture, a subject that materialises the aforementioned distortions and deformations: 'Intentionality is still generated in a Euclidean space that prevents it from understanding itself, and must be surpassed by another, "topological", space which establishes contact between the Outside and the Inside, the most distant, the most deep.'[37]

To return to the point of departure, which concerned the scope of *analysis* of the soul. The great merit of psychoanalysis remains that it detached the subject both from the metaphysical soul and from the intentional consciousness. Freud's main gesture consisted not so much in the hypostasis of the subjective split, but in the elaboration of decentralised model of thinking. The Freudian unconscious resides entirely in this ungraspable, undetectable, interrupted line, precisely a fold, which both links and delimits the inside and the outside, the subject and the Other. Lacan's return to Freud through structural linguistics strives to show that Freud's initial works contained an anticipation of structuralism, namely an anticipation of its decentralisation of language. This decentralisation, however, did not imply that the science of language should treat language beyond the subject. Therefore, the first move of the return to Freud intensified the materialist potentials of classical structuralism, which already envisaged language beyond its exclusively organonic, pragmatic and communicative context; while the second one revealed the form of subjectivity that corresponds to the 'emancipation of language' from 'its' tool-model.

In the end one could say that both Deleuze and Lacan subscribed to the Heraclitian challenge to philosophy, a dynamic structure of becoming versus a static structure of endless permutations of the same. The choice is then not between structure and becoming, but between structure-as-constellation and structure-as-becoming. The vulgarised version of Heraclitus claims that for him 'everything flows' and consequently that the only permanent thing is movement. Yet Heraclitus did not merely invent the first philosophy of becoming but also the first materialist philosophy of *logos*, the name of negativity (or multiplicity of differences) in being. Deleuze wrote that being clamours – but this clamour, this 'ontological scream', is precisely the birth hour of *logos*, a manifestation of the structural real, which can subsequently become the object of *logos* in the sense of rationalisation through rigorous geometrisation and formalisation.

Notes

1. Deleuze, Gilles and Guattari, Felix, *A Thousand Plateaus* (Minneapolis: University of Minnesota Press, 1987), pp. 75, 85, 92, 100.

2. The subtitle of Deleuze and Guattari's book on *Kafka* indicates something similar in relation to writing, opposing major and minor literature.
3. It is more than ironic that Nietzsche saw in this notion the greatest invention of Deleuze's most hated philosopher of negativity, Hegel: 'Let us take, thirdly, Hegel's astonishing move, with which he struck through all logical habits and indulgences when he dared to teach that species concepts develop out of each other. With this proposition the minds of Europe were preformed for the last great scientific movement, Darwinism – for without Hegel there could be no Darwin. [. . .] We Germans are Hegelians even had there been no Hegel, insofar as we (as opposed to all Latins) instinctively attribute a deeper meaning and greater value to becoming and development than to what "is"; we hardly believe in the justification of the concept "being" – and also insofar as we are not inclined to concede that our human logic is logic as such or the only kind of logic . . .' (Nietzsche, Friedrich, *The Gay Science* (Cambridge: Cambridge University Press, 2001), p. 218). I thank Nathaniel Boyd for drawing my attention to this fabulous passage.
4. Deleuze, quoted in Lecercle, Jean-Jacques, *Deleuze and Language* (Basingstoke and New York: Palgrave Macmillan, 2002), p. 62.
5. Lecercle, *Deleuze and Language*, p. 67.
6. Milner, Jean-Claude, *Le périple structural: figures et paradigme* (Paris: Verdier, 2008), pp. 263, 277.
7. Lacan, Jacques, *Autres écrits* (Paris: Seuil, 2001), p. 225.
8. Lecercle, *Deleuze and Language*, p. 98.
9. Lacan, *Autres écrits*, p. 483.
10. Ibid. p. 314.
11. Ibid. p. 313.
12. See Žižek, Slavoj, 'Hegel versus Heidegger', available at <http://www.e-flux.com/journal/hegel-versus-heidegger/> (last accessed 1 April 2016). The expression 'house of being' comes from Heidegger.
13. Lacan, Jacques, *The Seminar of Jacques Lacan, Book XX: Encore* (London and New York: W. W. Norton, 1999), p. 37; translation modified.
14. Lacan, *Encore*, p. 3.
15. Lacan, Jacques, *Le séminaire de Jacques Lacan, livre XVI: D'un Autre à l'autre* (Paris: Seuil, 2006), p. 30.
16. Lacan, *Encore*, p. 20.
17. Ibid. p. 18; translation modified.
18. Stalin, quoted in Jakobson, Roman, *Poetry of Grammar and Grammar of Poetry* (The Hague: De Gruyter, 1981), p. 95.
19. Lacan, *Encore*, p. 20.
20. Ibid. p. 20.
21. Lacan, Jacques, *Television: A Challenge to the Psychoanalytic Establishment* (New York and London: W. W. Norton, 1990), pp. 5–6.
22. Ibid. p. 6.
23. Deleuze, Gilles, *Desert Islands and Other Texts 1953–1974* (Los Angeles: Semiotext(e), 2004), p. 173.
24. Ibid. p. 177.
25. Ibid. p. 174.
26. Ibid. p. 179; original emphasis.
27. Foucault, Michel, *The Order of Things* (New York: Vintage Books, 1994), p. 342.
28. Deleuze, *Desert Islands*, p. 190.
29. Lacan, *Encore*, pp. 104–5; translation modified.
30. Could we not see in the couple baroque–suprematism that Lacan alludes to a peculiar reflection of the conceptual couple *lalangue–mathème*, the intrusion of *jouissance* into the language, on the one hand, and the pure formal language evacuated of all *jouissance*, on the other – literature and mathematics, two realisations of the absolute

autonomy of the signifier and two royal roads into a materialist science of language? So structuralism should also become baroque and thus break once and for all with the representational and communicative conception of language.

31. Ibid. p. 113.
32. Ibid. p. 116.
33. Ibid. p. 116.
34. 'Baroque Art and Architecture', *Encyclopædia Britannica*, available at <http://www.britannica.com/art/Baroque-period> (last accessed 1 April 2016).
35. Deleuze, Gilles, *The Fold: Leibniz and the Baroque* (London: The Athlone Press, 1993), p. 29.
36. 'Baroque Art and Architecture'.
37. Deleuze, Gilles, *Foucault* (Minneapolis: University of Minnesota Press, 2006), p. 110.

Chapter 9

Exalted Obscenity and the Lawyer of God: Lacan, Deleuze and the Baroque

Lorenzo Chiesa

I

It is well known that both Deleuze and Lacan pay considerable attention to the baroque. Deleuze centres his 1988 book *The Fold* on this
topic. Lacan dedicates to it some intense passages of a crucial lesson of his
1972–3 Seminar *Encore*, which could rightly be regarded as a summary of
this work, if not of his late teaching.

For Deleuze, the baroque takes an interest in all the places 'where what
is seen is inside: a cell, a sacristy, a crypt, a church, a theatre, a study, or a
print room', and extracts power and glory from them.[1] As such, however, it
does not point at any hidden essence, but at a basic 'operative function',
namely folding; the baroque 'does not stop creating folds'.[2] Ultimately,
the fold amounts to power, a power inseparable from the infinite act of
folding, whereby being as multiple and thus non-universalisable remains
nonetheless univocal.[3] What is at stake both aesthetically and ontologically
is in the end a 'new harmony'.[4] The philosopher who has fully grasped the
theoretical implications of the baroque as folding is Leibniz. Deleuze's
own thought proposes itself as a contemporary resumption and expansion
of the baroque and of Leibniz. Quite explicitly: 'we are discovering new
ways of folding, akin to new envelopments, but we remain Leibnizian
because it is always a matter of folding, unfolding, refolding'.[5]

On the other hand, for Lacan, the baroque amounts to the 'exhibition of bodies evoking jouissance'.[6] This aesthetical dimension works as
a cipher for a fundamental characteristic of being in general: being does
not think. Or specifically: it is incorrect to think that 'what is thought of
is in the image of thought, in other words, that being thinks'.[7] Even more
precisely: 'being by speaking enjoys', yet what it enjoys is 'insufficient

jouissance'.[8] In knowing this insufficient *jouissance*, and enjoying this very knowledge, the speaking/thinking being does not want to know anything else about it. Thus, the being that in speaking supposedly thinks does not itself really think. Thanks to its visual and plastic orgies of suffering bodies, the art of the baroque counters this state of generalised repression – which ultimately amounts to knowledge *tout court*, or even civilisation *tout court*. The baroque evidences a 'filthy truth':[9] the truth that 'there is no sexual relationship'; that being is not-One; that the speaking being normally does not think, since it rather prefers to *evoke* a *jouissance* that, however, is *not*. This truth is nothing else than the obscene but most fundamental kernel of Christianity. In turn, psychoanalysis shares such an approach to truth, but, as we will see, also takes a step further.

II

It seems to me that these apparently distant, if not contrasting, formulas (inside versus exhibition; being as univocal versus being as not-One; new harmony versus highlighted suffering; neo-Leibnizianism versus post-Christianity) overshadow a number of otherwise significant convergences between the two authors. Both Deleuze and Lacan deem that the aesthetics of the baroque elicits a new ontological understanding of the link between the body and the soul. Both read this against the background of a problematisation of what we mean by 'world', 'cosmos' and 'universe'. Both believe this problematisation is strictly related to the emergence of the modern notion of infinity. Both do not fail to dwell on the consequences all the above has in rethinking the philosophical status of the subject and the object.[10]

Let us start with what is at first sight most striking, especially for a reader who is more at home with Lacan than with Deleuze: the latter's definition of the subject as proposed in *The Fold* in strict connection with his discussion of the baroque. According to Deleuze, or according to Deleuze's reading of Leibniz, which is in any case not merely exegetical, but propositional:

1. There is no 'subject defined beforehand', no 'sub-ject'.[11]
2. What is rather at stake in understanding the subject on the basis of the function of the fold is 'a place, a position', or better, a 'point of view': 'a subject will be what comes to the point of view, or rather what dwells in the point of view'.[12]
3. This perspectival take on the subject should not be confused with the idea of a 'missing center' ('centre défaillant').[13] Perspectivism is no

doubt a form of relativism and pluralism, but not in the sense that it would entail a 'relativity of what is true'.[14] Quite on the contrary, the point of view where the subject dwells – a subject without whom, importantly, 'the point of view would not be'[15] – is a *power of ordering cases/events* ('*puissance d'ordonner les cas*'), and as such a 'condition for the manifestation of what is true' ('condition de la manifestation du vrai').[16]

4. Such an appearing of truth to the subject, a truth of *variation* against a background of chaos that could not as such appear without the subject's assumption of a point of view, corresponds to 'the very idea of baroque perspective'.[17]

Most of this strongly resonates with Lacan's own notion of the subject. Limiting ourselves to a brief survey of Seminar XX, but bearing in mind that Lacan already made many of these points much earlier in his work, we can in fact ascertain that:

1. Our conscious knowledge constantly 'supposes' the subject; *sub-ponere* literally means 'to put under', 'to under-lie'. But actually the subject comes into existence only as 'barred'. Supposing the subject veils this truth. Such 'discordance between knowledge and being', Lacan writes, 'is my subject'.[18]

2. The barred subject and its veiling are a retroactive effect of the symbolic structure in which the speaking animal precariously positions itself. 'What speaks without knowing it makes me "I", subject of the verb', yet 'that doesn't suffice to bring me into being'.[19] This does not prevent the subject from existing. Or, more precisely, 'the symbolic cannot be confused with being – far from it'; at the same time, 'it subsists qua ex-sistence of the act of speaking'.[20]

3. The barred subject comes into existence only as relative to a point (*ponctuel*). He is thus always a vanishing (*évanouissant*) subject, 'for it is a subject only by a signifier and to another signifier'.[21] In addition, the subject that manifests himself in his gap (*béance*) does so in a place or locus (*lieu*) – that is, linguistic structure – that as such does not itself 'hold up'.[22]

4. This predicament neither exonerates the subject from clinging to a fictional notion of 'centre', nor dispenses him from dealing with truth. 'What remains at the center is the fine routine that is such that the signified always retains the same meaning [*sens*] in the final analysis'.[23] The meaning in question is, quite simply, nothing else than the feeling 'each of us has of being part of his world, that is, of his little family and of everything that revolves around it'.[24] The barred subject does not go

without a worldview.[25] And this is the case because the failing linguistic structure can be sutured through the phantasmatic production of another subject.

5. As for truth, from the point of view of the barred subject, it is a matter of 'minorising' ('minoriser') it, that is, of 'put[ting] it in its place'. Thus, truth 'is reduced, but indispensible'.[26] That is: the truth of contingency, of the not-One, does not fail to give rise through the subject to the discursive production of the One, and its fragile necessity. Or also: truth is the truth of the difference between not-One and One, which can only be half-said. If 'not-One' then 'One', but 'One' *is not* really One.

III

In the end, it is precisely his understanding of the subject along the lines we have just delineated that allows Lacan to state, when he introduces the baroque in Seminar XX, that 'I rather situate myself on the side of the baroque' ('je me range plutôt du côté du baroque').[27] Here, he does not go on to explain what specifically a baroque (understanding of the) subject amounts to, apart from insisting once again on the fact that in situating himself in the linguistic structure, the subject, 'I' – including the subject Lacan who says 'je me range' – is equally not 'active', that is, passively situated by structure.[28] Yet, there are passages from Seminars VII and XI where Lacan develops the perspectival status of the subject in much more openly aesthetical terms, and even links it with the way in which the baroque challenges the classical Renaissance perspective and its presupposing the subject.

We have seen that, for Lacan, the subject is a vanishing subject. Better said, the de-substantialised subject fleetingly appears as that which a signifier represents for another signifier. Juxtaposing Seminar XX with Seminar XI we can further specify this aesthetically: it is precisely insofar as the subject is *ponctuel*, that is, relative to a point or position in the linguistic structure, that the subject is *not* (or not simply) 'a punctiform being that gets his bearings at the geometral point from which the perspective is grasped'.[29] From Plato to Kant passing through Descartes (Lacan refers to all of them in the two lessons of Seminar XI he dedicates to these matters), geometral vision has in different ways always gone together with the idea of a substantial subject (or 'punctiform being') that underlies vision. Yet, 'the geometral dimension of vision does not exhaust, far from it, what the field of vision as such offers us as the original subjectifying relation'.[30] This non-exhaustion is precisely what the baroque highlights, which makes it a unique episode in the history of art and architecture.

Lacan focuses on such exceptionality of the baroque already in Seminar VII. Here, he sketches a grand paradigm that attempts to define what art is in general, and how it has varied throughout human history. The basic aim of artistic production, including architecture, is to 'indicate that what we look for in illusion is something where this very illusion somehow transcends itself and destroys itself'.[31] In so doing art ultimately renders visible the primacy of the domain of language and of a corresponding void over that of images. Lacan singles out four historical stages in this process:

1. 'Primitive architecture', which is conceived quite simply as 'something organised around a void'.[32] It includes every form of construction from the moment we stopped letting stones roll and erected them to the sophisticated forms of late-classical and Gothic architecture (Lacan mentions Saint Mark's Basilica in Venice).[33]
2. Medieval frescoes, where we 'learn to paint architecture on the walls of architecture'.[34] This painting is itself ultimately something organised around a void.
3. The Renaissance discovery of pictorial perspective. This is the outcome of the attempt to create something that resembles more and more closely the void of architecture.[35]
4. Neo-classical architecture, as epitomised by Palladio's theatre in Vicenza. Here, in adopting the perspectivism of painting, architecture ends up 'submitting itself to the laws of perspective'.[36] In this way the void is paradoxically repressed.
5. Baroque painting and architecture. The baroque uses the recently dis-covered 'properties of lines' but deforms them. It thus returns to the void as the veritable objective of any artistic research, or better 'makes something emerge that is precisely there where one has lost one's bear-ings, or, strictly speaking, nowhere'.[37]

Let us dwell on these last two stages. Lacan identifies the stage of neo-classical architecture as that in which 'one strangles oneself with one's own knots'.[38] Why? Because the very artistic process that aimed at the self-overcoming of 'illusion' and at the appearance of its reliance on the void and the signifier achieves the opposite result. Palladio's theatre places the laws of perspective inside a building that is regulated by them: the real arch constructed on the stage is entirely functional to the long streets receding to a distant horizon that are painted behind it; the ensuing trompe-l'oeil scenery dictates the bearings of the audience. This is the perfect setting for what in Seminar XI Lacan will call a 'bipolar reflexive relation'[39] in which the subject subsists as a 'punctiform being'. The distant horizon contained in Palladio's actual building stands as an 'unnamed substance from which I, the seer, extract myself', and I extract myself as the matching counterpart of that horizon.[40] This is precisely the supreme illusion that art intended to *contrast* by means of illusions. The subject now believes that 'as soon as I perceive, my representations belong to me', and I thus 'apprehend the world'.[41]

As for the baroque, for Lacan, it is in a sense a continuation of previous investigations on the laws of perspective. However, it also disrupts them and even marks their collapse. More precisely, it *shows* that geometral vision 'is situated in a space that is *not* in its essence visual'.[42] With regard to the process of subjectivation, this means that the baroque evidences how consciousness and conscious vision, as exemplarily orchestrated in Palladio's theatre, have their basis in the unconscious structure of the gaze as a point of subjective annulment.[43] If, as claimed in Seminar VIII, baroque artists manage to highlight the seductive power of images in an unprecedented way, they can achieve this, as indirectly suggested in Seminar XI, only by 'staining' perspective.[44]

What Lacan has in mind here is anamorphosis, which he identifies as a specifically baroque technique, and discusses in both Seminar VII and Seminar XI. The definition of anamorphosis provided in Seminar VII is particularly clear: 'It is a kind of construction that is made in such a way that by means of an optical transposition a certain form that was not visible at first sight transforms itself into a readable image.'[45] Lacan dwells on Holbein's painting *The Ambassadors*: there first seems to be an undecipherable stain at the feet of the two men in the portrait; it is only when we place ourselves at a certain angle that we see a skull appear. Importantly, as soon as the skull appears, the other figures of the painting – those supported by geometral vision – disappear because of the convergence of the lines of perspective. Lacan carefully distinguishes these two moments of anamorphosis, and by extension of the baroque: that of the emergence of the undecipherable stain within geometral vision, which he understands as an encounter with the void; and that of the satisfying experience of extracting a form from this very void, which nonetheless evokes death, 'the subject as annihilated', and is made possible only at the cost of temporarily losing one's geometral/conscious bearings.[46]

This fluctuation is further explored in another passage of Seminar VII devoted to baroque architecture. As seen, architecture in general is 'something organised around a void', which pictorial perspective veils. But as such it is at the same time 'something fixed' that points in the direction of the 'presentification of the pain' we suffer when we cannot move.[47] Against this background, the distinctiveness of baroque architecture would be its plastic 'effort towards pleasure', which, however, only makes baroque architecture 'shine' to the extent that it produces 'tortured forms'.[48] Using the terminology Lacan will adopt in Seminar XX, we could say that the paradoxical satisfaction provided by the tortured forms of baroque architecture and the anamorphic skull of baroque painting are nothing else than an evocation of *jouissance* as absent.

IV

Unlike Lacan, Deleuze is certainly not a thinker who gives ontological or aesthetical prominence to the void. As he observes in *The Fold*, voids are only 'apparent voids'; 'in the Baroque, folds are always full'; 'the Baroque Leibniz does not believe in the void, which seems to him to be always filled with a folded matter'.[49] This point is developed with specific reference to baroque architecture: 'the façade can have doors and windows – it is riddled with holes – although there is no void, a hole being only the site of a more rarefied [*subtile*] matter'.[50]

Here, there seems to arise an unsurpassable tension between Deleuze and Lacan. But we would be mistaken to use it as a pretext for stopping any further enquiry on the convergences between their investigations of the baroque. This is not only because Lacan's approach to the void is far more refined than is usually assumed (in short, the void does not amount to a lack in the very texture of being, or a fundamental derailment of nature as such), but especially because of the way in which Deleuze himself treats the baroque *object*. Just as for Lacan the void 'stain' of baroque paintings stands as a concrete indicator of what he calls object *a*, so for Deleuze the apparent void of baroque façades circumscribes a 'new object', which he calls 'objectile'.[51] The critique of the supposition, or subposition, of the subject is matched in both authors by a correlative attempt to think, in Deleuze's own words, a 'non essentialist' object.[52] Deleuze further defines the 'objectile' as an object that 'becomes an event'.[53] On his part, in Seminar XI, Lacan stresses how the emergence of something that is nowhere (atopia) according to geometral vision should be considered as an 'encounter with the real'; he then speaks of it as a 'meaningless event'.[54]

Last but not least, the reference to anamorphosis remains present also in Deleuze: the objectile is, quite bluntly, 'something = x (anamorphosis)'. More precisely, as seen, a subject will be what comes to the point of view, and any point of view is a point of view on a variation, or difference. But this does not simply mean that the point of view – of baroque perspective – is what varies with the subject, following a superficial understanding of relativism: the point of view is rather 'the condition under which a potential [*éventuel*] subject grasps a variation (metamorphosis), or: something = x (anamorphosis)'.[55] As we have also seen, such a mutual implication of the anamorphic object and the retroactive subject, or truth of variation, ultimately provides a perspectival 'power of *ordering* events' against an otherwise chaotic background.

In this context, we should not lose sight of two key arguments Lacan makes in Seminar XI, since they profoundly resonate with what we have just said about Deleuze. I only hint at these intricate issues so as to set the ground for further research. First, for Lacan, the meaningless event, that of encountering object *a*, is after all itself in turn responsible for giving the subject nothing less than the coordinates of the world:

> if the function of the stain is recognized in its autonomy and identified with that of the gaze, we can see its track, its thread, its trace, at every stage of the constitution of the world in the scopic field. We will then realize that the function of the stain and of the gaze is both that which governs the scopic field most secretly and that which always escapes from the grasp of that form of vision that is satisfied with itself in imagining itself as consciousness.[56]

In other words, atopia and the point of view are inextricable; this is one of the great lessons of the baroque.

Second – and this is very significant in terms of an overall comparative assessment of Lacan's and Deleuze's respective ontologies – object *a* and its privileged embodiment in the baroque stain is the object of a 'desire to obtain absolute difference'.[57] Later on I will argue that this absolute difference does *not* correspond to Deleuze's 'truth of variation' as 'the difference that differentiates itself' ('la différence qui se différencie')[58] – as such epitomised by the folds of the baroque – but it would be absurd to overlook their contiguity in the name of a simplistic opposition between a philosophy of the void and a philosophy of fullness.

V

For Deleuze, the transformation of the object into an 'objectile' is correlative to the transformation of the subject as sub-posed into a 'superject'.[59] Infinite folding is the operational function responsible for this. Folding thus calls into question any essence. By the same token, inflexion itself, that is, the 'genetic element' of the fold, cannot be regarded as a being that is 'in the world', because it is rather 'the World itself, its beginning' in terms of a 'non-dimensional point'.[60]

Lacan's stance is initially analogous. As he spells out in short succession in an underestimated passage of Seminar XX, 'the reciprocity between the [barred] subject and object *a* is total'.[61] Moreover, this reciprocity is such, quite surprisingly, in the sense of a 'folding' ('pliure').[62] Elsewhere in

Seminar XX, Lacan also adds that psychoanalytic discourse 'never resorts to any substance'.[63] *Yet,* the fold as the reciprocity between the barred subject and object *a* should not be considered, as in Deleuze, in terms of an instantiation of a pre-subjective cosmogenetic factor, or 'Fold',[64] but, quite on the contrary, as the specific structure of the subject qua *fantasy.* Throughout Seminar XX, and in the same passage in which Lacan speaks of the *pliure,* fantasy is often presented very plainly, without recourse to any psychoanalytical jargon: it is the structural fiction that makes us believe that 'the world is symmetrical to the subject', or also, that the world 'is the equivalent, the mirror image, of thought'. This invariably also deludes the subject into believing that 'the world kn[ows] as much about things as he d[oes]'.[65]

We could perhaps suggest that Lacan stresses the subjective 'power of ordering events' aspect of the Deleuzian fold, where Deleuze ultimately favours what he sees as its being a pre-subjective 'pure Event'.[66] But we should not forget that the Lacanian *pliure* itself originates as a meaningless event. And I add: a meaningless event that as such *is,* while the fantasy it gives rise to is semblance. Before returning to this contrast and seeing how, in spite of the common terminology, a basic ontological disagreement is indeed at stake here, we should first tackle Deleuze's and Lacan's treatment of the notion of the world in *The Fold* and Seminar XX. Along with the closely linked notions of the body and the soul, the world is arguably one of the leitmotivs of both texts.

VI

According to Deleuze, the baroque should be understood in terms of an incipient 'collapse of the world'.[67] This amounts more precisely to a 'crisis and collapse of all theological Reason'.[68] The world started to accumulate evidence against Reason, and, consequently, against itself as an ordered universe. Deleuze does not hesitate to define this predicament, made possible also by the scientific revolution, as a 'psychotic episode'.[69] Better said, the baroque would offer, in Deleuze's own words, a 'schizophrenic' and temporary solution to the collapse of classical reason.[70] It is as such a 'transition'[71] exemplified paradigmatically by Leibniz's theodicy of the best of all possible worlds.

The important point of this theodicy is, for Deleuze, not that God always chooses the best of possible worlds, since this 'best' is already a consequence of the demise of the Platonic Good: 'If this world exists, it is not because it is the best; it is rather the inverse: it is the best because it is, because it is the one that is.'[72] Rather, Leibniz's crucial point – whereby the baroque should be seen more generally as the last attempt to reconstruct classical reason – is that 'the only irreducible dissonances are between different worlds'.[73] Incompossibility is confined to the borders that divide possible worlds. Harmony and the consistency of this world are thus preserved. The philosopher is neither a judge (Kant), nor an investigator (empiricism), but God's lawyer.[74] In other words, the principle of the world is maintained by a proliferation of principles: 'We can always slip a new [principle] out from under our cuffs'; 'we will not ask what available object corresponds to a given luminous principle, but what hidden principle responds to whatever object is given, that is to say, to this or that "unsolved case".'[75]

Deleuze's analysis of the baroque approach to the question of the world via Leibniz also allows him to mark a key *distinction* between the baroque and the *neo*-baroque, to which Deleuze's own philosophy belongs. In fact, for the neo-baroque paradigm 'divergent series [appear] in the same world'; there is an 'irruption of incompossibilities on the same stage'.[76] In short, we experience the end of any possible theodicy, which is replaced, starting from Nietzsche and Mallarmé, by 'a world without principle'.[77] The latter should be understood as a 'Thought-world that throws dice', where the roll of the dice is 'the power of affirming Chance' by thinking it, and Chance is not a principle, but the absence of any principle.[78] Deleuze also calls this Thought-world 'chaosmos' and proceeds to sketch what has rightly been defined as a neo-baroque 'metaphysics of chaos',[79] indebted to Whitehead but also highly original.

Let me sketch the contours of this metaphysics. Its main coordinates are: chaos, the event, and the sieve (*crible*).[80] The event is produced in the midst of a chaotic multiplicity, a 'pure Many', only thanks to a sieve. As such chaos does not exist; it is just the other side of what is produced thanks to the sieve. The something that is produced is a One that is initially a singularity yet not a unity. There are three conditions for an event to take place: first, there must be extension. Second, extended matter must present intensions, that is, intensities or degrees. Third, an individual unity must emerge through a concrescence of (extended/intensive) elements, or 'prehension'. The individual unity is 'creativity, formation of the New'.[81] Individual unities do as such somehow anticipate the advent of psychic life. Things are themselves prehensions and together with the subject (as 'superject') they 'prehend a world'.[82] Most significantly, the world is a 'motley world' that can no longer be expressed as one and the same world by its individual unities (as was instead still the case with Leibniz's compossible monades). The reason for this is, again, that according to the neo-baroque paradigm, or metaphysics of chaos, 'bifurcations, divergences, incompossibilities, and discord belong to the same motley world'.

The world can therefore only be continuously 'made or undone according to prehensive unities and variable configurations'.[83] Variation is the truth of the world.

As will be clear by now, the metaphysics of chaos revolves around a two-layered interrogation, which Deleuze makes explicit: first, 'how can the Many become a One?'; second, 'in what conditions does the objective world allow for a subjective production of novelty, that is, of creation?'[84] There are then two other and even more crucial questions, which Deleuze does not ask, and which condense in my view both the proximity and the distance between Deleuze's and Lacan's speculation: in what sense does the singular yet pre-individual One, or something, that is extracted from the chaos *differ only slightly*[85] – as Deleuze writes in italics – from the chaos? How can we avoid turning the absence of any principle in the cha-osmos, that is, the fact that the world is not-One, into chaos as a supreme *principle*?

VII

Similarly to Deleuze, Lacan believes that the baroque is a transitional yet exceptional period in the history of the arts and human thought in general. It should be seen as an attempt to cope with the fact that, by the sixteenth century, 'the world is in a state of decomposition'[86] due to the collapse of classical *episteme* and the influence it exercised on medieval Christian theology, as well as to the concomitant rise of modern science. Like Deleuze, for Lacan, the baroque *both* participates in the decomposition of the world and contradictorily slows it down. Like Deleuze, Lacan sees this paradoxical process as strictly linked with the question of truth.

On the one hand, the baroque goes back to the roots of Christianity: 'the Counter-Reformation was ultimately a return to the sources and the baroque the parading thereof'.[87] The baroque returns to the 'essence of Christianity' by communicating a 'filthy truth' ('vérité d'immondice'):[88] the truth that the world is not-One, that the universe as uni-verse is a 'flower of rhetoric'[89] – as Lacan states in another lesson of Seminar XX – fundamentally because there is no sexual relationship, that is, because sex does not have a meaning for the speaking being. Lacan is as always very careful in choosing his words: the truth *d'immondice* is literally *im-monde*, from the Latin *immundus*, where the prefix *im* negates the *mundus*, or world.

In other words, the not so good 'good news' of the Gospels is simple:[90] there is no *jouissance*. However, even Christians found that hard to digest ('Christians abhor what was revealed to them'[91]). The filthy truth of Christianity certainly 'inundated what we call the world', destroyed the 'miraculous, universal balance' founded by the Romans (including their 'baths of jouissance sufficiently symbolized by those famous thermal baths'),[92] yet by the late Middle Ages and the Renaissance it was compromised. Thomas Aquinas reinjected Aristotle into the 'good news', and the cult of saints could be regarded as the rebirth of polytheism and its strictly linked supposition of a sexual knowledge that would give access to *jouissance*.[93] The baroque, especially its visual arts, reacted to this through a virulent exhibition of tortured and suffering bodies. Lacan goes as far as suggesting that 'those representations are themselves martyrs. You know that "martyr" means witness – of a more or less pure suffering.'[94]

On the other hand – and this is crucial – Lacan equally states that the baroque's return to the sources of Christianity 'revives the religion of men'.[95] This is a tricky specification that deserves particular attention. The baroque certainly revived Christianity as a religion, but Lacan's assumption here is that Christianity goes together with a filthy truth (the truth of incompleteness) that is as such disavowed by religion. We can follow Lacan's reasoning only if we dwell on his suggestion, repeated several times in this lesson, that Christianity is the 'true religion' ('that it is the true religion, as it claims, is not an excessive claim'; 'the Gospels [. . .] you can't speak any better of the truth'[96]). As I have argued elsewhere, claiming that Christianity is the true religion actually means claiming that the religion of Christ is *less false* than other religions.[97] Christianity still disavows its filthy truth. It does so by giving it an unprecedented *meaning*: Christ has become one of us to spread the good news that the love of God can eventually save us, but, as Lacan does not fail to add, he can save us only if we concomitantly save *him* from *his* filthy truth.[98] Salvation is preserved by replacing the classical illusion of *jouissance* with the 'abjection' of *this* world, while opposing the latter to *another* world of eternal life. Christianity thus recuperates meaning (salvation and eternal life) precisely thanks to the disclosure of truth as meaninglessness (the abjection of this world). It turns incompleteness into the definitive reason to believe in completeness.

How does all this apply more concretely to baroque art? I think the key here is to carefully ponder why Lacan refers to it as 'obscenity – *but* exalted'.[99] The baroque is literally ob-scene, that is, 'out of place', precisely in that its martyrised bodies portray the filthy truth of the insufficiency of *jouissance* qua the absence of the sexual relationship. Concurrently, the baroque is also plainly ob-scene since it shows that sex is 'out of representation' for the human animal: fundamentally, language cannot represent it. However, as seen, the baroque is as such equally an 'exhibition of the body *evoking* jouissance'. The mirage of absolute *jouissance* is still there, yet in a new way, that is, through an exaltation of ob-scenity; the *im-monde* of the *immondice* communicated by Christianity does not only witness to the not-One of *this* world and its abjection, but equally points in the direction of an 'outside of the world' (following another acceptation of the prefix *im*). Is this not what Bernini's Saint Teresa indicates? Her quasi-orgasmic spasms ob-scenely exclude copulation – 'If copulation isn't present, it's no accident. It's just as much out of place there as it is in human reality.'[100] Yet, at the same time, her contorted body is exhibited as exalted towards the otherworldly dimension of the rays of God – which is not a 'dit-mension', the dimension of speech where *jouissance* is never enough. Even in the Christian baroque, the prospect of divine copulation, albeit portrayed as absent, 'nevertheless provides sustenance with the fantasies by which reality is constituted'.[101]

VIII

Lacan explicitly sides his psychoanalysis with the baroque. However, similarly to Deleuze, he needs to specify how a neo-baroque paradigm differs from the baroque. In fact, he speaks of his 'baroquism': 'I coincide with the "baroquism" with which I accept to be clothed.'[102] Just like Deleuze stops vetriloquising Leibniz when he has to concede that the latter does not admit incompossibilities in the same world (and hence Deleuze's truth of variation), so Lacan has to distance himself from the Christian notion of truth revitalised by the baroque. Christianity as the least untruthful religion is also psychoanalysis's worst enemy: incompleteness provides in Christianity the ultimate reason to believe in completeness. The Christian approach to truth is noteworthy insofar as it evidences that truth can only be half said. Incompleteness, the not-One, and the absence of any metalanguage cannot really be maintained, or thought, without at the same time promulgating completeness, the One, and the existence of a metalanguage. For Lacan, there remains a logical and even biological necessity for the speaking animal to rely on the mirage of absolute *jouissance*: this fundamental fiction, sustained by fantasy, is what Lacan calls 'love'. Yet, Christianity transforms such a predicament into a dogma, that is, the neat separation between the abjection of our world and the perfection of the world to come.

Lacan therefore points out that psychoanalysis needs to 'minorise' the truth of incompleteness brought about by Christianity and successively obscured by its being nonetheless a true *religion*. It is first certainly a matter of 'displacing', or 'dislodging', any notion of completeness – as Christianity initially does with its 'filthy truth' of abjection – but we should then also be careful not to 'disturb' it too much, Lacan says.[103]

Even outside of a Christian direct and openly dogmatic transvaluation of incompleteness into completeness, promulgating the former as truth always goes together with a return to the latter, that is, 'saving God',[104] in spite of one's alleged atheism. What psychoanalysis rather needs to be doing is 'putting truth in its place', that is, acknowledging that, at least with respect to our dit-mension, incompleteness and completeness are structurally inextricable.

More to the point, for Lacan, psychoanalysis should ultimately 'take truth as a simple *function*'.[105] Truth as a function is the truth of what Seminar XIX calls the 'bifidity of the One', that is, to put it simply, the structural oscillation between One and not-One for the speaking animal, where *both* One and not-One have truth-value. Truth is thus only a 'knowledge of truth' ('savoir sur la vérité') that never gives rise to a 'truth of knowledge' ('vérité sur le savoir').[106] Or also, truth as a function is *not* as such a *true* function.[107]

IX

There is a third and final definition of the baroque in Seminar XX: 'the baroque is the regulation of the soul by corporal radioscopy'.[108] This should be read in line with the two other definitions of the baroque and the double movement of its art as a transitional phase we have been discussing so far – in short, a movement from completeness to incompleteness and back. The important addition here is Lacan's focus on the notions of the body and the soul, whose pregnancy for the entirety of Seminar XX has so far been underestimated by critics. If, as widely accepted, this work primarily deals with the absence of the sexual relationship and the way in which love (as a 'desire to be One'[109]) endeavours to stand in for it, then one should also pay attention to the fact that the former amounts to the absence of a 'soul of copulation',[110] Lacan says, and the latter should more correctly be written as 'âmour', that is 'soul-love' (as a conjunction of *âme*, soul, and *amour*, love).[111] Moreover, Seminar XX – and even the very lesson on the baroque – abounds with discussions of Aristotle's *De Anima* and the Christian adaptation of its notion of the soul.

In short, by exhibiting tortured and suffering bodies, the baroque would offer a scopic exploration that operates a 'reduction of the human species' ('espèce humaine') to an 'unhealthy humor' ('humeur malsaine') precisely by pinpointing 'the gap peculiar to the sexuality of speaking beings' (i.e. the absence of the sexual relationship).[112] Yet, this movement is intended as and results in a 'regulation of the soul', or, we could specify, an updating of the soul by means of love. The Christian revelation of our species' 'misfortune' ('malheur') eventually sustains the Church's intention 'to carry the species [. . .] right up to the end of time'.[113] The baroque exaltation of ob-scenity – which has never been admitted more nakedly in any cultural milieu, Lacan adds – is simultaneously put to the service of fabricating artistic 'utensils' that aim to 'one-up each other'.[114] In other words, by evoking an absolute *jouissance* that is off the screen of this abject world but scopically summoned as such in absentia (think again of the divine rays in Bernini's Saint Teresa), the art of the baroque would encourage the 'beings whose nature is to speak [. . .] to engage in amorous diversions'[115] that partly supplement for the absence of the sexual relationship. Copulation is diagonally recuperated through love and the species preserved up to the end of time.

X

Lacan's overall treatment of the relation between the soul and the body in Seminar XX and throughout his Seminars of the early 1970s is ambitious and far-reaching. It overlaps with his critique of ancient *episteme* and the way it still influences the process of subjectivation today, in spite of the Galilean revolution and the subsequent evolution of modern and contemporary science. I can here only provide a summary of the most salient arguments:[116]

1. Classical science and philosophy (*episteme*) assume that the body can function only if it 'suffices unto itself',[117] which means that it must be self-contained. In other words, the body is taken for One body.
2. From this standpoint, 'the soul is nothing other than the supposed identity of this body'. Or, better: the soul is the supposed identity of the body 'with everything people think in order to explain' it. 'The soul is what one thinks regarding the body' as enclosed and self-sufficient.[118]
3. The reciprocal necessity that the One is and that Being is One, onto-totology, arises directly from the inextricability between the body and the soul as what one thinks the enclosed and self-sufficient body *is*. In other words, 'if there is something that grounds being, it is assuredly the body':[119] the One-Being, God, follows from the One-body as identified by the soul.
4. The parallelism between onto-totology and the One-body qua soul allows the alleged bipolarity of the male and female sexual values to be taken epistemologically 'as sufficient to support, suture that which concerns sex'[120] (i.e. the absence of the sexual relationship as absence of meaning), and consequently to set up a theory of knowledge. As long

as the Other sex is taken as one's soul qua the supposed identity of one's body, knowledge always revolves around the assumption that the power of knowing relates to the world just as man relates to woman.
5. To love amounts exactly to mis-taking the Other sex for one's soul.

For Lacan, Christianity's message about human abjection disrupts this comforting paradigm, which he sees as Aristotelian and animistic. The fragmented body of Christ on the cross vehemently opposes the foundation of being on the One body, and hence also the soul as the identity of the body, as well as the possibility of setting up a (sexual) theory of knowledge on their correspondence. The ob-scenity of the baroque only reinforces this anti-ontotological imagery. But, at the same time, as Lacan stresses, the resurrected Christian God then returns primarily as a *body*: 'Christ, even when resurrected from the dead, is valued for his body, and his body is the means by which communion in his presence is incorporation.' And crucially: 'Christ's wife, the Church as it is called, contents itself very well' with that.[121] Animism and the occultation of the absence of the sexual relationship are thus apparently restored.

Psychoanalysis as a neo-baroque praxis aimed at 'separating severely'[122] the One from being emerges precisely out of the false solution with which Christianity intends to join onto-totology again. The Christian God's health remains 'precarious', Lacan quips. This is already evident at the level of his supposed being at once one and trine. 'Either he becomes a count' – 'one-two-three' – 'only retrospectively after Christ's revelation', and in this case 'it is his being' – his being also trine – 'that suffers a blow'. Or, alternatively, 'the three is prior to him, and it is his unity that takes a hit'.[123] In other words, in spite of resurrection, Christianity either saves being at the expense of the One, or saves the One at the expense of being.

With specific regard to the baroque, its full scopic assumption of the incarnation of God in the body of an animal ravaged by the word and subsequent crucifixion and death can no longer really sustain an (Aristotelian) uni-verse. Nor can it consistently defend the (already Platonic) division between the derelict world of the many and the redeemed world of the unitary being. Exalted ob-scenity still evokes absolute *jouissance*, but this does not suffice. Luther's claim that we are waste matter falling into the world from the devil's anus cannot be counter-reformed.

XI

The question of how to articulate a new thinking of the body and the soul is also very prominent in *The Fold*'s analysis of the baroque through the philosophy and the theodicy of Leibniz, as well as their legacy to the neo-baroque paradigm. The second chapter of the book is entitled 'The Folds in the Soul'; the entirety of part III is entitled 'Having a Body'. Without going into the details of Deleuze's lengthy and fascinating discussions, we can single out two main arguments:

1. Leibniz's baroque philosophical theodicy promotes a tentative 'new harmony', or resolution of 'tension', made possible precisely by the *distinction* between 'two levels', that of the soul and that of the body: 'That one is metaphysical and concerns souls, and the other is physical and concerns bodies, does not prevent the two vectors from composing one and the same world.'[124] There is here a 'superior correspondence' ('correspondance supérieure') that endlessly relates one level to the other.[125] The two levels thus do not amount to a Platonic (or early Christian) distinction between two worlds, but to the function of the fold, which 'reverberates on the two sides following a different regime'.[126] In short, the fold passes between souls and bodies; it is a virtuality that is internally 'actualised' in the intimacy of souls and externally 'realised' in the material partition of bodies. The distinction between inside and outside should be understood as expressing on two levels the same 'expressed', or fold, or best of possible worlds, where 'the expressed does not exist outside its expressions'.[127]

2. Beyond the Leibnizian 'transformation of the cosmos into a "mundus"',[128] Deleuze's neo-baroque philosophy of the chaosmos and its assumption of incompossibility as applicable to one and the same world – which would overthrow any remaining harmony – need to take a step further. That is, Deleuze postulates that as soon as the function of the fold is no longer anchored to God by his lawyer (Leibniz), the distinction between the two levels (body and soul) should be thought in itself as *Difference*: 'a Difference that does not stop unfolding and folding over from each of its two sides, and that unfolds the one only while refolding the other'.[129] The fold becomes the *Fold* ('the distinction between the two levels' ultimately 'refers to the Fold'[130]). This Fold 'differentiates and differentiates *itself*'.[131] It amounts to the truth of variation, whereby being is univocal as a 'pure Event'.[132]

XII

We could argue that Deleuze's and Lacan's surprisingly similar treatment of the baroque and its legacy is first and foremost philosophically important because it allows us to pinpoint the general ontological disagreement on which this specific convergence rests. In the same passages of *The Fold* we have just discussed, Deleuze himself conveys very clearly how his ontology of Difference neatly diverges from the sporadic, yet far-reaching, ontological pronouncements Lacan makes when he investigates the logic of sexual difference (and the truth of the absence of the sexual relationship that goes with it). According to Deleuze, the Fold that 'differentiates and differentiates itself' means primarily that 'differentiation does not refer back to a pregiven undifferentiated, but to a Difference'.[133] While I can here only hint at these complex matters – to which I have dedicated considerable attention in my recent work, using extensive textual evidence – it would not be incorrect to suggest that, for Lacan, differentiation (ultimately the symbolic oscillation between One and not-One, or also, what he calls 'the not-two') *does* refer to *indifference*. It is, in Deleuze's own words, 'the differentiation of an undifferentiated'.[134] But this referring of difference to indifference is not a referring *back*. Indifference is not superseded by the contingent emergence of sexual/symbolic difference, but persists irrespectively of the symbolic order and *in* the symbolic order itself.

To put it very succinctly, according to Lacan, sexual/symbolic difference *is*. It is real. But to think of this difference as in itself *Difference* would reintroduce a transcendent dimension of being, whereby for Difference to be there must also be that which differs from difference, that is, the One. To state unproblematically that the not-One is, or that the whole truth is 'there is no sexual relationship' (or 'there is no metalanguage'), amounts to an unpardonable strategic mistake that paves the way to a new 'triumph of religion'. This warning sums up in my view Lacan's lesson to contemporary materialisms and realisms, which all too often forget it.

Deleuze has in this context the great merit of developing an ontology for which the not-One (chaos) as Difference *admittedly* corresponds to univocal being. In *The Fold*, he even concedes that this should also be understood in terms of God as a 'Process' ('God desists from being a Being who compares worlds and chooses the richest compossible. He becomes Process, a process that at once affirms incompossibilities and passes through them'[135]). The problem, which we cannot tackle here, is that Deleuze also – contradictorily in my view – posits the not-One as differential yet univocal Process/God as a plane of *immanence*. If, according to Deleuze, the baroque Leibniz instructed himself as God's lawyer – and Lacan agrees that the baroque is ultimately a last attempt at 'saving' God – we could say that, following the 'death of God', the neo-baroque Deleuze nonetheless continues to work as his unofficial pro bono legal adviser.

In the end, for Lacan, being does not think, whether in an orderly or chaotic fashion. 'Asymmetry in nature is neither symmetrical nor asymmetrical – it is what it is', he says.[136] On the other hand, a chaos that 'chaotizes',[137] or, which is the same, an infinite Fold that is, for Deleuze, 'Power',[138] still remains a transcendent Principle. We can speak of a Deleuzian chaotic 'Thought-world' only to the extent that the being that speaks and thinks (because there is no sexual relationship) is real. Yet, in thinking, the thinking being thinks *and* does not think. Thus, the basic ontological principle of Lacan's speculation is not even indifference, which is as 'abstract' as Deleuze's chaos,[139] but in-difference. In-difference is what Seminar XI called 'absolute difference'.[140]

Notes

1. Deleuze, Gilles, *The Fold: Leibniz and the Baroque* (London: The Athlone Press, 1993), pp. 27–8.
2. Ibid. p. 3; translation modified.
3. See ibid. pp. 18, 3, 9.
4. See, for instance, ibid. p. 35.
5. Ibid. p. 137; translation modified.
6. Lacan, Jacques, *The Seminar of Jacques Lacan, Book XX: Encore* (London and New York: W. W. Norton, 1998), p. 113.
7. Ibid. p. 105.
8. Ibid. p. 105.
9. Ibid. p. 107.
10. Here I will not analyse the question of infinity. Suffice it to stress that it is already implicitly present in the titles of both Deleuze's and Lacan's respective works. For Deleuze, the fold is an infinite unfolding that is also a refolding. Moreover, Leibniz's philosophy and theodicy can only be accurately conceived if we give the right weight to his infinitesimal calculus (see especially *The Fold*, pp. 96–8). For Lacan, the *encore* ('again!' or 'more!') of 'insufficient jouissance' goes together with a 'realm of the infinite' (*Encore*, p. 103) – or better, as François Récanati has it, an 'infinitisation of infinites' ('Intervention au séminaire du Docteur Lacan', *Scilicet*, 4 (1973), pp. 55–73) – that lies on the side of the not-all of woman and her specific *jouissance*.
11. Deleuze, *The Fold*, pp. 19–20; translation modified.
12. Ibid. p. 19; translation modified.
13. Ibid. p. 21.
14. Ibid. p. 21.
15. Ibid. p. 22.
16. Ibid. p. 21; translation modified. Here as elsewhere, the English translation is unreliable: 'condition de la manifestation du vrai' is rendered as 'condition for the manifestation of reality'.
17. Ibid. p. 20.
18. Lacan, *Encore*, p. 120.
19. Ibid. p. 119.
20. Ibid. p. 119.
21. Ibid. p. 142.
22. Ibid. pp. 11, 28.
23. Ibid. p. 42.
24. Ibid. p. 42.
25. Ibid. p. 42.
26. Ibid. p. 108.
27. Ibid. p. 106; translation modified.

28. Ibid. p. 106.
29. Lacan, Jacques, *The Four Fundamental Concepts of Psycho-analysis* (London: Vintage, 1998), p. 96.
30. Ibid. pp. 86–7.
31. Lacan, Jacques, *The Seminar of Jacques Lacan, Book VII: The Ethics of Psychoanalysis* (London: Routledge, 1992), p. 136; translation modified.
32. Ibid. p. 135; translation modified.
33. Ibid. pp. 60, 136.
34. Ibid. p. 136.
35. Ibid. p. 136.
36. Ibid. p. 136.
37. Ibid. p. 136.
38. Ibid. p. 136.
39. Lacan, *Four Fundamental Concepts*, p. 81.
40. Ibid. p. 82.
41. Ibid. p. 81.
42. Ibid. p. 94; my emphasis.
43. See ibid. p. 82.
44. See Lacan, Jacques, *Le séminaire de Jacques Lacan, livre VIII: Le transfert, 1960–1961* (Paris: Seuil, 2001), p. 198. On the 'stain', see, for instance, *Four Fundamental Concepts*, pp. 74, 273.
45. Lacan, *The Ethics of Psychoanalysis*, p. 135.
46. Ibid.; *Four Fundamental Concepts*, p. 88.
47. Lacan, *The Ethics of Psychoanalysis*, p. 60.
48. Ibid. p. 60; translation modified.
49. Deleuze, *The Fold*, p. 36; translation modified.
50. Ibid. p. 39; translation modified.
51. Ibid. p. 19.
52. Ibid. p. 19; translation modified.
53. Ibid. p. 19.
54. Lacan, *Four Fundamental Concepts*, pp. 53, 69.
55. Deleuze, *The Fold*, p. 20; translation modified.
56. Lacan, *Four Fundamental Concepts*, p. 74; translation modified. The English translation reads: 'the function of the stain and of the gaze is both that which governs *the gaze*', which is nonsensical given the context.
57. Ibid. p. 276.
58. Deleuze, *The Fold*, p. 10; translation modified. The English translation misleadingly renders this as 'a difference is being differentiated'.
59. Ibid. p. 20.
60. Ibid. pp. 14–15.
61. Lacan, *Encore*, p. 127.
62. Ibid. p. 127. Fink prefers to translate *pliure* as 'bending'.
63. Ibid. p. 11.
64. Deleuze, *The Fold*, p. 30.
65. Lacan, *Encore*, p. 127.
66. Deleuze, *The Fold*, p. 15.
67. Ibid. p. 68.
68. Ibid. p. 67.
69. Ibid. p. 67.
70. Ibid. pp. 68, 82.
71. Ibid. p. 81.
72. Ibid. p. 68; translation modified.
73. Ibid. p. 82.
74. See ibid. p. 68.

75. Ibid. p. 67; translation modified.
76. Ibid. p. 82.
77. Ibid. p. 67; translation modified.
78. Ibid. p. 67.
79. Tarizzo, Davide, 'La metafisica del caos', in Deleuze, Gilles, *La piega. Leibniz e il Barocco* (Turin: Einaudi, 2004), pp. vii–xli.
80. Deleuze, *The Fold*, p. 76. The English translation renders *crible* as 'screen'; I think 'sieve' is in this context more accurate.
81. Ibid. p. 77.
82. Ibid. p. 78. On this entire process, see pp. 76–8.
83. Ibid. p. 81.
84. Ibid. pp. 76, 79.
85. Ibid. p. 76; original emphasis.
86. Lacan, *Encore*, p. 36.
87. Ibid. p. 116.
88. Ibid. pp. 109, 107.
89. Ibid. p. 56.
90. 'That is reported by four texts said to be "evangelical", not so much because they bore good news as because (their authors) were announcers who were good at propagating that sort of news' (ibid. p. 107).
91. Ibid. p. 114.
92. Ibid. p. 107.
93. See ibid. pp. 114, 116.
94. He continues: 'that was what our painting was about, until the slate was wiped clean when people began to seriously concern themselves with little squares' (ibid. p. 116).
95. Ibid. p. 113.
96. Ibid. p. 107.
97. Most recently, in Chiesa, Lorenzo, 'Psychoanalysis, Religion, Love', in *Crisis and Critique*, 2: 1 (2015), pp. 57–71.
98. See Lacan, *Encore*, p. 108.
99. Ibid. p. 116; my emphasis.
100. Ibid. p. 113.
101. Ibid. p. 113.
102. Ibid. p. 113.
103. Ibid. p. 108; translation modified.
104. Ibid. p. 108.
105. Lacan, Jacques, *Le séminaire de Jacques Lacan, livre XIX: . . . ou pire* (Paris: Seuil, 2011), p. 200; my emphasis.
106. Ibid. p. 195.
107. I have analysed and problematised this understanding of truth in Chiesa, Lorenzo, *The Not-Two: Logic and God in Lacan* (Cambridge, MA: MIT Press, 2016); see especially the Conclusion.
108. Lacan, *Encore*, p. 116.
109. Ibid. p. 6.
110. Ibid. p. 113.
111. See, for instance, ibid. pp. 84–5.
112. Ibid. p. 116.
113. Ibid. p. 116.
114. Ibid. p. 113.
115. Ibid. p. 113.
116. For a more detailed analysis of these issues, see *The Not-Two*, ch. 2, sec. 2.
117. Lacan, *Encore*, p. 109.
118. Ibid. p. 109.
119. Ibid. p. 110.

120. Lacan, . . . *ou pire*, p. 40.
121. Lacan, *Encore*, p. 113.
122. Lacan, . . . *ou pire*, p. 30.
123. Lacan, *Encore*, p. 108; translation modified.
124. Deleuze, *The Fold*, p. 29.
125. Ibid. p. 29; translation modified.
126. Ibid. p. 29; translation modified.
127. Ibid. pp. 29, 35.
128. Ibid. p. 29.
129. Ibid. p. 30; translation modified.
130. Ibid. p. 30.
131. Ibid. p. 30; translation modified; my emphasis.
132. In Badiou's words, this is 'the very action of the One as self-folding' (Badiou, Alain, *Deleuze: The Clamor of Being* (London and Minneapolis: University of Minnesota Press, 2000), p. 89).
133. Deleuze, *The Fold*, p. 30; translation modified.
134. Ibid. p. 10.
135. Ibid. p. 81.
136. Lacan, Jacques, *The Seminar of Jacques Lacan, Book II: The Ego in Freud's Theory and in the Technique of Psychoanalysis* (London: W. W. Norton, 1991), p. 38.
137. Deleuze, Gilles and Guattari, Félix, *What is Philosophy?* (New York: Columbia University Press, 1994), p. 42.
138. Deleuze, *The Fold*, p. 18.
139. Ibid. p. 76.
140. However, there is also an aspect of Lacan's speculation that points in the direction of Deleuze's chaosmos. Nature is as such Difference, and it is then a question of thinking the 'becoming variegated [. . .] against a variegated background'. See Chiesa, *The Not-Two*, ch. 2, secs 4 and 5.

Chapter 10

The Death Drive

Alenka Zupančič

In the beginning of his famous essay 'Beyond the Pleasure Principle' Freud
introduces the problem of the compulsion to repeat, thus opening one of
the most interesting as well as most controversial conceptual chapters in
psychoanalysis, summed up by the hypothesis of the so-called death drive.[1]
Freud proposes a range of different examples. We come across people, he
writes, all of whose human relationships have the same outcome: such
as the benefactor who is abandoned in anger after a time by each of his
protégés, however much they may otherwise differ from one another; or
the man whose friendships all end in betrayal by his friend; or the man
who time and again in the course of his life raises someone else to the position of great private or public authority and then, after a certain interval,
himself upsets the authority and replaces him with a new one; or the lover
each of whose love affairs passes through the same phases and reaches the
same outcome. There is also the case that became notorious under the
name of *fort-da* [gone-there] – the words used by a small child playing
with a wooden reel with a piece string tied round it, repeatedly casting
it away and puling it back to himself. Even more intriguing are the cases
where the subject seems to have a *passive* experience, over which he has no
influence, but in which he comes across the repetition of the same fatality.
There was the case of the woman who married three successive husbands
each of whom fell ill soon afterwards and had to be nursed by her on their
deathbeds. Even at the level of dreams which are supposedly governed by
the pleasure principle and guided by a 'wish fulfilment', psychoanalysis
discovered a surprising compulsion to repeat some particularly traumatic
incidents. The basic problem presented to psychoanalysis by the compulsion to repeat is thus the following: if one starts from – as Freud did at
some point – the primary character of the pleasure principle which aims to

maximise pleasure (and whereby pleasure is defined as '*lowering of tension*') or minimise displeasure, then the phenomena of the compulsion to repeat contradict this framework. Why would somebody be compelled to repeat a distinctly unpleasant experience?

Two divergent accounts of the mechanisms and the logics of the repetition can be discerned already in Freud. According to the first, what we find at the origin of repetition is a repression of a traumatic event – repetition appears at the place of remembering, one repeats something that one cannot remember. Repetition is thus fundamentally the repetition (in different 'disguises') of a concrete, originally traumatic event or experience. Although Freud preserved the basic outline of this explanation, he also saw that it nevertheless leaves several problems and questions unanswered, suggesting that the whole story may be more complicated. Practically all interesting and productive readings of Freud on this point emphasise the necessity of another turn which complicates the above scheme and puts the repetition in a new perspective. Despite some important differences these readings all agree on one point, which recently has been made again by Ray Brassier in the context of his take on negativity and nihilism: what the compulsion to repeat repeats is not some traumatic and hence repressed experience, but something which *could never register as experience to begin with*. The trauma that is being repeated is outside of the horizon of experience (and is rather constitutive of it). This is how Brassier reads the intriguingly speculative part of 'Beyond the Pleasure Principle', where Freud ventures into a speculation about the genesis of organic individuation. A primitive organic vesicle (that is, a small bladder, cell, bobble or hollow structure) becomes capable of filtering the continuous and potentially lethal torrent of external stimuli by sacrificing part of itself in order to erect a protective shield against excessive influxes of excitation. In doing so, it effects a definitive separation between organic interiority and inorganic exteriority. The separation between the organic inside and the inorganic outside is thus achieved at the price of death of a part of the primitive organism itself.[2] As Brassier put it:

> Thus, individuated organic life is won at the cost of this aboriginal death whereby the organism first becomes capable of separating itself from inorganic outside. This death, which gives birth to organic individuation, thereby conditions the possibility of organic phylogenesis, as well as of sexual reproduction. Consequently, not only does this death precede the organism, it is the precondition for the organism's ability to reproduce and die. If the death-drive qua compulsion to repeat is the originary, primordial motive force driving organic life, this is because the motor of repetition – the repeating instance – is this trace of the aboriginal trauma of

organic individuation. [. . .] The death-drive is the trace of this scission: a scission that will never be successfully *bound* (invested) because it remains the *unbindable* excess that makes binding possible.[3]

This is a crucial point, and we shall return to it. Yet this important emphasis notwithstanding, Brassier's reading still remains within the classical Freudian scheme, according to which the compulsion to repeat is in the service of mastering the unbound 'erring surplus' (the excess of excitation), related to the aboriginal trauma, even though the latter could not have been *experienced* as such. The compulsive repetition is thus explained as the mechanism through which 'the psyche is striving to muster the anxiety required in order to achieve a successful binding (*Besetzung*) of the excess of excitation released by the traumatic breaching of its defenses. It is this binding that lies "beyond the pleasure principle".'[4] In other words: when the usual mechanisms of defence (including repression) – which can still master the excessive excitement within the register of the pleasure principle – no longer work, anxiety is brought in as the last resort in order to perform this work of binding, which in this case takes place beyond the pleasure principle. And the role of the compulsive repetition (of the unpleasant) is to give rise to this anxiety. In spite of its unpleasant character, anxiety is still a defence (against an even bigger displeasure); and the repetition providing this drastic defence is ultimately still in the service of the pleasure principle qua lowering of tension, it is a paradoxical extension of the pleasure principle itself. And so is the death drive. Or else one would need to distinguish between the death drive as such, and the *compulsion* to repeat this or that (empirical) traumatic experience. What suggests a move in this last direction is that Brassier is brought to separate the repetition itself from the excess of excitation and to put them, so to speak, on two opposite sides: the excess is the trace of the aboriginal trauma (prior to any experience), and the compulsion to repeat an *empirically* traumatic experience is a means of awakening anxiety in order to master and 'bind' the excess. But this would then imply that the (death) drive itself is not intrinsically related to repetition.

These considerations and difficulties could be a good starting place from which to look at the perhaps surprising proximity between Lacan and Deleuze in their readings of Freud on this point, which will then bring us to examine the relationship between their respective ontologies.

In relation to Freud both Lacan and Deleuze first vigorously reject the principle of 'lowering of tension' as a fundamental principle and, second, they insist that there is a direct connection between the 'erring/unbound excess' and repetition. As to the first point, they reject the hypothesis of two competing principles (pleasure as 'Eros' and death drive as 'Thanatos'), as well as the possibility of relating the death drive to a homeostatic tendency ('return to the inanimate')[5] and hence its subjection – in the last instance – to the pleasure principle as the primary principle. This last emphasis and the ontological primacy of the death drive it implies, which is not so surprising in the case of Lacan, is certainly much more so in the case of the allegedly 'vitalist' Deleuze. In the introductory part of *Difference and Repetition*, where he develops one of the most lucid readings of Freud's death drive ever proposed, he explicitly suggests that the death drive 'is the transcendental principle, whereas the pleasure principle is only psychological'.[6] Or: 'Eros and Thanatos are distinguished in that Eros must be repeated, can be lived only through repetition, whereas Thanatos (as transcendental principle) is that which gives repetition to Eros.'[7] In other words, Eros is but part of the logic (of the appearing) of Thanatos or of the death drive, and does not have the status of another, complementary (or primary) principle. Death drive is the fundamental (and only) principle, and it has nothing to do with any kind of lowering of tension.

In the same way Lacan argues against the duality of the drives, claiming that 'every drive is virtually a death drive',[8] as well as against what he perceives as a remainder of the Aristotelian metaphysics in Freud. He thus argues strongly against:

> backing the primary process up with the principle which, if pleasure were its only claim, would demonstrate nothing, save that we cling to the soul like a tick to a dog's hide. Because what else is the famous lowering of tension with which Freud links pleasure, other than the ethics of Aristotle?[9]

One should add to this, however, that to think of the death drive as fundamental does not amount to positing the primacy of some obscure *will* or tendency to aggression, destruction, death. As Deleuze perspicuously pointed out, Freud did not discover the death drive in the context of destructive and aggressive tendencies, but in the context of considering the phenomena of repetition. According to Deleuze, repetition itself is precisely the place of original affirmation. Which is why for him the true question is: 'How is it that the theme of death, which appears to draw together the most negative elements of psychological life, can be in itself the most positive element, transcendentally positive, to the point of affirming repetition?'[10]

For both Lacan and Deleuze repetition is essentially related to the death drive as the fundamental matrix of the drive. What the logic of the latter demonstrates could well be, to borrow the sharpened formulation of this by Slavoj Žižek:

> that the most radical tendency of a living organism is to maintain a state of tension, to avoid final 'relaxation' in obtaining a state of full homeostasis.

'Death drive' as 'beyond the pleasure principle' is the very insistence of an organism on endlessly repeating the state of tension.[11]

One should also emphasise that Lacan's and Deleuze's criticism of Freud is probably closer to the spirit of Freud, to his crucial findings and insights, than the simple acceptance of the claim about an original tendency to lower the tension.

The other crucial point concerns the relation between the 'erring excess' and repetition. Both Lacan and Deleuze insist that the excess (of excitation) does not exist somewhere independently of repetition, but only and precisely in repetition itself and through it. In other words, the thing in defence against which repetition mobilises anxiety exists only through the repetition itself. Repetition is to be found on both sides of this movement: repetition is what brings in the excess 'bound' by anxiety through repetition. The death drive already involves repetition, so that the repetition itself could be seen as split, or two-sided.

In Deleuze, this is the split between repetition as 'transcendental principle' and repetition as 'empirical'. With every empirical repetition something else is at stake (and repeated) as well, namely the difference as such: it is only through and in relation to this repetition as pure difference that the things exist which we can described as different, similar or the same.[12] This is why one should not understand repetition here solely in the narrow sense of repeating an identical configuration, but as something no less at work in the colourful variety of differences. The point is that 'something' can be repeated in very different forms, while it does not exist somewhere outside these forms. This 'something' has no independent existence, yet at the same time it is not simply reducible to the elements which it repeats. Or, in a longer but crucial passage from Deleuze:

> Death has nothing to do with a material model. On the contrary, the death instinct may be understood in relation to masks and costumes. Repetition is truly that which disguises itself in constituting itself, that which constitutes itself only by disguising itself. It is not underneath the masks, but is formed from one mask to another, as though from one distinctive point to another, from one privileged instant to another, with and within the variations. The masks do not hide anything except other masks. There is no first term which is repeated [. . .]. There is therefore nothing repeated which may be isolated or abstracted from the repetition in which it was formed, but in which it is also hidden. There is no bare repetition which may be abstracted or inferred from the disguise itself. The same thing is both disguising and disguised.[13]

We must be attentive to Deleuze's wording, which is very precise here. The point is not simply that all that exists are masks/appearances/disguises *and nothing else*. The point is (1) that there is no substance that would repeat itself in different disguises and could be deciphered as such, pointed out and separated from them; and (2) that *there is* something besides the masks, yet the ontological status of this something is paradoxical: we are dealing with something that only exists in repetition of different masks, and which calls for redoubling in its formulation ('The same thing is both disguising and disguised'). Moreover, not only does that what is repeated only exist through the 'masks' with which it is repeated, these masks themselves exist only (and literally) through what they repeat: 'The masks or costumes, do not come "over and above": they are, on the contrary, the internal genetic elements of repetition itself, its integral and constituent parts.'[14] These, then, are the two sides of repetition.

In Lacan a similar inherent split could be established between two levels of the drive: drives as involved in all kinds of partial satisfactions, following the well-known list (oral, anal, scopic), and the drive as purely disruptive pulsating negativity that propels them. In Seminar XI, for example, he emphasises the difference between object *a* as marking a negativity (loss or gap) as such, around which the drive circulates, and all forms of objects *a*, which 'are merely its representatives, its figures',[15] and which constitute different partial drives. As in Deleuze, these two levels cannot be separated. Death drive does not exist somewhere independently of these multiple figures, but only with them and through them. This also means, however, that the supposedly original chaotic, fragmented (empirical) multiplicity of the drives is already a *result* of some 'unifying' negativity – as opposed to the rather romantic and much too simple idea about an original chaotic freedom of the drives.[16] However, this fundamental negativity is 'unifying' in a very specific sense which, again, bears some surprising resemblance to the Deleuzian notion of 'univocity'.

In Deleuze the notion of the univocity of being is directly linked to the singular and central relation between two levels of difference involved in repetition:

> We must show not only how individuating difference differs in kind from specific difference, but primarily and above all how individuation properly *precedes* matter and form, species and parts, and every other element of the constituted individual. Univocity of being, in so far as it is immediately related to difference, demands that we show how individuating difference precedes generic, specific and even individual differences within being; how a prior field of individuation within being conditions at once the determination of species of forms, the determination of parts and their individual variations. If individuation does not take place either by form or by matter, neither qualitatively nor extensionally, this is not only because it differs in kind but because it is already presupposed by the forms, matters and extensive parts.[17]

This is a very dense passage. It invokes, among other things, the very beginning of metaphysics and the whole discussion by Aristotle (in Book VII of *Metaphysics*) of what is *being qua being*, where Aristotle attempts to decide whether this title should go to matter or to form.[18] What makes him eventually decide that the title does not go to his first candidate, which is the formless matter of which everything is ultimately composed, but to form, is precisely the question of individuation. He very briskly concludes that substance must be 'separate' (*chôriston*) and 'some this' (*tode ti*, sometimes translated 'this something'), and – implying that matter fails to meet this requirement – the title goes to form. Precisely what the requirement amounts to is still a matter of considerable scholarly debate. Yet one can plausibly say that it concerns the question of (a certain type of) individuation. And this is precisely the point (or the 'symptom') to which both Lacan and Deleuze respond with the argument that could be most concisely put in the following terms: Aristotle fails to distinguish between 'difference' and 'differentiating difference', and hence between two levels of individuation: one that can be seen as separate individual entities, and the one that only makes it possible for the latter to appear (or to count) as such. In his discussion of the ontological status and presuppositions of *one* (as unit) in the seminar . . . *ou pire* Lacan points out that Aristotle's logic is founded on 'the intuition of the individual posited as real'.[19] This means that, in a nominalist way, Aristotle takes empirical individuation (difference) as the foundation of the notion of One. In relation to this Lacan does not simply embrace a realist ('Platonic') stance according to which One would exist as such (the idea of One that would precede any empirical oneness). Instead, by drawing strongly on the contemporary mathematical logic and set theory,[20] he proposes his own way of thinking the difference and the relationship between the two levels of individuation, and comes up with formulations strongly consonant with Deleuze's. The One of individuation can only be founded on pure difference, it 'comes from' a negativity that is repeated in (and with) any countable one. 'One cannot be founded upon sameness. On the contrary, in set theory it is designated as something that has to be founded upon pure and simple difference.'[21]

The way Lacan reads the notion of the 'empty set' in modern mathematics echoes, almost word for word, the Deleuzian construction of the individuating difference as prior to all countable differences, while at the same time involved (as repeated) in each one of them. It is not that we have, say, first an empty set, then a set with one element, a set with two elements, and so on. The empty set appears only through its repetition, for – mathematically – it is already a set with one 'element' (this element being the empty set). The constitutive emptiness does not exist without the One with which it appears the first time (although it is not reducible to it) and, on the other hand, this One 'comes from' the empty set which it repeats.

'Emptiness', 'hole' and 'radical difference' are posited by Lacan at the core of repetition as constituting/generating what *there is*, and what is countable. This is the 'unifying negativity' which is always the 'same' only insofar as it is absolutely singular, *alone* (*un seul*).[22] This also applies to Deleuze. Albeit borrowing the notion of univocity (of being) from Duns Scotus and Spinoza, Deleuze nevertheless modifies it at a crucial point: we are not dealing with a configuration in which being or substance is One, and everything that exists is a modification of this One-Substance. Deleuze's claim is not that 'being is One', but that being is difference, which is one (alone), *singular*. The accent is on there being only one, *single* Difference, and not on the difference forming a One. This single, pure Difference is repeating itself with different entities, different 'ones' (and their differences), constituting them in this way, and constituting itself in this repetition.

Deleuze has two magisterial concepts with which he thinks this fundamental negativity: Difference (the radical, individuating difference as conceptualised in *Difference and Repetition*) and the 'crack', *fêlure*, which plays a most significant role in *The Logic of Sense*. Unsurprisingly, both are discussed by Deleuze as directly related to the 'death instinct'. He famously introduces the concept of the crack in relation to F. Scott Fitzgerald's novel *The Crack-Up* (translated in French as *La fêlure*), making a proper concept out of it, and developing it more extensively in his discussion of Zola that concludes – which is quite significant positioning – *The Logic of Sense*. Deleuze takes as his starting point the following extraordinary passage from *La bête humaine*:

> The family was really not quite normal, and many of them had some flaw [*fêlure*]. At certain times, he could clearly feel this hereditary taint [*fêlure*], not that his health was bad, for it was only nervousness and shame about his attacks that made him lose weight in his early days. But there were attacks of instability in his being, losses of equilibrium like cracks [*cassures*] or holes from which his personality seemed to leak away, amid a sort of thick vapor that deformed everything.[23]

Deleuze first carefully stresses that the crack does not designate the route along which morbid ancestral elements will pass, marking the body. 'Heredity is not that which passes through the crack, it is the crack itself – *the imperceptible rift or the hole*.'[24] He further distinguishes this 'grand', 'epic' heredity from what he calls 'small' heredity and which is what we usually mean by this term: the transmission of something determined, transmission as 'reproduction' of the same. Although they are in no way

reducible to one another, they are very closely related. A way of conceiving this relation would be (again following Zola) in terms of the relation
between the crack and its surroundings. Distributed around the crack
there are what Zola calls the temperaments, the instincts, the big appetites.
Deleuze takes the notion of 'instincts' (and their objects) to refer to the
corporeal ('empirical') appearance of the crack[25] – a corporeal appearance
without which the crack would remain but a 'diffuse potentiality'. He then
proposes the following formulation of the relation between the two levels,
which directly echoes the way he describes the relation between repetition
(as pure difference/being) and its masks (that which appears) in *Difference
and Repetition*:

> If it is true that the instincts are formed and find their object only at the edge
> of the crack, the crack conversely pursues its course, spreads out its web,
> changes direction and is actualized in each body in relation to the instincts
> which open a way for it, sometimes mending it a little, sometimes widening
> it [. . .] The two orders are tightly joined together, like a ring within a larger
> ring, but they are never confused.[26]

Whereas Deleuze arrives to this topology by way of literature, Lacan
sketches it with reference to modern mathematics. They can both be said
to 'force' their references to some extent (is Zola really saying this? Is
mathematics really saying this?) in order to come up with a wording of
their own which, again, is often astonishingly similar. Describing the relation between the empty set and the elements that can be counted (as one)
and said to exist, Lacan works his way to his principal thesis according to
which One (that could be said to be) emerges out of an ontological deficit,
a 'hole', posited as primary. Here are some highly suggestive formulations:
(countable) One 'only begins from its lack';[27] 'One emerges as effect of
the lack';[28] 'the fundament of One turns out to be constituted out of the
place of a lack'.[29] One emerges out of 'the entry door designated from the
lack, from the place where there is a hole'.[30] As one can see very clearly,
the 'hole' is not an effect or a result of a failed repetition or impossibility; rather, it is itself the impossible. The impossible is precisely what *is*
repeated, it is the repetition itself, and it is itself 'productive'. The proximity between this 'hole' or original lack (the negativity on which the death
drive is premised) and the Deleuzian *fêlure* becomes even more striking in
the following passage from Deleuze:

> The crack designates, and this emptiness is, Death – the death instinct. The
> instincts may speak loud, make noise, or swarm, but they are unable to cover
> up this more profound silence, or hide that from which they come forth and
> to which they return: the death instinct, *not merely one instinct among others*,
> but the crack itself around which all the instincts congregate.[31]

This is most interesting in relation to Lacan's discussion of the relation-ship between sexuality and the (always) partial drives: sexuality, consid-ered from a phenomenological point of view, appears to be composed of several different partial drives, to which it provides a more or less accom-plished unification. (And this was basically Freud's view of the matter.) What Lacan adds to this – and we are clearly on a speculative level here – is that we could also see sexuation as prior to the partial drives: not as a kind of primary substance, but as a pure negativity, hole/crack (and in this sense as the real) around which the drives 'congregate' (to use Deleuze's word-ing). There is no sexual drive: sexuality (as 'activity') appears at the point of its own fundamental lack. Taken at this level, sexuality 'unifies' the drives not by uniting them in a more or less coherent whole (of sexual activity), but precisely as the crack (of being) around which they circulate and to which they keep returning. 'Sexual' refers to the 'hole' or the 'crack' shared (and repeated) by different drives. Taken at this level, sexuality is indeed synonymous with the death drive, and not opposed to it, as Eros opposed to Thanatos. It is Thanatos insofar as the latter is, in Deleuzian terms, 'that which gives repetition to Eros'.

And, perhaps not so surprisingly any more, when discussing the 'crack' Deleuze also links it to sexuation: As opposed to '*some*' (the somatic cells, the biological cells forming the body of an organism), he writes, 'the "*germen*" is the crack – nothing but the crack'.[32] The 'germen' – that is to say the germ cells, the elements involved in sexual reproduction – is the very instance of *fêlure*.

It is of course well known how, in *Difference and Repetition*, Deleuze states emphatically that the motor, the mobile of repetition is not an impos-sibility (to repeat), a failure, a lack, a deficiency; there is nothing (outside it) that motivates repetition, repetition itself is the primary 'motivator' and motor. Yet we must not read this Deleuzian stance against 'negativity' and 'lack' too quickly. As we have seen in his consideration (and appropriation) of the death drive, things are more complicated and more interesting. The point is rather that 'negativity' (the crack, the hole) is the primary site of affirmation. Repetition is the hole/crack that repeats itself, and by this it repeats what is around it and related to it. Or, in other words, repetition is negativity taken in its absolute sense: not negativity in relation to some-thing, but original negativity, negativity that is itself productive of what is there and what can be differentiated, compared, said to fail, and so on. We could also say that he takes negativity as such to be the original positive force – as opposed to a secondary notion of negativity (and difference). And the whole question now becomes how to eventually separate this 'bad' neg-ativity from a 'good' one. It is with this question that some more significant differences between Lacan and Deleuze start to appear.

As we have seen, both Lacan and Deleuze emphasise the necessity to think the difference of difference, that is the necessity to distinguish between difference in a radical sense and the usual way in which the term is used and which already presupposes a prior Difference. And in both Lacan and Deleuze *repetition* is conceived as the form of the relationship between these two differences, or between these two levels of difference. If Deleuze can see in the Nietzschean eternal return an actualisation of the univocity of being, this is precisely because eternal return (as repetition) realises this relationship in its simultaneous, instant doubleness: 'The wheel in the eternal return is at once both production of repetition on the basis of difference and selection of difference on the basis of repetition.'[33] What does this mean? What is repeated comes from the pure negativity of difference which, in repetition, is always already something (that is to say something which comes under the categories of analogy, similarity, identity); at the same time this repetition itself is a 'centrifugal force' that expels all that which, of the difference, gets 'reified' into something in this same repetition.[34]

The centrifugal force of repetition in its most radical form thus not only introduces the difference at the very core of repetition, but also 'realises' this difference – it realises it by extracting the repetition itself from repetition, by extracting what is new from the mechanism of repetition that produced it. This is what could be described, in Deleuze, as concept-project, the latter being no less than the project of realised ontology: 'However, the only realized Ontology – in other words, the univocity of being – is repetition.'[35] Difference is the only and the original being, yet at the same time it (still) needs to be realised, that is to say *repeated* and thus separated from all the metaphysical and dialectical attendance that constitutes the history of Being and of its thought. This task can be accomplished by the 'centrifugal force' of the repetition itself. Yet what this amounts to is not only a 'realised ontology', but also an 'ontologisation of the Real' – the Real in the Lacanian sense.

In order to see what is at stake here, we could look at the Deleuzian argument from the perspective of the classical difference between Being and appearing. The Deleuzian revolution in philosophy consists in proposing that Being qua being is the very relationship (difference) between Being and appearing. In other words, Deleuzian ontology does not simply differentiate from others by what he poses (conceives) as Being. When he claims that Being is pure difference, his claim is precisely that it is the pure difference as that which repeats itself as the relation between (what has so far been called) 'being' and 'appearing'. In other words, and if we may use this topological metaphor: it is the placing of Being that changes, and not simply its referent. The *relation* between Being and its appearing (the Difference, or the 'crack' between them) is now what is called

Being. At the same time, the ontological primacy of the Difference means that (1) the Difference, the rift between (what has traditionally been conceptualised as) being and appearing precedes both; and that (2) 'realised ontology' does away with the difference between being and appearing, because all that remains is the Difference itself (pure difference, and not a difference between this and that). This Difference is pure being qua being in its univocity. And it equals (pure) *movement*. In the same way that the *fêlure*, the 'crack', is finally not so much a rift as it is a pure movement or force. This shift from *topological* to *dynamical* tropes is indeed crucial for Deleuze: the topological non-coincidence of being and appearing is 'liquefied' into Being as pure *movement* of Difference.

Lacan's conceptual manoeuvre is different. As we have seen, he shares with Deleuze the insight that what is problematic in the classical metaphysical difference between Being and appearing is the fact that it misrecognises how this difference actually always involves *three* terms and not just two. There is Being, there is appearing, and *there is* the non-coincidence of the two. The relationship between Being and appearing is never just about these two terms: the fact that they are two (or that Being '*needs*' to appear) bears witness to the fact that something third is at stake.

In order to illustrate more 'plastically' this tripartite structure that both Deleuze and Lacan recognise as the hidden truth of the classical metaphysical couples and distinctions, we can refer once more to the Freudian presupposition of the 'aboriginal death' discussed by Brassier: presupposed by the distinction between life and death is a death that precedes both life and death and makes their distinction possible. Presupposed by the distinction between inside and outside is something that paradoxically falls 'out' before the distinction between 'in' and 'out' can actually appear.[36] What this singular logic illustrates is a division (difference) that does not come from something (some whole) being cut into two, but comes as a result of a *subtraction*, of something being taken away (the concept of the one-less, *l'un-en-moins*, that appears in late Lacan corresponds to this, precisely). This tripartite topology is crucial for both Lacan and Deleuze at their starting point. And the whole question now becomes what one makes out of this third term.

It is at the point of this third term that Lacan introduces his concept of the Real, not to be confused with being. Deleuze, on the other hand – and in a genuinely Nietzschean sense – *revaluates* it, and with it the entire landscape: he makes (of) it the true Being qua being. For Lacan, what is at stake can only be rendered by insisting on the tripartite topology, which is that of the Borromean knot. For Deleuze, this third term is finally nothing but the *double* movement of Being in its univocity. This is why he will say: 'The two orders are tightly joined together, like a ring within a larger ring, but they are never confused.'[37] For Lacan, on the other hand, for the two orders to be tightly joined together, yet never confused, one needs to think this topology in terms of *three* rings, and not just two – hence the Borromean knot.

With the concept of the Real, Lacan gives a conceptual support to the rift, the crack, implied by, yet invisible in the deployment of differences, and repeated with them. He extracts it from its invisibility, claiming that psychoanalysis is in the position to actually assign to it some minimal consistency.

Whereas Deleuze moves to ontologise this Real, and makes it the real Being qua being, it is essential for Lacan to keep them apart. This Lacanian holding of Being and the Real apart does not suggest that Being is not real – the Real is precisely not a predicate. Lacan's reluctance towards something like a psychoanalytic ontology is well known. He is not after developing his own ontology. Yet the reason does not lie perhaps in his conviction that ontology is meaningless (after the transcendental turn) and necessarily 'metaphysical'; on the contrary. If there is someone who has always refused to consider psychoanalysis as exempt from ontological interrogations, it is Lacan. His point is rather that the very notion of ontology (as science of Being qua being) has to be expanded by an additional concept (the Real) that holds and marks the place of its inherent contradiction as the very place from which Being can be thought.

Why is Lacan so reluctant to ontologise this Real? Because the Real for him is not simply something that is out there (not even as a 'diffused potentiality' yet to be realised), it is not to be confused with reality: the Real is what is necessary in order for what is (out) there to be *thought*, and for this thought to have any consequences for what is out there. Thought, in the emphatic sense of the term, is the prerogative of the Real (and in this precise sense the Lacanian theory is very far from any kind of nominalism). The Real is not an Idea – it is the conceptual name for what must go wrong in reality for an idea to appear at all. And this is also what relates thought to the political dimension proper, instead of confining it to the act of 'understanding', 'reflecting', 'analysing' reality. It is also a genuinely 'political' point in Lacan.

The Real is not so much something that we have to strive for (or hope for, or trust in its capacity to eliminate everything else), as it is a possible weapon in the struggle with what is. It is also bound to the idea of an intervention as conceived in psychoanalysis: an intervention with a 'weapon' produced by the very configuration that one aims at changing. This is the central idea of analysis:

> Psychoanalytic intervention should in no way be theoretical, suggestive [. . .] Analytical interpretation is not made in order for it to be understood; it is made

in order to make waves [. . .] I learn everything from my analysands; [. . .] I borrow my interventions from them, and not from my teaching [. . .] And if you choose your words well – the words that will haunt the analysand – you will find the elected signifier, the one which will work.[38]

It is not out of (false or sincere) modesty that Lacan says 'I learn every-thing from my analysands', 'I borrow my interventions from them'. The psychoanalyst is not an expert treating patients with his or her expertise, which he or she would be applying to the symptoms of a given concrete case; symptoms in the psychoanalytic sense are something very different from organic symptoms or symptoms in the medical sense. If one wants to shift something in the thing (in the unconscious structure), one has to give the word to it, for it alone can come up with, produce the word that eventually 'works' and moves things.

Thought is not simply on the side of the subject, it is out there. Yet for it to become effective (to become a material force), something else/new has to occur – a new signifier with which one thinks (differently), and which triggers a new subjectivation. This is where Lacan and Deleuze seem to be the furthest apart: whereas for Deleuze materialism of thought implies radical de-subjectivation, for Lacan (the effect of) subjectivation is the very instance of the materialism of thought.

But what exactly is this new signifier, ideally produced at the end of analysis, the one signifier that makes/is the Difference?[39] It is the formula, the algorithm of the enjoyment that defines, paves the route of the repeti-tion in a concrete configuration. It is the signifier that kills the (compul-sive) repetition because it successfully repeats its enjoyment.[40] It is the algorithm that disorientates the drive by cutting off the well-established routes of its satisfaction. It is the letter to be inserted at the very core of the double face of the drive and of its 'satisfaction'. In itself, the drive is quite indiscriminate, indifferent towards what it satisfies along the way of pursuing its one and only goal, which is simply to 'return into circuit',[41] that is to repeat itself, as Deleuze reads this. This is the 'affirmative' force of repetition (repetition for the sake of repetition) related to the drive: not something that failed, but the repetition itself is the sole drive of the drive. The drive is always satisfied. However, in its very indifference it is also always supportive of whatever complicated paths and extraordinary objects our enjoyment may choose under the sign of repression. It does not care one way or the other. By itself, the drive does not work against repression. In this precise sense the death drive is as much an accomplice of repression as it is utterly indifferent to it. Which also means that one cannot simply count on it to make the 'right' selection (which is what is implied in the Nietzschean/Deleuzian perspective). There is absolutely no guarantee that, left to itself, the death drive will expel the right (that is the wrong) things. One needs something else, or more: it is only a new signifier (and the subjectivation triggered by it) that can effect and sustain the separation at the very heart of the drive. Not a force (be it centrifugal or other), only a letter can disentangle what only exists in entangled form, and hence eventually change this form itself. This is why for Lacan the only vital politics of the drive is that of a dead letter. (And of the thought that it carries and transmits.)

This is an important conceptual feature that separates Lacan from Deleuze: the surplus ('the erring/unbound excess') is not in itself the real scene of emancipation, but the means of production of that which eventually realises this 'emancipation'; the eventual tectonic shift does not take place at the level of this surplus, but thanks to the newly produced *signifier*. This signifier is not about any signification, nor is it a kind of Deleuzian sign that acts directly upon matter: it marks the dead end of signification, its '*ab-sense*'.

The Deleuzian perspective, on the other hand, could be said to merge politics and ontology. The Deleuzian ontology is a political ontology. Or, put differently: realised ontology looks very much like a political project. And one could ask: does emancipation (as political project) have a brighter future in the hands of a dead letter (a new signifier) than in the hands of ontology (to be realised)? This question is of some relevance today.

Several decades ago the decline of politics proper (and of conceiving politics as effective thought) was accompanied by the rise of 'ethics'. The (philosophical and social) success of the latter was linked to its promise to carry out the task of politics better than politics. This is how the rising ethical discourse presented itself. The new ethics to replace the old politics. Concepts like 'antagonism', 'class struggle', 'emancipation' and 'politics' itself were generally replaced by notions of 'tolerance' and 'recognition of the Other', and by the self-imposed rules of political correctness.[42] Ever since the beginning of the last economic and political crisis, starting in the early 2000s, the limits of this 'ethics as politics' were becoming more salient, and the notion of politics as politics started to re-enter the stage. At the same time we were (and still are) witnessing an astounding rise of the so-called new ontologies and new materialisms (to a large extent, albeit not exclusively, inspired by Deleuze), which paradoxically advance by making a very similar kind of promise as ethics did a while ago: to be able to carry out the task of politics better than politics. The massive use (and popularity) of the word 'ontology' is symptomatic in this respect. The point I am trying to make is not, of course, that ontology should be a-political. That would indeed be a stupid point to make. The point, and the (Lacanian) question, is simply this: what if this reinscription of the Real into Being is a way of foreclosing its gap? For Lacan this is precisely the gap where truth holds on to the Real, and where truth preserves and maintains a political dimension, the question of how we situate ourselves in it. Hence:

> We cannot confine ourselves to giving a new truth its rightful place, for the point is to take up our place in it. The truth requires us to go out of our way. We cannot do so by simply getting used to it. We get used to reality. The truth we repress.[43]

Notes

1. Freud, Sigmund, 'Beyond the Pleasure Principle', in *The Penguin Freud Library Vol. 11: On Metapsychology* (Harmondsworth: Penguin, 1991).
2. See ibid. p. 299.
3. Brassier, Ray, *Nihil Unbound* (New York: Palgrave Macmillan, 2007), pp. 237–8.
4. Ibid. p. 234.
5. According to this (Freudian) hypothesis, the occurrence of life corresponds to a disturbing arousal of tension, and the death drive can serve as the basis of the explanation of destructive tendencies because it is itself nothing other than the tendency to return to the inanimate, to re-attain the supposedly zero-level tension ('nirvana') of lifeless, inorganic, inanimate matter.
6. Deleuze, Gilles, *Difference and Repetition* (New York: Columbia University Press, 1994), p. 16. Deleuze uses the term 'death instinct', following the then current French translation of the Freudian *Todestrieb*.
7. Ibid. p. 18.
8. Lacan, Jacques, *Écrits* (New York and London: W. W. Norton, 2006), p. 719.
9. Lacan, Jacques, *Television: A Challenge to the Psychoanalytic Establishment* (New York and London: W. W. Norton, 1990), p. 19.
10. Deleuze, *Difference and Repetition*, p. 16.
11. Žižek, Slavoj, *Organs without Bodies: On Deleuze and Consequences* (London: Routledge, 2004), p. 24.
12. Hence Deleuze writes, for example, that even when dealing with something that appears as a repetition of the same (such as, for instance, the rituals in obsessional neurosis), we have to recognise in the element that is being repeated, that is in the repetition of the same, the mask of a deeper repetition (Deleuze, *Difference and Repetition*, p. 17).
13. Ibid. p. 17.
14. Ibid. p. 17.
15. Lacan, Jacques, *The Four Fundamental Concepts of Psychoanalysis* (Harmondsworth: Penguin, 1979), p. 198.
16. For a more detailed elaboration of this point, see Zupančič, Alenka, 'Die Sexualität innerhalb der Grenzen der blossen Vernunft', in Härtel, Insa (ed.), *Erogene Gefahrenzonen* (Berlin: Kulturverlag Kadmos, 2013), pp. 41–56.
17. Deleuze, *Difference and Repetition*, p. 38.
18. See Aristotle, *The Metaphysics* (Harmondsworth: Penguin, 1999).
19. Lacan, Jacques, *Le séminaire de Jacques Lacan, livre XIX: . . . ou pire* (Paris: Seuil, 2011), p. 139.
20. Which are decidedly not Deleuzian references.
21. Lacan, *. . . ou pire*, p. 144.
22. Ibid. p. 165.
23. Quoted in Deleuze, Gilles, *The Logic of Sense* (London: The Athlone Press, 1990), p. 331.
24. Deleuze, *The Logic of Sense*, p. 321; my emphasis

25. Ibid. p. 322.
26. Ibid. p. 325.
27. Lacan, . . . *ou pire*, p. 146.
28. Ibid. p. 158.
29. Ibid. p. 158.
30. Ibid. p. 147.
31. Deleuze, *The Logic of Sense*, p. 326; original emphasis.
32. Ibid. p. 322.
33. Deleuze, *Difference and Repetition*, p. 42.
34. See ibid. p. 297.
35. Ibid. p. 303.
36. And this is also the status of the Freudian unconscious: the unconscious is not the opposite of the conscious, it is not that of which we are not conscious, it is also what disappears from the conscious before the difference between what we are conscious of and what not, can appear.
37. Deleuze, *The Logic of Sense*, p. 325.
38. Lacan, Jacques, 'Conférences et entretiens dans des universités nord-americaines', *Scilicet*, 6–7 (1976), pp. 5–63, pp. 32, 34.
39. 'The One at stake in the S_1 which the subject produces, so to say, at the ideal point of analysis, is, differently from the One at stake in repetition, the One as only One [*Un seul*]. It is the One so far as, whatever the difference that exists, of all the differences that exist and that all have the same value, there is only one, and this is the difference' (Lacan, . . . *ou pire*, p. 165).
40. Ibid. pp. 151–2.
41. Lacan, *Four Fundamental Concepts*, p. 179.
42. This point was made by Slavoj Žižek.
43. Lacan, *Écrits*, p. 433.

Chapter 11

Repetition and Difference: Žižek, Deleuze and Lacanian Drives

Adrian Johnston

Over the course of many years now, Slavoj Žižek repeatedly has emphasised that the fundamental underlying concern and main overriding ambition of his intellectual efforts in their entirety is to argue for a counterintuitive identity between, on the one hand, the *Cogito*-like subject of German idealism and, on the other hand, the death drive (*Todestrieb*) of Freudian and Lacanian psychoanalysis.[1] Consistent with this emphasis, the short circuit of this coincidence of apparent antagonists (i.e. subject and death drive) also features centrally in the pages of *Less Than Nothing: Hegel and the Shadow of Dialectical Materialism* and *Absolute Recoil: Towards a New Foundation of Dialectical Materialism*.[2] In these two philosophical works from 2012 and 2014 respectively, Žižek is concerned with confronting G. W. F. Hegel in particular with Sigmund Freud's and Jacques Lacan's theories of libidinal economics (as involving the death drive). Both the *Todestrieb* as well as a Lacanian distinction between drive (*Trieb, pulsion*) and desire (*désir*) are presented by Žižek as requiring of Hegel's philosophy certain revisions and changes while simultaneously being foreshadowed by this same philosophy.

In *Less Than Nothing*, Žižek goes so far as to put forward the death drive as the extimate nucleus of Hegelianism, as that which this philosophy, as it were, neither can live with nor can live without. In line with a stress on groundless contingency as the *Ur*-modality of Hegelianism's absoluteness,[3] Žižek identifies as 'the core of Hegelian dialectics' (i.e. the main engine of Hegel's System) nothing other than 'the death drive or the compulsion to repeat' in its brute, dumb facticity – that is, a recurrent circling movement exhibiting an acephalous, idiotic character resembling a mechanical automaton rather than a human subject.[4] Žižek's move here displays a convergence of (seeming) opposites in which the heights of meaning/sense (Hegel's dialectically systematic absolute Idea as the entire integrated network of categories and concepts both logical and real) coincide with the depths of meaninglessness/nonsense (a non-dialectical repetitiveness making possible the Hegelian System and yet, at the same time, perpetually evading this System's comprehension). Of the four post-Hegelians Žižek, at this point in *Less Than Nothing*, mentions by name as targeting this extimate dimension of Hegel's philosophy (i.e. Søren Kierkegaard, Freud, Lacan and Gilles Deleuze), it is, unsurprisingly, Lacan who is most important for his purposes. A Lacanian psychoanalytic Owl of Minerva permits an *après-coup* making explicit of (as a raising to the dignity of its Notion) a Hegelian philosophical presupposition (as *an sich*) waiting to be delivered by its belated positing (as *an und für sich*). Lacan's psychoanalytic conceptions of drive and repetition are put forward by Žižek as the keys to 'positing the presuppositions' that are, precisely, Hegel's implicit conceptions of the contingent Absolute and its dialectical developments propelled along by a non-dialecticisable negativity interminably reiterating itself. I also will take up much later Žižek's reference to Deleuze in conjunction with Lacan's own scattered references to Deleuze's philosophy.

Properly appreciating and assessing Žižek's identification of psychoanalytic drive theory as, to paraphrase Lacan appropriately in this context, 'in Hegel more than Hegel himself' obviously requires examining how Žižek himself conceptualises *Trieb* generally and the *Todestrieb* specifically. Throughout the rest of what follows, I will be tacitly but heavily relying upon my reconstruction of Freud's, Lacan's and Žižek's accounts of drives and libidinal economies in my 2005 book *Time Driven: Metapsychology and the Splitting of the Drive*. I further explore Žižek's pre-2012 parsings of metapsychological drive theory at various moments in my 2008 book *Žižek's Ontology*, explorations likewise in the background of what ensues below. Now, the best place to start this particular examination in the present intervention is with Žižek's distinction, based on a certain interpretation of Lacan, between *pulsion* and *désir*. Indeed, the Žižekian conception of drive is utterly dependent upon this distinction.

In *Less Than Nothing*, the drive–desire contrast is invoked by Žižek multiple times. Therein, the first and most substantial articulation of this difference, an initial articulation upon which subsequent returns to this topic in both *Less Than Nothing* and *Absolute Recoil* draw, begins thusly:

> What does drive mean from a *philosophical* standpoint? In a vague general sense, there is a homology between the shift from Kant to Hegel and the shift from desire to drive: the Kantian universe is that of desire (structured around the lack, the inaccessible Thing-in-itself), of endlessly approaching the goal, which is why, in order to guarantee the meaningfulness of our

ethical activity, Kant has to postulate the immortality of the soul (since we cannot reach the goal in our terrestrial life, we must be allowed to go on *ad infinitum*). For Hegel, on the contrary, the Thing-in-itself is not inaccessible, the impossible does happen here and now – not, of course, in the naïve pre-critical sense of gaining access to the transcendent order of things, but in the properly dialectical sense of shifting the perspective and conceiving the gap (that separates us from the Thing) as the Real. With regard to satisfaction, this does not mean that, in contrast to desire which is constitutively non-satisfied, the drive achieves satisfaction by way of reaching the object which eludes desire. True, in contrast to desire, the drive is by definition satisfied, but this is because, in it, satisfaction is achieved in the repeated failure to reach the object, in repeatedly circling around the object.[5]

Žižek's opening question is motivated by his above-discussed thesis that drive theory à la Lacanian psychoanalysis is the best means for retroactively positing a pivotal presupposition in speculative dialectics à la Hegelian philosophy (i.e. the ceaseless restlessness of dialectical negativity). Moreover, his manner here of aligning Immanuel Kant and Hegel with desire and drive respectively reinforces the heterodoxy of his Hegelianism. In other words, and in a gesture familiar to connoisseurs of the Žižekian *oeuvre*, Žižek's Hegel abruptly transubstantiates Kantian epistemological defeat (as equated with the 'That's not it!' of the 'hysteria' of Lacanian *désir*) directly into ontological victory (as equated with the 'That's it!' of the 'perversion' of Lacanian *pulsion*).[6] Put differently, Žižekian Hegelianism involves a kind of interminably and compulsively repeated enjoyment of negativity, an automatic, inhuman and senseless orbiting around certain centres of gravity akin to black holes in physics and/or attractors in mathematics (i.e. Žižek's '*eppur si muove* of the pure drive').[7]

Many other passages in *Less Than Nothing* and *Absolute Recoil* embellish upon this fashion of linking Kant and Hegel with desire and drive.[8] For this Žižek, the central motor mechanism powering the kinetics of Hegelian dialectical negativity is a meta-dialectical 'parallax' between drive and desire.[9] Put differently, Žižek's psychoanalytic, drive-theoretic revisitation of Hegel's philosophy quite deliberately suggests that something non-dialectical (i.e. a *Verstand*-type binary opposition) generates and underlies the dialectical (i.e. *Vernunft* as speculative dialectics). Similarly, when Žižek speaks of 'the very "drive" to *break* the All of continuity in which we are embedded, to introduce a radical imbalance into it',[10] this sympathetically can be heard as accurately capturing Hegel's post-Spinoza, anti-Schelling insistence on 'grasping and expressing the True, not only as *Substance*, but equally as *Subject*',[11] with subjectivity (identified by Žižek as equivalent to (death) drive) being an excrescence of substantiality (i.e. 'the All of continuity in which we are embedded') disrupting this very substantiality from within and out of itself (with the latter therefore being, in proper Hegelian fashion, self-sundering and auto-dialecticising).[12] Hence, in Žižek's discourse, 'subject' and 'drive' are two names, in German idealism and psychoanalysis respectively, for the same thing, namely an existent negativity both produced by and simultaneously interfering with grounding *Substanz* qua a chain of (rough) equivalences including: the Absolute, the One, the All, the Infinite, the Totality, the Whole, and so on.

In *Less Than Nothing*, Žižek further enriches the concept of drive by contrasting it with instinct (in addition to the contrasts already drawn with desire).[13] Although Hegel is not mentioned directly by name in the drawing of this contrast, Žižek's manner of doing so fundamentally expresses an ambivalence with respect to him. On the positive side of this ambivalence, Žižek characteristically corrects certain standard, commonplace (mis)interpretations of Hegelianism. Apropos Hegel's conception of the distinction between human and non-human animals, Žižek's remarks warn against construing this specific philosophical anthropology as the straightforward progress narrative of a teleological development in which simple animality is superseded by comparatively more complex humanity ('the zero-degree of "humanization" is not a further "mediation" of animal activity, its reinscription as a subordinated moment of a higher totality (for example, we eat and procreate in order to develop our higher spiritual potentials)'[14]). With such instances as the famous discussion of habit in the *Encyclopedia of the Philosophical Sciences'* treatment of the human 'soul' (*Seele*) clearly in mind,[15] Žižek contends that human animals become properly human (qua (partially) de-animalised) by passing through a concentration into the more, rather than less, rudimentary (i.e. the repetitive, the narrow, the habitual, the fixed, the driven, etc.).

Additionally, when Žižek asserts 'man perceives as a direct goal what, for an animal, has no intrinsic value',[16] this alludes to aspects of Freud's and Lacan's accounts of distinctive features of specifically human libidinal economies (in addition to its allusions to Hegel's philosophical anthropology). As regards Freud, one could take as an exemplary illustration here the Freudian oral drive: whereas the hunger of an instinct (*als Instinkt*) to obtain nourishment would, in the case of a human infant, invest in milk as the nourishing substance *an sich*, the oral drive (*als Trieb*) parasitically accompanying this instinct cathects (*als Besetzung*) instead such not-directly-nourishing objects and activities as the sensory-perceptual representatives of the breast and the repetitive motor movements of the mouth involved in sucking (i.e. in Žižek's terms, 'mere by-products'[17] of sating instinctive hunger). As regards Lacan, I cannot help but recall a humorous moment during his early 1950s elaborations of the mirror stage in 'Some Reflections on the Ego'. Therein, he contrasts human and non-human primate responses to reflective surfaces: While the non-human primate quickly realises that the mirror image is nothing but a semblance, the flat, superficial illusion of a conspecific who is not really there, and then quite reasonably loses interest in it as unreal, the human being becomes permanently enthralled by this image, getting lured into the spectral vortex of a virtual reality in which appearances, fictions, semblances, and the like become more valued and important than anything 'real'. On this occasion, Lacan is not only engaging in a bit of tongue-in-cheek human self-deprecation (with human idiots stupidly falling again and again for mirages and deceptions readily and wisely turned away from by humanity's closest animal relatives) – he also is taking a swipe at his arch-enemies, the pseudo-Freudian ego psychologists, for whom 'adaptation to reality' is a gold standard of human mental health. Lacan's counterpoint is that a hallmark feature of humanity is an original dis/mal-adaptation to reality, a preference for the unreality of illusory images and fictitious phantasms instead of the reality adaptationally favoured by non-human animals, including the other primates. One implication is that ego psychology's insistence on patients 'adapting to reality' is literally dehumanising, stunningly blind and deaf to essential facets of the so-called 'human condition'.[18]

But, returning to Hegel, and on the negative side of Žižek's ambivalence towards him, Žižek views Hegel's philosophy as sometimes lapsing into precisely the pseudo-Hegelianism Žižek's positive, pro-Hegel remarks at this same moment in *Less Than Nothing* seek to rectify. This should not, despite the likelihood of the contrary, come as a shock, since Žižek, in both *Less Than Nothing* and *Absolute Recoil*, explicitly makes clear that his general interpretive *modus operandi* with respect to his chosen cardinal points of reference (such as Hegel, Karl Marx, Freud and Lacan) is, at least when suitable, to play them off against themselves, thereby bringing to light that which is extimately in 'x' (Hegel, Marx, Freud, Lacan . . .) more than 'x' him- or herself ('What characterizes a really great thinker is that they misrecognize the basic dimension of their own breakthrough'[19]). Žižek describes this critical-exegetical procedure as 'thinking with Freud against Freud, or with Hegel against Hegel'[20] and similarly maintains that 'the only way beyond Lacan is through Lacan'.[21] *Less Than Nothing* pinpoints a number of topics, such as rabble-rousing poverty, mathematised experimental science, the psychoanalytic unconscious and Freudian–Lacanian drives (especially the *Todestrieb*), arguably addressable and assimilable by Hegelianism only if the latter undergoes significant metamorphoses involving immanent self-critiques (i.e. Hegelian critiques of Hegel(ianism)).[22]

For Žižek, Hegel mishandles human sexuality as something quasi-animalistic to be subordinated to the socio-symbolic mediations of the family as itself an element of *Sittlichkeit*.[23] But, the analytic Owl of Minerva, with the benefit of hindsight afforded specifically by its conceptualisation of the largely unconscious, drive-centred, sexual-libidinal economy of human psychical subjects, accurately sees that this sexuality, with its everyday and not-so-everyday obsessions and fixations, fits elsewhere in Hegel's System than Hegel realises (namely, in the 'Anthropology' of the 'Philosophy of Subjective Spirit', with the soul and its habits so near to and yet so far from animality, rather than much later in the subsequent 'Philosophy of Objective Spirit'). From Žižek's perspective, it is not that Hegel's System cannot accommodate at all such post-Hegelian developments as the psychoanalytic theory of human sexuality, being rendered obsolete by them. Instead, this System allegedly can accommodate them, but in ways other than those that Hegel himself might favour. Fidelity requires a certain amount of betrayal – a dialectical truth that applies as much to relations with dialectical thinkers as to those with non-dialectical ones.

As seen, Žižek's rendition of the Lacanian distinction between drive and desire non-dialectically opposes them, treating this opposition as a meta-dialectical motor of dialectical processes. At this juncture, I would propose that Žižek's Lacanian difference between *pulsion* and *désir* is itself the fallout of, in human beings, the failure of evolved instincts, themselves symptoms of nature's weakness, its lack of strong principles, its careless sloppiness, its negligent laxness permitting proliferations of just-functional-enough malformations. To go into more precise details, I can begin by observing that the natural history of evolution has eventuated in *Homo sapiens* equipped with central nervous systems involving emotional, motivational and cognitive functions highly distributed neurophysiologically over a diverse neuroanatomical landscape spanning the breadth from the brain stem to the neocortex. What is more, epigenetics and neuroplasticity make this same evolved brain naturally inclined to the dominance of nurture over nature, pre-programmed in somatic-biological-material terms for reprogramming in and by psychical-social-symbolic terms. These natural variables specific to human evolutionary neurobiology – thanks to these variables, evolutionarily older instinctual-type motivational and emotional functions get connected with and mediated by evolutionarily newer cognitive functions – consequently result in, within individual human beings, what would be animal instincts always-already being transubstantiated into human drives as per Freudian psychoanalytic metapsychology.

To be even more exact apropos Lacan and Žižek in particular, drive and desire can be understood in light of the immediately preceding as the dividing and becoming-antagonistic of two sides of what remains, in non-human animals, internally un-conflicted instinct. The instinctual would involve both the repetitive and the teleological. That is to say, instincts both demand recurrences of set patterns of intending and acting (as does the repetition operative in Freudian *Trieb*) as well as impel in the direction of certain ends (as does the Freudian *Lustprinzip*, with its twin aims of attaining pleasure and avoiding pain). Moreover, such animal instincts qua organic (by contrast with the kludgy 'anorganicity' of the peculiar human organism and its kaleidoscopic, patched-together drives) generally tend to embody harmonious syntheses of repetition and teleology. These syntheses occasionally break apart in non-human animals due primarily to interferences of exogenous origins. In other words, instinctually dictated repetitions cease functioning effectively toward certain *teloi* if and when environmental changes cause these instincts to go from being adaptive to becoming maladaptive in relation to their changed surroundings.

But, maladaptation at the levels of motivational/libidinal forces and factors is the endogenous rule, rather than the exogenous exception, in human (instead of non-human) animals. To be more specific, Žižek's version of the Lacanian drive–desire distinction can be recast as reflecting a coming-apart of the repetitive and the teleological (i.e. of what, in the instincts of non-human animals, are organically coupled unless interfered with by external contingencies). Arguably, this rift is opened precisely by neurobiological evolution widely distributing animal-instinctive emotional and motivational functions across humans' heterogeneous, variegated emotional, motivational and cognitive neuroanatomy and neurophysiology. Such distribution is perhaps a stretch too far, bringing about rips and tears in the fabric of human libidinal economies, splits and wounds that come to be organising principles of these economies.

Put simply enough, Lacanian-Žižekian *pulsion* could be said to entail repetition-without-teleology and Lacanian-Žižekian *désir* teleology-without-repetition. According to Lacan's distinction between a drive's 'aim' and its 'goal' (a distinction closely related to that between drive and desire), an aim-inhibited drive can achieve satisfaction, as per Freud's main characterisation of sublimation as the satisfaction of an aim-inhibited drive, precisely because it has an 'aim' (i.e. Lacan's 'goal') other than the aim inhibited. Lacan reasons, on the basis of Freud's own claims, that if all drives aim at satisfaction and yet can and do achieve 'satisfaction' via sublimation even when these same aims of theirs are inhibited, then there must be an 'aim'–'satisfaction' circuit wired into *Trieb* separate from the one calibrated by the dialectical push and pull between the see-sawing pleasure and reality principles. The inhibitable Freudian-Lacanian (drive-) aim would involve 'satisfaction' à la the pleasure principle, namely 'pleasure' qua contentment, happiness, homeostasis, well-being, and so on. By contrast, the Lacanian (drive-)goal consists in another 'satisfaction' altogether than that of the pleasure principle's aim(s), this being nothing other than the idiotic *jouissance* of aimless repetition (i.e. repetition-without-teleology). In other words, Lacan, apropos *pulsion*, clearly contrasts the aim of pleasure as satisfaction with the goal of *jouissance* as, so to speak, an Other 'satisfaction'.

The latter, this enjoyment of and in Žižekian 'stuckness'[24] as repetition *sans* the teleology imposed by the instinct-like *Lustprinzip*, can be and is derived from interminably circling revolutions around, as it were, *idées fixes*. This is a *jouissance* of what sometimes even is, from the perspectives of instinct and desire alike (which, despite their significant differences, both involve teleologies), pointless, counterproductive, self-destructive, and the like. Such 'enjoyment' (often consciously unenjoyable) might be bio-materially made possible by (even if admittedly far from exhaustively explicable through) the neuro-evolutionary opening of a rift decoupling brain-stem-level emotional and motivational structures and dynamics (especially those of the so-called SEEKING system of affective neuroscience as per Jaak Panksepp and like-minded researchers[25]) from neocortex-level cognitive ones. The former side of this rift arguably supports affectively intense, *jouissance*-saturated repetitions without accompanying teleologies (i.e. Freud's source and pressure of drive, Lacan's drive-without-aim-but-with-goal, and/or my 'axis of iteration' as per *Time Driven*), while the latter side of this same rift arguably supports representational, signifier-like differences/differentiations with accompanying teleologies (i.e. Freud's aim and object of drive, Lacan's desire with its interrelated Thing (*das Ding, la Chose*) and object-cause (*objet petit a*), and/or my 'axis of alteration' as per *Time Driven*).

Within the ontogenies of singular human organisms, evolution, with its cold indifference to whether life flourishes or withers and somewhat low bar of 'good enough to survive long enough to reproduce' at the scale of populations rather than individuals, permits the emergence of this far-from-optimal gap fragmenting what otherwise would be organic animal instincts into the anorganic split drives characteristic of human beings. The natural-historical genesis of such a fissuring presumably brought with it certain evolutionary advantages, namely those accruing thanks to evolved neocortically enabled sapience (itself allowing sapient creatures much more finer-grained, longer-term and/or bigger-picture cooperating, planning, predicting, responding, etc. than sentient-but-not-sapient creatures). But, there also seem to have been many disadvantages attributable to this very same genesis. In neuro-evolutionary terms, these would be ones arising from the immanent nature- or evolution-generated de- and re-organisation of pre-neocortical instincts into what thereby become drives proper via the routing of these instincts through evolved neocortically enabled sapience. In psychoanalytic terms, they are the uniquely human libidinal dysfunctions detailed in *Time Driven* as symptoms of 'the splitting of the drive' referred to in that book's sub-title. However, so long as, on overall species-scale balance, such disadvantages do not result in *Homo sapiens* as a whole being driven to extinction through population-magnitude aggregates biologically failing to survive and reproduce, the sub-optimal, discontent-inducing mechanisms of drives are allowed to continue running their courses. What is not forbidden by natural evolution is permitted. Exemplary of what exists with this permission is a queer isolated species many of whose members are miserable wretches tirelessly but unwittingly working in myriad ways against their own happiness and flourishing – a species which, as Freud famously observes in *Civilization and Its Discontents*, appears counterintuitively to be getting less, rather than more, content even as it rapidly gains in adaptive powers by virtue of the modern progress of its interlinked, co-evolving scientific *savoir* and technological *savoir-faire*.

In addition to drive, what about desire as per Lacan and Žižek? As I indicated above, whereas Lacanian-Žižekian *pulsion* embodies repetition-without-teleology, Lacanian-Žižekian *désir* represents teleology-without-repetition. What I mean by the latter is that desire in this precise technical sense always is oriented toward select *teloi* in the dual guises of the always-already lost Real Thing (i.e. *das Ding*) of a time-before-time ontogenetic past and the eternally-yet-to-come fantasmatic object (i.e. *objet petit a*) of a forever-receding future. Furthermore, these two *teloi*, the irretrievably lost *jouissance* of *das Ding* and the expected-but-never-obtained *jouissance* of *objet petit a*, co-constitute each other such that object *a* is a projection forward into the future of a past Thing and, correlatively but conversely, the Thing is a retrojection backward into the past of the present and future unattainable object *a*. *Désir* à la Lacan is, among many other of its myriad features, inherently teleological, ceaselessly dissatisfied in its perpetual, restless straining beyond itself in the directions of impossible-to-reach ends. Whatever it does manage to attain, Lacanian desire's response, as Žižek rightly underscores, invariably is a disappointed 'Ce n'est pas ça' ('That's not it').

Interestingly, such desire looks as though it bears resemblances to different aspects of both instinct and drive. To be more precise, *Instinkt* and *Trieb* share in common repetitiveness, namely the basic imperative to think and behave in certain fixed manners again and again, a libidinal-motivational injunction Freud labels *Wiederholungszwang*. However, unlike the instincts of non-human animals – these ultimately are rooted in evolutionarily primitive mammalian brain-stem neuroanatomy and neurophysiology – the drives of human ones route such repetitious tendencies through the cognitive circuitries of evolutionarily advanced

neocortical neuroanatomy and neurophysiology. Such intra-neural mediation transforming animal *Instinkt* into human *Trieb* via (re)distribution
spanning the gaping distance from brain stem to neocortex, also brings
with it extra-neural mediations – and this because the epigenetics and
neuroplasticity of the neocortex, as a certain Real, hardwire/pre-program
this cortex for re-wiring/re-programming vis-à-vis more-than-corporeal,
non-biological, denaturalising dimensions both experiential-phenomenal
(i.e. Imaginary) and socio-structural (i.e. Symbolic). In and through these
somatically intra- and psychically extra-bodily distributions/redistributions
and mediations/meta-mediations at the tangled intersections of natural
and human histories, instincts are torn apart and become the split drives
distinctive of humanity and distinctively theorised by psychoanalysis.

Without pretending to offer an exhaustive or even thorough delinea-
tion of Lacanian *désir* in all its multifaceted complexity, I would propose
that this desire fairly can be depicted in the context of this present discussion as animal instinct transubstantiated (*als Aufhebung*) by having been
always-already derailed into human drive at the ontogenetic level of individual members of the species *Homo sapiens*. Lacan's consistent fashion
from the 1950s onward of characterising *désir* in an interrelated triad also
involving *besoin* (need) and *demande* (demand) can be construed with
early twenty-first-century (post-)Lacanian neuro-psychoanalytic hindsight as anticipating what I am proposing here. As per this Lacan, need
is very much akin to instinct as a natural physical imperative regularly
repeating itself. For a living being thrown even well before the actual
moment of biological birth into a pre-existent inter- and trans-subjective
set of matrices of mediation and destined thereby to become a 'speaking being' (*parlêtre*), these Real needs are forced, within the surrounding strictures imposed upon the little human being by both Imaginary
others and Symbolic Others, into being (mis)communicated in the form
of socially recognised, language-symbolised demands. Whether as Freud's
somatic drive-sources and drive-pressures (i.e. my axis of iteration) or
Lacan's bodily needs, aspects of the bio-material substance of the human
organism get colonised and overwritten by swarms of psychically inscribed
socio-symbolic rules and representations. Thereby, in Freudian terms, the
more-than-somatic ideational representations (*Vorstellungen*) of psychical
drive-aims and drive-objects (i.e. my axis of alteration) denaturalise and
divert drive-sources and drive-pressures. In Lacanian terms, Imaginary
phenomena and Symbolic structures involving both others and Others
constrain Real corporeal requirements to (mis)translate themselves into
signifier-like images and words (i.e. needs getting articulated as demands).

Both Freud's drive-sources and drive-pressures as well as Lacan's needs
are features of the libidinal economy that defensibly could be described

as, on their own in isolation, instinctual components of human nature. Of course, as always-already channelled through and filtered by representations and signifiers in creatures naturally inclined towards the dominance of nurture over nature, these instinctual features admittedly are never encountered and dealt with directly by analytic clinicians and metapsychologists in some state of undiluted purity (both Freud and Lacan acknowledge this in various different manners). Nonetheless, in both Freudian and Lacanian theoretical frameworks, they are posited to be unavoidable and compelling presuppositions. What is more, for any Freudian and/or Lacanian who also is a staunch, committed materialist (whether Žižek, myself, or whoever else), these biological forces and factors must be acknowledged and granted their appropriate place.

In connection with Lacan's recurrent denunciations of the mistranslation of 'drive' (*Trieb*) as 'instinct' (*Instinkt*), he sometimes maintains that *pulsion* might best be translated as *dérive* (drift). Indeed, drive is very well depicted as drift – as natural instinct set adrift by and on more-than-natural mediators (whether as Freud's somatic sources and pressures diverted into the psychical *Vorstellungen* of aims and objects or Lacan's corporeal needs forcibly expressed in and through the extra-corporeal signifiers of demands). But, again, what about *désir* à la Lacan?

The Freudian sources and pressures of drives as well as Lacanian needs all give rise to repetition, to a well-nigh irresistible *Wiederholungszwang* buffeting desire and pushing it into its ceaseless yet vain attempts and reattempts to grasp 'IT' (i.e. *das Ding/la Chose* as incarnated within and by *objet petit a*) always resulting in the disappointing sense of 'That's not IT!' In addition to these relentlessly reiterated 'demands for work' (to borrow Freud's phrase for the repetitious insistence of drive-sources and drive-pressures), Lacan's theory of the signifier, a theory integral to the account of desire, has it that the signifier is simultaneously a condition of possibility and impossibility for repetition. On the one hand (i.e. condition of possibility for repetition), signifier-like representations (whether as words or images) enable libidinal economies and their subjects to orient themselves towards the quest for, as Freud puts it, 're-finding lost objects', towards seeking out what are marked and identified as the 'same' things again and again (i.e. 'IT'). But, on the other hand (i.e. condition of impossibility for repetition), the structural dynamics of signifiers make it such that repetition itself engenders difference, that each re-finding is a re-losing, that each successive return to sameness liquidates this very same sameness (thus resulting in 'Ce n'est pas ça').

Lacanian desire arises from the forced (mis)translation of needs into the signifiers of demands. Hence, *désir* is, one could say, caught between two varieties of repetitiousness: first, the *Wiederholungszwang* of biological, instinct-like vital requirements as recurrently insisting upon labour at their behest; second, the iterability enabled and generated by the signifiers impressed upon a human animal who thereby becomes a *parlêtre*. I claimed earlier that desire as per Lacan defensibly can be described as involving teleology-without-repetition – and this by contrast with Lacanian drive as repetition-without-teleology. However, I now can and should nuance this by observing that desire's 'without-repetition' is, more precisely, without successful, satisfying repetition (or, as the Lacan of Seminar X (1962–3) would put it, desire nevertheless is 'not without' ('pas sans') repetition entirely). That is to say, Lacanian *désir*, whether thought of in relation to instinct, Freud's drive-source and drive-pressure, Lacan's need and/or Lacan's *pulsion*, constantly is pushed into futile, Sisyphean efforts at reaching *teloi* whose necessary unreachability tends to be misperceived by the desiring subject as contingent rather than necessary.

At least one of the tones audible in desire's cry of 'That's not IT!' is contributed by lingering vestiges of the teleological leanings inherent in animal instincts. Put differently, the 'Ce n'est pas ça' of desire can be heard as containing impotent (à la Hegel's *Ohnmacht der Nature* and my related 'weak nature') natural instinct's feeble protest against denaturalised drive's repetition-without-teleology, namely the latter's 'perverse' enjoyment (qua *jouissance*) of failure, of tirelessly and pointlessly skirting around never-attained aims. Whereas Lacanian drive is the enjoyment of veering off teleological course, Lacanian desire does not enjoy this, instead remaining fixated upon its ever-receding *teloi* past and future. Like intrinsically failed instincts always operating 'beyond the pleasure principle', desires are dissatisfied and dissatisfying stucknesses in impossible, doomed teleologies.

I am tempted to suggest that the ontogeny of desire emerging through need passing into demand partly involves a recapitulation of the phylogeny of instinct becoming drive (more precisely, the evolutionary genesis of the neocortex and its assumption of mediating roles in relation to emotional and motivational brain functions). Even more, the latter arguably is a necessary condition for the former. In other words, the denaturalising socio-symbolic suffusions and regulations of the libidinal economy (such as the overwriting of bodily needs by the signifiers of demands) are made possible in part by virtue of a neuroanatomy and neurophysiology in which a highly plastic neocortex genetically coded endogenously to be epigenetically re-coded exogenously plays a pivotal role in relation to emotional-motivational circuits. Thanks to such a cognitive cortex receptive to influences and inscriptions impressed upon it by the living being's surrounding environments of countless sorts, instinct becomes drive, with drive itself being split between a teleology-without-repetition (i.e. Freud's drive-aim and drive-object, Lacan's *désir* and my axis of alteration – all depending upon the evolved human brain's cognitive circuitry) and a repetition-without-teleology (i.e. Freud's drive-source and drive-pressure, Lacan's *pulsion* and my axis of iteration – all depending upon the human brain's emotional and motivational circuitry as well as the entire rest of the body).

The time has come to circumnavigate back to re-engaging directly with Žižek himself. I will end this intervention with an attempt to demonstrate why and how my revisitation of psychoanalytic drive theory resolves what I would contend are certain problems his fashions of redeploying Lacan's drive–desire distinction in *Less Than Nothing* and *Absolute Recoil* create for him. But, before closing thusly, Žižek's reflections on the already-mentioned notion of stuckness are worth considering.

Along with the *pulsion–désir* pair, and closely related to it, stuckness is a strikingly recurrent theme throughout both *Less Than Nothing* and *Absolute Recoil*.[26] Apropos this theme, Žižek implicitly relies upon a feature of the Lacanian logic of the signifier I underlined a short while ago, namely that, in a coincidence/convergence of opposites, repetition produces difference in and through signifier-like structures and dynamics. One of Žižek's central theses as regards Hegel in these 2012 and 2014 books is that Hegel's dialectical-speculative philosophy fundamentally relies upon repetitions producing differences:

> We can clearly see here what is wrong with one of the basic common-sense criticisms of Hegel: 'Hegel always presupposes that the movement goes on – a thesis is opposed by its anti-thesis, the "contradiction" gets aggravated, we pass to the new position, etc., etc. But what if a moment refuses to get caught in the movement, what if it simply insists in (or resigns itself to) its inert particularity: "OK, I am inconsistent with myself, but so what? I prefer to stay where I am . . ."' The mistake of this criticism is that it misses the point: far from being a threatening abnormality, an exception to the 'normal' dialectical movement, this – the refusal of a moment to become caught in a movement, its sticking to its particular identity – is precisely what happens as a rule. A moment turns into its opposite precisely by way of sticking to what it is, by refusing to recognize its truth in its opposite.[27]

This reversal of stubborn repetition into radical difference is entirely in line with the Lacanian logic of the signifier. Additionally, Žižek is quite correct that Hegel, contrary to various complaints and objections, indeed allows for resistances to and reactions against the dialectical-speculative trajectories he traces.

But, in *Less Than Nothing*, at the start of a chapter (the seventh) entitled 'The Limits of Hegel', Žižek indicates that the employment of a (Lacanian) dialectic between repetition and difference along the lines laid out in the preceding block quotation is a self-exonerating move not available to

Hegel himself.[28] The 'excess of purely mechanical repetition' Žižek here claims Hegel misses is nothing other than the Freudian-Lacanian death drive.[29] As observed, the *Todestrieb* is, in Žižek's view, an extimate core of Hegelianism, something 'in Hegel more than Hegel himself'. Clearly, Žižek is convinced that post-Hegelian psychoanalytic drive theory is both compatible with and even integral to a Hegelianism reinvented for the twenty-first century.

In this very vein, *Less Than Nothing* subsequently goes so far as to equate the repetition of death-drive-type stuckness with the negativity so central for Hegel himself.[30] Through a contrast with 'the Orient' broadly speaking – more specifically, Žižek likely has in mind first and foremost a favourite bête noire, namely 'Western Buddhism' – he presents his fusion of Hegelian dialectics with Freudian-Lacanian *Todestrieb* as emblematic of a 'Western negativity' overall (presumably in non-dialectical opposition to an Eastern, or pseudo-Eastern, positivity). Furthermore, and to refer back to my earlier discussions of (death) drive and desire à la Freud, Lacan and Žižek, it strikes me as more accurate to identify Žižek's Western negativity precisely with a death-drive-like dimension of Lacanian *désir* (rather than directly with, as per Žižek, *Todestrieb*/*pulsion de mort* proper). For Lacan himself, the unattainability of pure repetition (i.e. repeating as dialectically self-subverting) is associated with the logic of the signifier generally and signifier-mediated desire specifically. Admittedly, *désir* repetitiously perseverates in its unhappy pursuit of the impossible Real Thing wrapped in the fantasmatic disguises of *objet petit a*. Thus described, Lacan's desire indeed exhibits a *Wiederholungszwang* 'beyond the pleasure principle'. Hence, Žižek is not without his justifications for recurring to a death drive originating with Freud in 1920. However, given that Žižek's Western-Hegelian negativity in *Less Than Nothing* hinges entirely on a repetition sublating itself into difference/newness, the psychoanalytic inspiration for this contemporary (neo-)Hegelianism looks to be not so much the Freudian *Todestrieb* as the Lacanian *désir* of the *parlêtre*.

Of course, speaking of the words 'repetition' and 'difference' in connection with each other in a context in which psychoanalysis and twentieth-century French philosophy/theory also are in play cannot but conjure up the figure of Deleuze and his 1968 masterpiece *Difference and Repetition*. As is well known, Lacan himself has the highest praise not only for *Difference and Repetition*, but also for Deleuze's 'Coldness and Cruelty' (1967) as well as *The Logic of Sense* (1969).[31] Despite the tensions and incompatibilities between Lacanian and Deleuzian orientations – as I will address shortly, the Žižek of both *Less Than Nothing* and *Absolute Recoil* pointedly mobilises these frictions between Lacan and Deleuze as regards repetition, difference, drive and desire – Lacan's enthusiasm for the non-Guattarianised Deleuze of 1967–9 is not misplaced. Certain facets of Deleuze's philosophy indeed cross-resonate strikingly with Lacanian psychoanalysis. Relatedly, Žižek, given his equation of Hegel's negativity with the stuckness of Freud's and Lacan's drives, views the account of repetition in *Difference and Repetition* as ironically quite Hegelian on the part of its avowedly anti-Hegelian author.[32]

The first of these facets appropriate to highlight in this specific context is the Deleuzian thesis according to which repetitions are inseparably immanent to their unfurling series of difference-inducing iterations – a thesis Deleuze articulates, in *Difference and Repetition*, via a revisitation of Freud from 1920 onwards (i.e. when *Wiederholungszwang* and the *Todestrieb* become explicit preoccupations).[33] Furthermore, at one point in *The Logic of Sense*, Deleuze states that 'the death instinct' ('l'instinct de la mort') is '*not merely one instinct among others*, but the crack itself around which all of the instincts congregate' ('*qui n'est pas un instinct parmi les autres*, mais la fêlure en personne, autour de laquelle tous les instincts fourmillent').[34] Despite the strangeness of Deleuze's rather un-psychoanalytic disregard for the Freudian and Lacanian distinction between *Trieb/pulsion* (drive) and *Instinkt/instinct* (instinct) displayed by his talk of 'l'instinct de la mort' (rather than *Todestrieb/pulsion de mort* (death drive)), this statement, already foreshadowed in 'Coldness and Cruelty',[35] condenses echoes of a number of lines of drive-theoretic thought (Freudian, Lacanian and/or Žižekian) touched upon by me earlier: the death drive is not a drive unto itself, but a trait of each and every drive, of *Trieb* as such (as per one of Freud's speculations regarding the *Todestrieb*); this death(ly trait of) drive involves repetitions disrupting the pleasure principle, following a *Wiederholungszwang* beyond, behind or beneath the *Lustprinzip*; the *Todestrieb*(-like nature of all drives) is the negativity of a 'crack' (*fêlure*) forming a centre of gravity within the libidinal economy (on the basis of the drive theories of Freud and Lacan, I divide drive qua drive into axes of iteration and alteration starting in *Time Driven*, and this arguably dovetails with both Deleuze's 'crack' as well as his pairings of difference (alteration) and repetition (iteration)). When Lacan, in Seminar XVI, favourably gestures at Deleuze's recourse to the figure of a 'blank' (*blanc*) or 'lack' (*manque*) as capturing the essence of what could be called 'structuralism'[36] (this being the Deleuze of *Logic of Sense* as well as the related essay 'How Do We Recognize Structuralism?'[37]), this hints that Deleuzian negativity (including what Deleuze, in *Logic of Sense*, associates with a deadly fissure shaping all drives) overlaps with the Lacanian Real as what immanently perturbs Imaginary-Symbolic reality (and, especially, the big Other of the symbolic order). Žižek approvingly reads this Deleuze similarly.[38]

Deleuze's 'Coldness and Cruelty', because of its focus on masochism, contains extended discussions of the *Todestrieb* as per Freudian psychoanalysis. Indeed, the tenth and penultimate chapter of it is entitled 'The Death Instinct' ('Qu'est-ce que l'instinct de mort').[39] Therein, Deleuze accurately maintains that Freud, in *Beyond the Pleasure Principle*, is not primarily concerned with this 'Jenseits' in terms of an utter and complete antithesis or nullification of the *Lustprinzip*, despite various impressions and interpretations regarding this 1920 book to the contrary. Instead, Deleuze's account, amply supported by the details of Freud's text, underscores that the repetitiveness (as compulsive repetition) with which Freud closely links the death drive is 'beyond' specifically as a transcendental dimension before or beneath the pleasure principle. That is to say, Deleuze associates the *Todestrieb* specifically with repetition as a condition of possibility for the consequent installation, via the 'binding' (*Bindung*) Freud identifies this repetition bringing about (or trying to bring about), of the *Lustprinzip* as the thereafter generally dominant governing tendency of psychical life. Such compulsive repetition is the groundless ground preceding and paving the way for a libidinal economy reliably leaning toward the pursuit of pleasure and the avoidance of pain. But, as a precondition for the pleasure principle, this *Wiederholungszwang* itself is not governed by the rule of law it precedes and helps establish. In other words, repetition, in enabling the *Lustprinzip*, does not necessarily obey this principle.[40] A year later, *Difference and Repetition* reiterates these points.[41]

In *Less Than Nothing*, Žižek, after rearticulating the Lacanian difference between drive and desire and associating the former with stuckness, favourably invokes Deleuze.[42] But, when the topic of Lacan's and Deleuze's positions on drive and desire resurfaces in *Absolute Recoil*, the latter fares much worse at Žižek's hands than he did in *Less Than Nothing*. Žižek leads into his critique of Deleuze by rehearsing the Lacanian distinction between *pulsion* and *désir*.[43] The interrelated references and themes fleshing out the drive–desire opposition at this point in *Absolute Recoil* are quite familiar components of the Žižekian theoretical repertoire: the Kant–Hegel relationship, examples from quantum physics, sexuation à la Lacan, and so on. Moreover, the motif of parallax splits (i.e. Hegelian-style ontologisations of Kantian-style antinomies) mobilised by Žižek in this 2014 context resonates with the thesis in his recent major philosophical works according to which the dialectical is animated by the non-dialectical, by impossible-to-sublate antagonisms and incompatibilities coming to function as the meta-dialectical conditions of possibility for any and all speculative dialectics. Along these lines, *Absolute Recoil*, like *Less Than Nothing* before it, treats the Lacanian *pulsion*–*désir* tension, an allegedly unbridgeable parallactic divide, as the meta-dialectical motor of the dialectics of the psychoanalytic libidinal economy.

Žižek begins addressing Deleuze by name apropos libidinal-economic matters.[44] Set against the wider background of the history of Western philosophy, Žižek's remarks implicitly stage a confrontation between (neo-) Spinozism (in the guise of the anti-Oedipal Deleuze's 'flux of desire, this endless productive movement [. . .] a positive assertion of life prior to all negativity' as akin to Baruch Spinoza's *natura naturans*, substance-as-S) and (neo-)Hegelianism (in the guise of Lacan's 'parallax unity of mutual exclusion' as akin to Hegel's *Negativ*, subject-as-$).[45] Žižek's quickly ensuing critical manoeuvre, in a nutshell, is to argue that Lacanian negativity (as symbolic castration, *manque-à-être*, *objet petit a*, and the like) is the disavowed condition of possibility for Deleuzian positivity (echoing Hegel's move of arguing that Spinoza presupposes without being willing and able to posit the subjective in his extreme monism of the substantial). What is more, when Žižek alleges that 'Deleuze remains within the paradigmatic modern opposition between production and (the scene of) representation', this alludes to the more precise charge of a regression back behind Kant to (again) Spinoza, with the latter's arguably *Verstand*-type (or, at least, insufficiently dialectical-speculative) dichotomy between *natura naturans* (i.e. Žižek's 'production' as the being of Spinoza's productive substance) and *natura naturata* (i.e. Žižek's 'scene of representation' as the appearances that are Spinoza's attributes and modes).[46]

From Žižek's Hegelian-Lacanian perspective, especially as per *Less Than Nothing* and *Absolute Recoil*, Deleuze's neo-Spinozism (especially à la *Capitalism and Schizophrenia*) suffers from two of the same shortcomings Hegel diagnoses in Spinoza's metaphysics: first, an inability and/or refusal to ask and answer ultimately unavoidable questions as to how and why the One of being (i.e. substance) gives rise to the Many of appearances (i.e. attributes and modes);[47] second, an incompleteness de-absolutising its ostensibly absolute (qua exhaustively infinite) ontology – and this due to a withholding of unqualified ontological weight from appearances.[48] Žižek resolves the first Spinozist shortcoming on Deleuze's part by, as I underlined a moment ago, positing the Lacanian negativity Deleuze himself presupposes but nonetheless avoids positing (just as Hegel posits the subjectivity Spinoza likewise presupposes without positing). Žižek's response to the second shortcoming of Deleuzian neo-Spinozism is, as I already have examined elsewhere,[49] to insist that any truly absolute ontology worthy of this adjective must admit and account for the strange being(s) of appearances as non-epiphenomenal. In this vein, Žižek's Lacan does to Deleuze what Žižek's Hegel does to Kant, namely fully ontologises structures and phenomena otherwise treated as ontologically secondary or sterile ('for Lacan, representation is never a mere screen or scene that mirrors the productive process in a limited and distorted way'[50]).

However, a slightly earlier moment in *Absolute Recoil* reveals that, despite above-seen appearances to the contrary, the negativity Žižek posits as the disavowed presupposition qua condition of possibility for Deleuze's neo-Spinozist positivity of the productive, deterritorialised flux of desiring machines falls on neither side of the Lacanian opposition between drive and desire. Instead, and in line with certain of the more philosophically abstract/speculative moments of both *Less Than Nothing* and *Absolute Recoil*,[51] Žižek muses about an *Urgrund*, an ultimate origin or source, out of which is generated the very distinction between *pulsion* and *désir*. He declares:

> Rather than defining the void of negativity around which the drives circulate as the 'pure' death drive, it would be more appropriate to posit a negativity/impossibility that precedes the very distinction between drive and desire, and to conceive of the drive and desire as the two modes of coping with this ontological impasse.[52]

Žižek's 'ontological impasse' would be a primordial Nothingness or Void as a zero-level baseless base for, among other things, drives, desires and their difference(s). In other contexts, I have expressed critical reservations (ones which Žižek mentions in *Absolute Recoil*[53]) apropos these moments in the Žižekian *oeuvre* when he looks to be indulging himself in what I dub (paraphrasing Wilfrid Sellars) 'the myth of the non-given', namely intellectual intuitions about the 'x' of an ineffable Negativity floating in an inaccessible time-before-time and from which all existent beings somehow emanate.[54] Now, I feel it to be appropriate and important to sharpen and specify these criticisms further in connection with the topic of drive and desire as explored throughout the preceding.

Žižek rightly underscores that both F. W. J. Schelling and Hegel take leave of the neo-Platonic and neo-Spinozist aspects of Friedrich Hölderlin's nonetheless pathbreaking critique of J. G. Fichte's quasi-Kantian subjectivist transcendental idealism (i.e. the critique sketched in 1795's 'Über Urtheil und Seyn').[55] Although this Hölderlin helps inspire and launch what becomes Schelling's objective idealism and Hegel's absolute idealism – both of these idealisms leave behind Kant's and Fichte's subjective idealism(s), departures initiated with 'On Judgement and Being' – Hölderlin's two friends from the *Tübinger Stift* come to consider his alternative to Kant and Fichte unsatisfactory due to its repetition of Spinoza's failures to ask and answer queries as to how and why substance manifests attributes and modes (or 'becomes subject', as the Hegel of the *Phenomenology of Spirit* would put it). That is to say, Schelling's and

Hegel's eventual dissatisfactions with this Hölderlin are ascribable to the latter's lack of explanations for how and why his 'Being' (the positive of a *Sein* akin to the One of neo-Platonism and the substance of Spinozism) breaks itself to pieces in and through 'Judgement' as Being judging itself (the negative of an *Urtheil* or *Ur-Teilung* akin to the Many of neo-Platonism and the attributes and modes of Spinozism, up to and including the reflexive, reflective metaphysical judgements of Spinoza's (intellectual) intuition). Interestingly, Lacan too, on one occasion, tacitly suggests that a neo-Platonic-, Spinozist- and/or Hölderlinian-style depiction of Freudian 'primary narcissism' (à la the libidinal-affective 'paradise lost' of symbiotic fusion, the 'oceanic feeling', prior to the negations disrupting this presumed harmony and establishing such differences as inside-versus-outside, me-versus-not-me, and self-versus-other) as the neonatal/infantile basis of ontogenetic subject formation renders this same formation (i.e. the emergence of subjectivity) incomprehensible and, indeed, seemingly impossible.[56] Žižek's own problematisations of (quasi-)Deleuzian 'new materialisms' knowingly echo these specific Hegelian, Schellingian and Lacanian objections against appeals to the pure positivity of a primordial plenitude.[57]

To take up again Žižek's musings in the previous block quotation from *Absolute Recoil*, his hypothesis about a single, sole *Ur*-source giving rise to the antinomic parallax gap between *pulsion* and *désir* strikes me as in danger of amounting to an inadvertent relapse into the neo-Platonism and Spinozism of Hölderlin with which, as Žižek himself correctly stresses, Hegel and Schelling split. It looks here as though some sort of (in a Schellingian phrasing) 'un-pre-thinkable being', the 'ontological impasse' of Žižek's (less than) Nothing, forms an indivisible, irreducible and unanalysable originary unity from which drives, desires and everything else in existence miraculously spring. To be more precise, this risks coming across as neo-Platonism and Spinozism merely with the signs reversed from positive (the surplus of the One or substance) to negative (the deficit of the not-One or negativity). It might similarly be said that this is neo-Spinozism under the sign of negation in the exact Freudian sense of *Verneinung*. As such Žižek's 'less than nothing' ends up being less than (fully) Hegelian.

An uncompromisingly Hegelian alternative to this perhaps compromised Hegelianism of Žižek's recent works, with the drive–desire distinction as a focal point, would be the replacement of the Žižekian primal Void as the groundless ground of this distinction with my grounding of this same distinction outlined above. My alternate account of the convergences and divergences between drive and desire as Žižek describes them mobilises biological evidence so as to provide a science-compatible, epistemologically responsible explanation of how these convergences and divergences evolve out of the dysfunctional, unreliable, collage-like instincts of a weak nature alone in its spade-turning facticity. This requires no intellectual intuitions of intangible Nothings. Whatever these thought experiments of mine might lack in aesthetic appeal or speculative sexiness they make up for in plausibility and justifiability.

To make explicit the biggest-picture ontological vision implicit in my specific version of drive theory, there are, at the outer limits of what can be discerned of 'in the beginning', the plural positivities of dispersed natural-material multiplicities as the ultimate factical bases of any and every negativity taking shape within and between these many givens (as the givenness of the Many). Combining this *Ur*-facticity with transcendental materialism's more-is-less principle, according to which negativities are generated in and through tensions and conflicts between positivities (such as, within the neuro-evolution of human instincts, the negativities of drives and/or desires arising partly from antagonisms and incompatibilities between the kludgy brain's stem and neocortex),[58] one has available an utterly non-mystical and thoroughly post-critical (rather than pre-critical) foundation for a dialectical-speculative theoretical edifice integrating philosophy, psychoanalysis and science. Although embracing the label 'transcendental materialism' in *Less Than Nothing*,[59] Žižek, two years later in *Absolute Recoil*, pointedly rejects it.[60] I am tempted to suggest that it perhaps is not entirely coincidental that, in this same 2014 book in which this rejection transpires, there also look to be lapses into a position discomfortingly resembling in modified terminological guise the basic metaphysical models of neo-Platonism, Spinozism and Hölderlinian Romanticism Hegel repudiates and Žižek himself likewise seeks to surpass despite these lapses of his. So, I close with proposing the following choice: either transcendental materialism (with its weak nature alone in the forms of, among other things, contingent material facticity and the dialectics of more-is-less) or regression back behind both dialectical materialism and Hegelian dialectical speculation into the darkness of a pre-Kantian night.

Notes

1. Žižek, Slavoj, *Looking Awry: An Introduction to Jacques Lacan Through Popular Culture* (Cambridge, MA: MIT Press, 1991), p. 37; *The Indivisible Remainder: An Essay on Schelling and Related Matters* (London and New York: Verso, 1996), pp. 121–2; 'Lacan Between Cultural Studies and Cognitivism', *Umbr(a): Science and Truth* (2000), p. 29; *The Puppet and the Dwarf: The Perverse Core of Christianity* (Cambridge, MA: MIT Press, 2003), pp. 79–80; Rasmussen, Eric Dean, 'Liberation Hurts: An Interview

with Slavoj Žižek' [29 September 2003], available at <http://www.electronicbookre-view.com/thread/endconstruction/desublimation> (last accessed 4 April 2016); Žižek, Slavoj and Daly, Glyn, *Conversations with Žižek* (Cambridge: Polity Press, 2004), pp. 61, 63–65; Johnston, Adrian, *Žižek's Ontology: A Transcendental Materialist Theory of Subjectivity* (Evanston: Northwestern University Press, 2008), pp. 109, 126, 166–7, 178–210, 222–3, 236–8.

2. Žižek, Slavoj, *Less Than Nothing: Hegel and the Shadow of Dialectical Materialism* (London and New York: Verso, 2012), p. 830; *Absolute Recoil: Towards a New Foundation of Dialectical Materialism* (London and New York: Verso, 2014), p. 89.

3. Johnston, *Žižek's Ontology*, pp. 123–268; Johnston, Adrian, 'Contingency, Pure Contingency – Without Any Further Determination: Modal Categories in Hegelian Logic', *Logos* (special issue: 'The New Life of German Idealism', Chepurin, Kirill (ed.)) (forthcoming, 2016); 'Absolutely Contingent: Slavoj Žižek and the Hegelian Contingency of Necessity', in Carew, Joseph and McGrath, Sean (eds), *Rethinking German Idealism* (Basingstoke: Palgrave Macmillan, forthcoming 2016), pp. 215–45.

4. Žižek, *Less Than Nothing*, pp. 492–3.

5. Ibid. p. 496.

6. Ibid. p. 550.

7. Ibid. pp. 496, 662.

8. Ibid. pp. 497–8, 638–9, 550, 639–40; Žižek, *Absolute Recoil*, pp. 89, 373–4.

9. Johnston, Adrian, 'Materialism Without Materialism: Slavoj Žižek and the Disappearance of Matter', in Hamza, Agon and Ruda, Frank (eds), *Slavoj Žižek and Dialectical Materialism* (Basingstoke: Palgrave Macmillan, 2015), pp. 3–22.

10. Žižek, *Less Than Nothing*, p. 498.

11. Hegel, G. W. F., *Phenomenology of Spirit* (Oxford: Oxford University Press, 1977), p. 10; Johnston, Adrian, '"Freedom or System? Yes, please!": How to Read Slavoj Žižek's *Less Than Nothing: Hegel and the Shadow of Dialectical Materialism*', in Hamza, Agon (ed.), *Repeating Žižek* (Durham, NC: Duke University Press, 2015), pp. 7–42.

12. Žižek, *Absolute Recoil*, p. 387; Johnston, Adrian, *Adventures in Transcendental Materialism: Dialogues with Contemporary Thinkers* (Edinburgh: Edinburgh University Press, 2014), pp. 13–64.

13. Žižek, *Less Than Nothing*, p. 499.

14. Ibid. p. 499.

15. Hegel, G. W. F., *Philosophy of Mind: Part Three of the Encyclopedia of the Philosophical Sciences with the Zusätze* (Oxford: Oxford University Press, 1971), §409–10, pp. 139–47.

16. Žižek, *Less Than Nothing*, p. 499.

17. Ibid. p. 499.

18. Lacan, Jacques, 'Some Reflections on the Ego', *International Journal of Psycho-Analysis*, 34 (1953), pp. 11–17.

19. Žižek, *Absolute Recoil*, p. 34.

20. Ibid. p. 34.

21. Žižek, *Less Than Nothing*, p. 18.

22. Ibid. pp. 440–2, 461–3, 484–5, 490, 492–3.

23. Žižek, *Absolute Recoil*, p. 499.

24. Žižek, *Less Than Nothing*, pp. 483, 499, 547, 549, 639–40, 884; *Absolute Recoil*, pp. 118–19.

25. Johnston, Adrian, 'Drive Between Brain and Subject: An Immanent Critique of Lacanian Neuropsychoanalysis', *The Southern Journal of Philosophy*, 51: supplement (2013), pp. 48–84; 'The Late Innate: Jean Laplanche, Jaak Panksepp, and the Distinction Between Sexual Drives and Instincts', in Godley, James (ed.), *Inheritance in Psychoanalysis*, Albany: State University of New York Press (forthcoming 2016).

26. Žižek, *Less Than Nothing*, pp. 499, 549, 639–40, 884; *Absolute Recoil*, pp. 118–19.

27. Žižek, *Less Than Nothing*, p. 294.

28. Ibid. pp. 455–6.
29. Ibid. pp. 492–3.
30. Ibid. pp. 482–3.
31. Lacan, Jacques, *Le séminaire de Jacques Lacan, livre XIV: La logique du fantasme* (unpublished typescript), sessions of 19 April 1967 and 14 June 1967; *Le séminaire de Jacques Lacan, livre XVI: D'un Autre à l'autre* (Paris: Seuil, 2006), pp. 134, 218–20, 245, 257; *Le séminaire de Jacques Lacan, livre XXI: Les non-dupes errent* (unpublished typescript, 1973–4), session of 19 February 1974.
32. Žižek, Slavoj *The Metastases of Enjoyment: Six Essays on Woman and Causality* (London and New York: Verso, 1994), p. 47; *Organs without Bodies: On Deleuze and Consequences* (London: Routledge, 2004), pp. 12, 33–93; *In Defense of Lost Causes* (London and New York: Verso, 2008), pp. 324, 396.
33. Deleuze, Gilles, *Difference and Repetition* (New York: Columbia University Press, 1994), pp. 17–18, 115, 274, 286, 289.
34. Deleuze, Gilles, *The Logic of Sense* (New York: Columbia University Press, 1990), p. 326 (*La logique du sens* (Paris: Minuit, 1969), p. 378); original emphasis.
35. Deleuze, Gilles, 'Coldness and Cruelty', in Deleuze, Gilles and Sacher-Masoch, Leopold, *Masochism: Coldness and Cruelty and Venus in Furs* (New York: Zone Books, 1991), pp. 30–1.
36. Lacan, *D'un Autre à l'autre*, p. 227.
37. Deleuze, *The Logic of Sense*, pp. 48–51, 66, 227–8; 'How Do We Recognize Structuralism?', in *Desert Islands and Other Texts 1953–1974* (Los Angeles: Semiotext(e), 2004), pp. 170–92.
38. Žižek, *The Metastases of Enjoyment*, pp. 131–2; *The Parallax View* (Cambridge, MA: MIT Press, 2006), p. 122; *Living in the End Times* (London and New York: Verso, 2010), pp. 304–5.
39. Deleuze, Gilles, 'Le froid et le cruel', in Deleuze, Gilles, *Présentation de Sacher-Masoch. Le froid et le cruel* (Paris: Minuit, 1967), p. 96.
40. Deleuze, 'Coldness and Cruelty', pp. 111–21.
41. Deleuze, *Difference and Repetition*, pp. 18–19, 111, 289.
42. Žižek, *Less Than Nothing*, p. 884.
43. Žižek, *Absolute Recoil*, pp. 372–3.
44. Ibid. pp. 373–4.
45. Žižek, Slavoj, *Enjoy Your Symptom!: Jacques Lacan in Hollywood and Out* (Abingdon: Routledge, 1992), pp. 192–3; *Organs without Bodies*, p. 52; *Less Than Nothing*, pp. 368–9, 374, 376, 611–12, 985; *Absolute Recoil*, pp. 8, 12, 387–8, 397; Johnston, *Adventures in Transcendental Materialism*, pp. 13–107.
46. Žižek, *Absolute Recoil*, p. 374; Johnston, *Adventures in Transcendental Materialism*, pp. 13–107.
47. Žižek, *Absolute Recoil*, p. 397.
48. Johnston, '"Freedom or System? Yes, please!"'
49. Johnston, *Žižek's Ontology*, pp. 269–287; *Adventures in Transcendental Materialism*, pp. 13–107, 111–38; '"Freedom or System? Yes, please!"'
50. Žižek, *Absolute Recoil*, pp. 374.
51. Žižek, *Less Than Nothing*, pp. 378–9, 712; *Absolute Recoil*, pp. 385, 391, 393–4, 410–15.
52. Žižek, *Absolute Recoil*, p. 207.
53. Ibid. pp. 225–6.
54. Johnston, Adrian, 'Reflections of a Rotten Nature: Hegel, Lacan, and Material Negativity', *Filozofski Vestnik*, 33: 2 (2012), pp. 23–52; 'Points of Forced Freedom: Eleven (More) Theses on Materialism', *Speculations: A Journal of Speculative Realism*, 4 (June 2013), p. 95; 'Materialism Without Materialism'; *Prolegomena to Any Future Materialism, Volume Two: A Weak Nature Alone* (Evanston: Northwestern University Press, forthcoming 2017).

55. Johnston, '"Freedom or System? Yes, please!"'
56. Lacan, Jacques, *Le séminaire de Jacques Lacan, livre VIII: Le transfert, 1960–1961* (Paris: Seuil, 2001), p. 410; Johnston, *Žižek's Ontology*, pp. 212–13; 'Reflections of a Rotten Nature', pp. 34–5; *Adventures in Transcendental Materialism*, p. 129.
57. Johnston, 'Materialism Without Materialism'.
58. Johnston, 'Points of Forced Freedom', pp. 95–6; 'Drive Between Brain and Subject'; *Prolegomena to Any Future Materialism, Volume Two*.
59. Žižek, *Less Than Nothing*, pp. 906–7.
60. Žižek, *Absolute Recoil*, p. 224; Johnston, Adrian, 'Confession of a Weak Reductionist: Responses to Some Recent Criticisms of My Materialism', in De Vos, Jan and Pluth, Ed (eds), *Neuroscience and Critique: Exploring the Limits of the Neurological Turn* (Abingdon: Routledge, 2016), pp. 141–70.

Chapter 12

Lacan, Deleuze and the Consequences of Formalism

Paul M. Livingston

There is a particular use of formalism in Deleuze and Lacan, essentially counterpoised to the thought of the signifier's adequate sense, but nevertheless decisive, for both, in witnessing its possible passage to a truth. This use of formalism is, as I shall argue, continuous both with twentieth-century developments of the attempt to found mathematics on a purely logical writing and with the original sense of 'form' (*eidos*) as the thinkable unity of 'one over many', with which Plato sought to capture the possible contact of thought with what is real in itself. It is to be distinguished, on the other hand, from any exterior translation of natural language into formal symbolism or, conversely, the simple 'application' of fixed formal-symbolic calculi to an already constituted field. It is also not simply a matter of 'structuralism'. For before the 'structuralist' reference to natural languages as systems of arbitrarily or conventionally posited differences lie, as its conditions of possibility and the grounds of its coherence, the problems to which formalism answers for both Deleuze and Lacan: those (for instance) of the *totality* of possible signification, the structure and genesis of the *possible* sense of signs, and the topological *position* from which these conditions can themselves be assayed. Thus rather than a simple regimentation or application of formal systems of signification, the use of formalism in Deleuze and Lacan involves finding the possible passage of signification to its specific limit: the place where, formalising the limits of its own mimetic or representational capacities, formalism itself marks, at its own impasse, a new possible inscription of truth. At this place, as I shall argue, it also witnesses the constitution of linguistic sense, the first entry of something like a 'one' into a world of otherwise pure multiplicity, and thereby the point, beyond possible representation, of thought's possible contact with being in itself.

In the following, I present this use of formalism, as it is developed most centrally in Lacan's Seminars XVII, XIX and XX, and in Deleuze's works of roughly the same period, especially his 1968 doctoral thesis, *Difference and Repetition*, and the closely related 1969 *The Logic of Sense*. This is not to prejudice, or presumptively exclude, the different or differently articulated positions that both thinkers would take with respect to formalism before or after the period I consider here. Nor do I treat here the problems of the complex biographical and critical relationship between the two themselves, problems which are further complicated in Deleuze's writings with Guattari beginning in 1972. I simply attempt, here, to extract a specific use of formalism which is held in common by Deleuze and Lacan at *one* stage of their itineraries, and which remains useful, as I shall argue, in confronting central problems of thought and action today. In the last section, I distinguish this from other contemporary uses of formalism in the wake of Deleuze and Lacan, specifically ones which either miss the specific level on which formalism here bears witness to this passage of the real by substituting for it a direct ontologisation of mathematics, or relapse to what is essentially a *pre*-formal thought of the logic of contradiction under the mandate of a (post-)structuralist renewal of the Hegelian dialectic.

Real, imaginary, symbolic

In Seminar XX, in the context of a discussion of the specific capacity of psychoanalytic discourse to produce a possible signification of truth, Lacan briefly clarifies the use of mathematical formalisation, in relation to what he writes as the object-cause of desire ('a'), the 'barred' subject ($\$$), the Other (A) and the phallic function (Φ), in allowing the 'very articulation of analysis' as such:

> This is where the real distinguishes itself. The real can only be inscribed on the basis of an impasse of formalization. That is why I thought I could provide a model of it using mathematical formalization, inasmuch as it is the most advanced elaboration we have by which to produce signifierness. The mathematical formalization of signifierness runs counter to meaning – I almost said '*à contre-sens*.' In our times, philosophers of mathematics say 'it means nothing' concerning mathematics, even when they are mathematicians themselves, like Russell.
>
> And yet, compared to a philosophy that culminates in Hegel's discourse – a plenitude of contrasts dialecticized in the idea of an historical progression, which, it must be said, nothing substantiates for us – can't the formalization of mathematical logic, which is based only on writing (*l'écrit*), serve us in the analytic process, in that what invisibly holds (*retient*) bodies is designated therein? [. . .]

That is why I do not believe that it was in vain that I eventually came up with the inscriptions (*l'écriture*) *a*, the $ of the signifier, A, and Φ. Their very writing constitutes a medium (*support*) that goes beyond speech, without going beyond language's actual effects. Its value lies in centering the symbolic, on the condition of knowing how to use it, for what? To retain [*retiner*] a congruous truth – not the truth that claims to be whole, but that of the half-telling (*mi-dire*), the truth that is borne out by guarding against going as far as avowal, which would be the worst, the truth that becomes guarded starting with (*dès*) the cause of desire.[1]

Lacan here exploits the crucial distinction among three 'orders' or 'registers' – those of the 'real', the 'imaginary' and the 'symbolic', which he had long propounded as irreducibly essential to understanding, not only the genesis, aetiology and development of the individual subject or psyche, but also the whole problematic field of the relations of being, truth, language and sense in which it constitutively takes root and finds its specific existence.[2] If the 'real', in the discourse devoted to the articulation of this field, can have the value of a primary mode of being, existence or truth, it can do so nevertheless only insofar as it also operates essentially as an obscure underside and constitutive limit, itself positively articulated only in the problems and impasses of the other two orders of the imaginary and symbolic. For Lacan, the 'imaginary' picks out the realm of the representational doubling characteristic of the (accurate or inaccurate) image, and the essential place of fantasy that this doubling engenders, including essentially (though not exclusively) the fantasy that sustains the imaginary production of the ego or 'I', insofar as it is thought as having any kind of substantial existence. The 'symbolic', by contrast, is the order of the specific structural functioning of language and signs, without essential reference to any pre-existing representational or mimetic meaning: here, following a decisive motif of Saussure's structuralism, the only articulation is provided by systems of differences, lacking in themselves the value of positive terms.

Yet if the real is thus sharply distinguished from either of the other two orders, and accordingly admits neither of imaginary representation nor of symbolic articulation within a linguistic system of differences, then how is an inscription of it – a writing *of* the real that maintains, as Lacan says, the possible speaking of a truth – possible nevertheless? Here, Lacan's formulation is precise. His motto – that the 'real can only be inscribed on the basis of an impasse of formalization' – does not say that the real *cannot* be written in any way at all. But neither does it say that it can be *simply* or *directly* inscribed, for instance by means of a directly representational or symbolism, or by means of the resources of an already given natural language. Rather, it is to be written *only* by means of a formalisation that articulates, in the specific mode of impasse, the essential capture of bodies in symbolic language, wherein the symbolic itself encounters the resistance of the material which would nevertheless withdraw from complete signification by it. The role of formalism, thought in this way, is specifically to *model* the real, without resemblance, by formally capturing the character of what Lacan calls 'signifierness': the pure character of signs *as such* insofar as they can indeed touch on such a real, without (yet) being able to capture it completely or convey from it an adequate sense. This point of possible contact that is to be modelled is, indeed, basically independent of (and at first, entirely without) meaning, at least if meaning is construed as the adequate sense of a sign, or of any combination thereof. Rather, as Lacan says, it is exactly because formalisation here operates *without* sense, as an operation of symbolisation that 'means nothing', that it can model just this phenomenon of the real's capture in the symbolic, by passing to its own specific limit of impasse.

This precise use of formalism at the limits of possible signification should be sharply distinguished from the simple inscription of any signifier *within* an already constituted natural language or conventional symbolic order. As Lacan says, it is not a matter of symbolic differentiation, but rather of 'centering the symbolic' itself and in this way, of indicating the structural place, necessary to *any* language, from which any signification is, as such, alone possible. And this centring is carried out, not in order to attain this or that symbolising effect, but rather in order to maintain a truth, the kind of truth to which a subject itself essentially constituted by its lacking or barred relationship to signification can nevertheless aspire. The particular mathemes that Lacan creates and schematises within his characterisation of the analytic discourse ($, *a*, etc.) are themselves situated in the structural and topological place of this truth in order to articulate the discourse that attempts to intervene at it. The formal articulation of their relationships, both in the 'analyst's discourse' and in the other three discourses of the hysteric, the university and the master which Lacan distinguishes from it starting in Seminar XVII, serve to indicate the structural or topological possibilities of the situation of a subject in relation to knowledge, signification as such and this specific truth.

The signifiers that articulate the discourses are not in themselves mathematical, though: why, then, is specifically *mathematical* formalisation privileged here, in Lacan's statement from Seminar XX, as alone granting access – the only kind of access we can have – to the specific writing of the real, and thereby to the only possible passage of the signifier to its truth? The answer is to be found in the universal and integral character of mathematical signification, which is, as a writing, capable of being transmitted without loss, regardless of the particular natural language one speaks, or of the particular meanings it makes available.[3] It is only as such a writing, separated from natural languages and indeed from any specifically constituted linguistic system, that mathematical formalism can capture formally the structural constitution of *any* such system, and thereby formulate, even if only at the point of impasse, the constitutive dynamics of its possible contact with being as it is in itself. This contact is, again, not to be thought in terms of mimetic representation or similarity, and neither is it to be specified by means of the limitation or articulation of an already existent conceptual generality of sense. It is rather to be indicated by the precise means of a formalisation bearing the universality and integrality of mathematics in treating the pure structure and dynamics of the signifier as such, and thereby alone capable of bearing theoretical witness to the fragile possibility of its conveyance of a truth.

It is in view of the same constitutive and formally indicated relationship of signifierness as such to the Real, beyond or before representational adequacy or conventionally constituted sense, that Deleuze, in his 1967 manifesto 'How Do We Recognize Structuralism?', identifies the radical novelty of the structuralist project, then shared by theorists as diverse as Lévi-Strauss, Foucault, Althusser and Lacan himself. He begins by considering how existing projects have been determined, almost without exception, by the dual of the real and the imaginary, thereby confining themselves to the unilinear and oscillatory dialectic of the true or false image and its accurate or inaccurate representation of what is, without yet bringing the 'third' dimension of the symbolic as such fully into view:

> We are used to, almost conditioned to a certain distinction or correlation between the real and the imaginary. All of our thought maintains a dialectical play between these two notions. Even when classical philosophy speaks of pure intelligence or understanding, it is still a matter of a faculty defined by its aptitude to grasp the depths of the real (*le réel en son fond*), the real 'in truth,' the real as such, in opposition to, but also in relation to the power of imagination. [. . .]
>
> The first criterion of structuralism, however, is the discovery and recognition of a third order, a third regime: that of the symbolic. The refusal to confuse the symbolic with the imaginary, as much as with the real, constitutes the first dimension of structuralism.[4]

For Deleuze, the importance of Lacan's introduction of the third order of the symbolic, and with it the proper definition of structuralism, lies in the way that it offers to clarify the actually deeper structural and formal underpinnings of the dual between the real and the imaginary that has formed the analytic and critical horizon of earlier theoretical projects. Even psychoanalysis, with Freud, continues to presuppose this bipolar principle, opposing the real effectivity of the reality principle to the imaginary one of the pleasure principle. With Lacan's discovery of the symbolic, however, the underpinnings of these relationships are revealed by means of an elaboration that takes on the value of a demonstration of their actual structural genesis:

> We already had many fathers in psychoanalysis: first of all, a real father, but also father-images. And all our dramas occurred in the strained relationship between the real and the imaginary. Jacques Lacan discovers a third, more fundamental father, a symbolic father or Name-of-the-Father. Not just the real and the imaginary, but their relations, and the disturbances of these relations, must be thought as the limit of a process in which they constitute themselves in relation to the symbolic. In Lacan's work, in the work of the other structuralists as well, the symbolic as element of the structure constitutes the principle of a genesis: structure is incarnated in realities and images according to determinable series. Moreover, the structure constitutes series by incarnating itself, but is not derived from them since it is deeper, being the substratum both for the strata of the real and for the heights [*ciels*] of imagination.[5]

By contrast with what are supposed as the given elements of the real or their (accurate or inaccurate) doubling in the imaginary, the elements of the symbolic have, for Deleuze 'neither extrinsic designation, nor intrinsic signification'.[6] They are not to be defined either by pointing to such pre-existing realities as they might designate, or to the 'imaginary or conceptual contents which [they] would implicate'.[7] What is left when these aspects of designation and implication are removed is merely their 'topological' and 'relational' sense, a sense that is, Deleuze says, 'necessarily and uniquely "positional"'.[8] Here, in particular, the investigation of individuals and subjects cedes to the investigation of the 'topological and structural space' defined by the system of their relations; in this way, structuralism points to a 'new transcendental philosophy, in which the sites prevail over whatever occupies them'.[9] This structural combination of elements that do not in themselves have signification provides the basis for a new understanding of the origin and genesis of *sense*: here, therefore, sense is no longer understood as founded on an originally conventional designation or a basic imaginary reduplication, but rather as produced as a secondary effect in the recombination of places in the structure.[10] The study of the relationships of structure, and of the basis of sense it indicates, provides the possibility, as Deleuze argues, for a transformation of the guiding principles and units of analysis for fields as diverse as psychology, economics, mythology, sociology and history. And in each case, the topic of the analysis is not the particularity of a specific empirical domain – for instance, a particular language or culture – but rather the elaboration of the formal and universal characteristics and relations that determine structurality as such by demonstrating and determining its points of articulation, differential and reciprocal relations, and singular points of differentiation and possible transformation.

These relations are accessible, if at all, only to a mathematical formalism which defines and articulates them on the level of the structural problems posed by each field. Deleuze makes reference in particular to the differential calculus as a 'pure logic of relations'.[11] Here, specific points of relation, differentiation and inflection characteristic of particular empirical domains are themselves formalised, at a higher level, in terms of the pure mathematics of differential relations as such, yielding a non-specific and overarching theory of variations and differences. This use of mathematical formalism thus has immediate application to the clarification of structure as a 'multiplicity of virtual coexistence'.[12] Its point is not to make a metaphorical or analogical use of mathemes or concepts drawn from mathematical praxis, but directly to *use* mathematics in the determination of the structurality of structure as it is realised or 'incarnated' in each domain:

> The question, 'Is there structure in any domain whatsoever?,' must be specified in the following way: in a given domain, can one uncover symbolic elements, differential relations and singular points which are proper to it? Symbolic elements are incarnated in the real beings and objects of the domain considered; the differential relations are actualized in real relations between these beings; the singularities are so many places in the structure, which distributes the imaginary attitudes or roles of the beings or objects that come to occupy them.
>
> It is not a matter of mathematical metaphors. In each domain, one must find elements, relationships, and points.[13]

In this way, the modelling that mathematical formalisation provides allows for the articulation of the general and universal structural relationships and differences that find their particular configurations in the real, imaginary and symbolic elements and relations constitutive of any specific structural domain. It is this sense that, for Deleuze as for Lacan, mathematical formalisation alone can elicit the underlying and determining real that is proper to structure as such, and thereby maintain the truth that is thinkable in it.

Paradox and impasse

Both Deleuze and Lacan thus appeal to mathematical formalism, in its integral transmissibility, its structural universality and its essential meaninglessness to capture the more general relationships that permit an understanding of structure as such with reference to a wide variety of domains, or articulate the position from which the real of structure works within these domains to achieve its specific effects. But beyond this, Deleuze and Lacan also both invoke a specific *way* of using logical-mathematical formalism to elicit the real of structure in itself. It can be specified as the *reflexive* use of formalism with respect to *itself* and up to its own specific *limit*, in order to elicit the precise point where it demonstrates in the form of *impasse* or *paradox* its own relationship to whatever irreducibly resists it. This use turns on the introduction of formally demonstrable structures of limit-paradox, aporia, and the necessary limitation of regular procedures of deduction or decision at the limits of language and at the basis of sense. As we shall see, the requirement that the real be inscribed *only* in these forms itself results from a positional commitment which Lacan repeatedly announces on behalf of the analyst's position, and which also determines the thoroughgoing immanence of Deleuze's critical thought to the field in which it intervenes. This is the axiom of the *non-existence of a metalanguage*, or of the radical impossibility of a simply exterior position with respect to the total constitutive logic of signification and its possible sense, from which the connection of language and being could be unproblematically assured.

In *The Logic of Sense*, Deleuze analyses propositions, in each of their essential functions of indexical denotation, expressive manifestation and conceptual signification, as resting on a series of closely related original paradoxes of seriality or presupposition. These paradoxes in fact constitute, as Deleuze argues, of the underlying fourth stratum or phenomenon of sense itself, which is at the structuring basis of all of the other phenomena of propositional language. At this structurally foundational level, each of the paradoxes demonstrates an essential and undecidable oscillation between an *infinite foundational regress* and an *unknowable point of foundation* which, if assumed as real, is demonstrably elusive to any positive intra-systematic inscription.

First, there is a paradox of *logical or conceptual inference*, given originally by Lewis Carroll in 1895.[14] Rule-governed logical inference to a conclusion, which articulates the conceptual meaning of propositions and their terms, presupposes the applicability of more general logical or inferential rules. But then the particular way these rules themselves are applied must apparently be licensed by further premises, which must themselves be introduced explicitly to the argument. The application of these premises will depend on further premises, and so forth. The infinite regress can only be blocked by the assumption of an absolute and necessarily unstated point of the automatic or self-licensing applicability of logical rules themselves.

Second, there is a formally similar paradox of *denotation* or *naming*.[15] The assumption that each name, in order to perform its designative function, must be endowed with a sense or meaning, necessarily invokes the question of the name for *this* sense, and hence of a further sense for the second name, and so forth. Once again, the infinite regress that results can only be blocked by the assumption of a kind of absolute point of assured correspondence or identity between names and their sense, a point at which it is no longer possible to ask for the sense of a name since the name simply names itself.

Finally, given these two structures, there is the third structural paradox of the necessary infinite *alternation* of signifier and signified, whereby each new signifier itself becomes a possible signified, and thus engenders the necessity of another distinct signifier, and so forth.[16] Again, the regress can only be avoided by the positing of an absolute point of fixed correspondence between signifier and signified, a kind of absolute signifier that already is its own signified, and which thus captures the total structural order of signification and forecloses its necessary regress only by paradoxically signifying itself.

The structural necessity of such a paradoxical place for any formal characterisation of sense points, according to Deleuze, to the necessary existence of certain 'paradoxical elements' in any structurally constituted language. These are elements which, rendering undecidable the oppositions between signifier and signified, denotation and denoted, and rule and instance, paradoxically capture the total structure of a signifying system and focus it at a singular, precise point. Closely related to what Lévi-Strauss termed the 'floating signifier', such 'paradoxical entities' are decisive for the formal theory of sense because of the way they themselves reflect, without resolution, the essentially paradoxical structure of the totality of signification at a determined point within it. In particular, it is characteristic of the paradoxical entity, according to Deleuze, that it circulate endlessly between the two parallel series of signifiers and signifieds, and thereby assures, beyond any assumption of mirroring, parallelism or term-by-term correspondence, the only relationship these two series can have. Making reference to Lacan's treatment of the structural effectivity of just such an element in his 1955 seminar on Poe's 'The Purloined Letter', Deleuze characterises the paradoxical element as:

> at once word and thing, name and object, sense and *denotatum*, expression and designation, etc. It guarantees, therefore, the convergence of the two series which it traverses, but precisely on the condition that it makes them endlessly diverge. It has the property of being always displaced in relation to itself. If the terms of each series are relatively displaced, *in relation to one another*, it is primarily because they have in themselves an *absolute* place; but this absolute place is always determined by the terms' distance from this element which is always displaced, in the two series, *in relation to itself.*

We must say that the paradoxical entity is never where we look for it, and conversely that we never find it where it is. As Lacan says, *it fails to observe its place (elle manque à sa place)*. It also fails to observe its own identity, resemblance, equilibrium, and origin. [. . .] It behooves it, therefore, to be in excess in the one series which it constitutes as signifying, and lacking in the other which it constitutes as signified: split apart, incomplete by nature or in relation to itself. Its excess always refers to its own lack, and conversely, its lack always refers to its excess.[17]

According to Deleuze, it is only by occupying this paradoxical place with respect to the totality of signification that the paradoxical element can not only found its structural sense, but also locate the precise point of the possibility of its radical transformation. This is the point of the intra-systematic and formally locatable promise not only (as Deleuze says quoting Lévi-Strauss) of 'all art, all poetry, all mythic and aesthetic revolutions', but also (Deleuze adds) of 'all revolutions'.[18]

As Deleuze points out, both the structure of the paradoxical element and the systematic series of paradoxes from which it results can further be formalised by reference to the foundational paradox that historically doomed the project of a consistent logicist reduction of arithmetic, namely Russell's paradox of the set of all sets not members of themselves. In particular, the inevitable generation of a regress in each case of the serial paradoxes necessarily invokes the question of a point of totality at which the regress could be halted, for example a name that would be able to name itself, or a conceptual signification that would be able to stand for itself. The confusion of formal levels which would alone yield such a point is then formally identical to the inclusion of a set within itself, and also invokes the question of the possibility of a set of all sets and accordingly (if this question is answered in the affirmative) to the contradictory Russell set itself. The paradoxicality of the paradoxical element with respect to the totality of signification that it captures is thus formally the same as that of the Russell set itself, which is a member of itself if and only if it is not.[19] In this way, according to Deleuze, once we consider the possibility of an intra-systematic element that reflects the total constitution of structural sense, we must ascribe to it the contradictory properties of the Russell set: those of both referring and not referring to itself, and of thereby witnessing the necessary contradiction of any location of the basis of the total structure of signification within that structure itself.

Why, though, can both the paradoxical element and the contradictions it witnesses not be avoided by means of the formal devices that standardly preclude Russell's paradox itself within axiomatic presentations of arithmetic and set theory, namely devices of foundation, serial ordering with respect to the referential powers of language, or a hierarchy of logical types? Within these presentations, following a suggestion originally made by Russell himself, the requirement is imposed that a set can only be included within another if the second is at a structurally higher level than the first: thus, both the possibility of a set belonging to itself and the possibility of a *total* set of all sets (and with this, the possibility of the paradoxical Russell set as well) are regulatively precluded in advance. These devices of foundation and hierarchy have a legitimate employment in such axiomatic theories as can legitimately refer to an essentially *open* domain of ever-higher stratified levels with no 'highest' type or *total* unification into a single total set. Conceived in terms of their implication for the structural characterisation of language or languages, these devices would require, in the case of each constituted language, a 'higher' or 'stronger' one from the perspective of which it would be possible to assay and describe the total structure of the first; whereas the second language would then require, for its own complete description, a third, even stronger one, and so forth.[20] But the reason that these devices cannot be used to preclude paradox in reference to the constitution of linguistic sense itself can be found in an axiom which Lacan repeatedly formulates, and makes a formal basis of his own consideration of the specific kind of Real which is shown at the point of the kind of formalising impasse to which Russell's paradox witnesses. This is the axiom that 'there's no such thing as a metalanguage': there is, in other words, no *outside* perspective or position from which it would be possible, with respect to the totality of language, to assay its structure and delimit its power without contradiction.

Given the radical nonexistence of such an exterior position, the formalisation of the basis of sense is determined as, necessarily, the internal formalisation of the paradoxical point of impasse, or the limitation of the formalism of sense with respect to the nonsense of the paradoxical element it must inscribe, in which alone can formally appear the total character of signification at a precisely signified (but necessarily absurd) point within it. As Deleuze puts the point, again drawing on Lévi-Strauss, the possibility of any positive knowledge already depends on the pre-existence, and possibility of reference to, a 'virtual totality of langue or language', a 'completeness of [the] signifier' which is always already 'there' in advance despite the necessary obstruction, to be overcome progressively by the advance of positive knowledge, of its progressively segmented allocation to the signified.[21] The necessity that (as Lévi-Strauss puts it) 'Man, since his origin' already has had this completeness 'at his disposal' – but yet without being able to situate himself *outside* the total field of the possible signified to which it gives meaning – is the necessity that sense as a whole be formally reflected, within this field, by the paradoxical element or structurally necessary point of the impasse of consistent formalisation.[22] It is just here that the Real of structure proposes itself, in connection with the constitutive ideas of totality, reflexivity and contradiction or inconsistency, to the only symbolic access that is possible to it, that of the formalisation of constitutive and foundational paradox.

If there is no metalanguage, and yet the subject of signification thus always already in advance relates itself to the total structure of signification as such, then the structure of the subject of signification is irreducibly consigned to situate itself in the paradoxical gap that thereby formally opens up between this totality and itself. A formally similar reference to the constitutive impasse of formalisation at its own limit is again the basis, in Lacan, for clarifying the structure of the subject as it results from the inherent gap between being and knowledge. Whereas, for Lacan, there is explicitly no way for the 'one' of totality to enter into the world except by means of the signifier itself – no source, that is, for this unity in a fusional principle of synthesis, or an intuitive givenness of unity as such – it is nevertheless crucial that, as he often puts it, through the agency of the symbolic and its proper mode of causality, there is nevertheless '[something of] oneness'. (*Y a d' l'Un*).[23] If, then, there is no metalanguage, and hence, as Lacan emphasises in Seminar XX, no 'language of being' capable of adequately expressing its totality, then the subject of the signifier is consigned to exist in the gap that thereby opens up between the 'oneness' that thus subsists on the level of structure and the unity of such a total (meta) language of being, which is not.

In Seminar XX, Lacan clarifies this situation by reference to its formal implication for the subject's relation to truth:

> There is some relationship of being that cannot be known. It is that relationship whose structure I investigate in my teaching, insofar as that knowledge – which, as I just said, is impossible – is prohibited (*interdit*) thereby. This is where I play on equivocation – that impossible knowledge is censored or forbidden, but it isn't if you write 'inter-dit' appropriately – it is said between the words, between the lines. We have to expose the kind of real to which it grants us access.
>
> We have to show where the shaping (*mise en forme*) of that metalanguage – which is not, and which I make ex-sist – is going. Something true can still be said about what cannot be demonstrated. It is thus that is opened up that sort of truth, the only truth that is accessible to us and that bears on, for example, the non-savoir-faire.[24]

As Fink notes in a footnote, Lacan's reference here is to Gödel's Incompleteness Theorems. The first of these shows that, for any adequately strong axiomatic, consistent formal system of arithmetic, there will be some sentence which demonstrably cannot be proven by the system, but is nevertheless evidently true. In this sense, the theorem itself witnesses the possibility of a sort of truth – a relationship to being, as Lacan says – that exceeds the order of systematic knowledge and the correspondence it presupposes between signs and their objects. Beyond this assumed correspondence, it bears witness to the truth that opens up at the limit-point of possible formalisation, in and through the very formalisation of the internal deductive structure of a language as such. At this point of essential impasse, the systematically suspended demonstration of a truth, and with it the proper situation of the subject in relation to the real of its being, exposes its proper unity and hence the real of which it is capable, substituting itself for the one of an adequate (that is, consistent and complete) metalanguage of being, which is not.[25]

Formalism, one, critique

I have argued for the existence of a specific use of formalisation in Lacan and Deleuze, one which functions as an elaboration of the total character of signification in relation to the constitutive formal (or meta-formal) ideas of completeness, consistency and reflexivity.[26] On the suggestion that is common to both thinkers, this use of formalisation articulates any possible position of a subject whose specific being is conditioned by the signifier, thereby inscribing at the point of paradox and formal impasse the truth that is proper to it. All of the specific formalisms which indicate the place of this truth, for Lacan and Deleuze, stand in determinative and formally tractable relation to the kind of unity – the one – that is introduced by signification as such. This is not the one of a self-enclosed and consistent totality of beings, accessible to a metalanguage position capable of assaying the total correspondence of words and things. It is rather the one that 'subsists', takes place, or is said in default of such a position – but is thus said only, as I have argued, on the basis of a problematic formalism of formalisation itself, which there indicates, at the point of formalism's own reflexive impasse, the proper mode in which alone the symbolic allows a thinkable access to being. This one that subsists at the point of impasse is what Lacan indicates with the motto that 'there is oneness'; again, it is the one of what Deleuze calls, early in *Difference and Repetition*, the sole ontological proposition that has ever been, that of the *univocity* of Being.[27] As Deleuze argues, the formally articulated claim that 'Being is said in one and the same sense' of all its distinct designators, modes and differences is sufficient to oppose to the analogical or equivocal senses of being invoked by Aristotle, Aquinas or Hegel in the service of an ultimately conceptual unification of beings under the sign of identity the formal unity affirmed by another tradition, the one represented by Scotus, Spinoza and

Nietzsche, which rather allows the full restoration of the ontological rights of difference.[28] And as I have suggested, the formalisation of this problematic unity or univocity, up to the point of paradox, operates for both Lacan and Deleuze as the sole possible indication of the problematic point of contact of symbolic thought with being in itself.

Although the formalisation of this problematic unity in both Lacan and Deleuze is thus continuous with the pursuit of the function in which Plato, at one point in his career, located in the idea or form – namely that of capturing the specific real of whatever is thinkable in being in itself – it has nothing to do with the positing of supersensible entities, timeless universals, or a transcendent dimension of reality of the kind that one associates with a vulgar 'Platonism'. For as we have seen, it is not in the transcendence of forms, but rather in the formalisation of symbolic formalism itself, that Lacan and Deleuze locate this specific real and find its own properly paradoxical structure. Accordingly, it is not in the transcendence of the supersensible, but in the immanence of what is proper to the symbolic as such, that Lacan and Deleuze find the real indicated by formalising thought, and there locate the specific structure of a being constitutively subject to it. It is also in this immanence, and at the specific point of impasse which formally locates the gap between being and knowledge introduced by the virtual totality of signification, that this use of formalism locates the point of possible critique, or transformation, of this totality as such. Indeed, as we have already seen in connection with what Deleuze calls the 'paradoxical element', whether it is a question of the transformation of an individual psyche, the innovation of new collective practices of art, science or culture, or critical intervention at the point of the spontaneous ideology of the community or the social whole, it is always, from this position, the point of the paradoxical impasse that provides the specific hope of transformation and the promise of the new.

Elsewhere, I have attempted to describe, under the heading of the 'paradoxico-critical' orientation of thought, the critical and political implications of this singular position with respect to the symbolic, its paradoxical impasse of formalisation, and the specific real of contradiction, antinomy or constitutive antagonism that shows up just there.[29] Here, in closing, I shall just attempt to indicate briefly how this formally grounded position, embodied in common by Lacan and Deleuze, differs from that of two other contemporary projects that also claim to draw on formalism, in substantial continuity to Lacan, to situate what are actually very different critical claims with respect to contemporary ideology and praxis.

First, it cannot be disputed that the ontological and political project of Alain Badiou certainly represents one of the foremost considerations of formalism and its implications in our time. Moreover, Badiou develops his account of being, the event and the possibility of subjectively grounded transformation in substantial continuity with Lacan. This is clear (for instance) in both the opening and closing pages of *Being and Event*, where he invokes the possibility of a new 'post-Cartesian' doctrine of the subject developing from (but also critical of) Lacan's, or indeed already in the motivation of the interventionist activism of the *Theory of the Subject*, where, invoking and reversing Lacan's motto about the real as the impasse of formalisation, he calls instead for a theory of the forced 'pass of the real, in the breach opened up by formalisation'.[30] This is the theory which he would then later find in the apparatus of Paul Cohen's technique of forcing, and its potential to inscribe the initially indiscernible, with radical structural consequences, at the infinite limit of the procedure of a faithful subject.

But although Badiou's development of forcing is thus itself continuous, in one respect, with the Lacanian thought of the relationship between the Real and the structural impasse, its way of conceiving of the location and consequences of impasse is in fact completely different. For while Deleuze and Lacan both suspend, at the specific point of the impasse of formalism with respect to itself, the paradoxical 'one' which offers for both the only possibility of an ontological inscription of the real, Badiou's direct ontologisation of mathematics invokes, by contrast, an ontology of pure multiplicity predicated on the presumptive denial of any 'one' or 'one-all' of signification as such. At the same time, a mandate of consistency is here to be maintained, at least with respect to that in Being which is presentable as such, by means of a problematic operation of 'counting as one' which operates, as if from outside language or indeed any possible presentation, both to constrain and to produce the kinds of novelty that can then appear there. As I have argued in more detail elsewhere, this has the effect of officially displacing the locus of truth, outside any determinative connection to language or its structure, but raises once more the deep problem of the problematic position of a metalanguage, from which it would be possible formally to articulate both what is ontologically presentable and what can (on Badiou's theory) transform it from the exterior position of an event.[31] In a more critical and practical register, these displacements yield, in turn, Badiou's activist and decisionist account of the potential consequences of an event, an account which, despite its clear uses with respect to certain problems of identification, also tends to abandon any specific register of immanent critique.[32]

Another contemporary position which claims substantial continuity with Lacan's, but in fact ultimately misplaces the level and critical force of the appeal to formalism which he shares with Deleuze, is Žižek's. The problem here is not, as with Badiou, that of a direct ontologisation of formalism that bypasses the specific significance of the symbolic in relation to the Real, but rather that of the distortions produced by a forced unification of the proper *impasse* shown by formalism for Lacan with the problematic and officially generative core of the Hegelian dialectic in the contradiction of terms. In texts such as the recent *Less Than Nothing: Hegel and the Shadow of Dialectical Materialism*, Žižek's zeal to force such a marriage of Lacan's structuralism and Hegelian dialectic indeed allows him, while clearly recognising how Lacan's formalism points to a constitutive and formally demonstrable inadequacy of the One of signification with itself, misleadingly to identify this inadequacy with the Hegelian contradiction. Accordingly, Žižek writes as if the (actually imaginary rather than symbolic) Hegelian 'unification of opposites' were itself sufficient not only to capture but indeed to traverse this proper 'deadlock' of the symbolic, thereby repeatedly yielding a greater ontological positivity to be reinscribed on a higher level.[33] This has the further effect, in terms of the specific terms of critique which Žižek can accordingly propose, of reinscribing the resource of positive transformation in the activity and agency of a once again substantialised subject, the subject able repeatedly to supplement the basic ontological inconsistency of the world itself by means of the kind of imaginary unification its agency can provide. With this, the essential formal impasse that Lacan and Deleuze both recognise, and place at the core of the possible access of a signifying subject to truth, is misplaced, and the specific possibilities of immanent critique and transformation it offers again missed.[34]

Notes

1. Lacan, Jacques, *The Seminar of Jacques Lacan, Book XX: Encore* (London and New York: W. W. Norton, 1999 [1973]), p. 93.
2. There are important changes and developments (which I pass over here) in Lacan's sense of the 'real', as well as its relations to the other two orders, over the course of his career For a helpful recent account, see Eyers, Tom, *Lacan and the Concept of the 'Real'* (London: Palgrave Macmillan, 2012).
3. 'Mathematical formalization is our goal, our ideal. Why? Because it alone is matheme, in other words, it alone is capable of being integrally transmitted Mathematical formalization consists of what is written, but it only subsists if I employ, in presenting it, the language (*langue*) I make use of' (Lacan, *Encore*, p. 119).
4. Deleuze, Gilles, 'How Do We Recognize Structuralism?', in *Desert Islands and Other Texts 1953–1974* (Los Angeles: Semiotext(e), 2004 [1967]), pp. 170–92, p. 171.
5. Ibid. p. 172.
6. Ibid. p. 173.
7. Ibid. p. 173.
8. Ibid. p. 174.
9. Ibid. p. 174.
10. Ibid. p. 175.

11. Ibid. p. 176.
12. Ibid. p. 179.
13. Ibid. p. 177.
14. Deleuze, Gilles, *Difference and Repetition* (New York: Columbia University Press, 1994 [1968]), p. 16. Interestingly, the paradox is also used by Quine decisively to criticise Carnap's conventional picture of logic and linguistic rules: see Quine, W. V., 'Truth by Convention', in *The Ways of Paradox and Other Essays* (New York: Random House, 1966 [1936]). For some discussion, see Livingston, Paul M., *The Politics of Logic: Badiou, Wittgenstein, and the Consequences of Formalism* (New York: Routledge, 2012), pp. 88–9. The original source is Carroll, Lewis, 'What the Tortoise Said to Achilles', *Mind*, 4: 14 (1895), pp. 278–80.
15. Deleuze, *Difference and Repetition*, pp. 28–31.
16. Ibid. pp. 36–8.
17. Deleuze, Gilles, *The Logic of Sense* (New York: Columbia University Press, 1990 [1969]), pp. 40–1; original emphasis.
18. Ibid. p. 49.
19. Ibid. pp. 68–9.
20. I proceed somewhat quickly and loosely here, blurring over distinctions between set-membership, referential power and structures of logical types, and invoking in passing also the close relationship between Russell's paradox and what has been called 'Tarski's paradox' of the indefinability without contradiction of a truth-predicate for a language, L, within that language itself, calling for (on Tarski's classical interpretation, at any rate) an open hierarchy of ever-stronger metalanguages. For a fuller and more detailed treatment of the relevant formal structures and their interrelationships, see Livingston, *The Politics of Logic*, ch. 1.
21. Deleuze, *The Logic of Sense*, p. 48.
22. Ibid. p. 48.
23. 'We know of no other basis by which the One may have been introduced into the world if not by the signifier as such, that is, the signifier insofar as we learn to separate it from its meaning effects' (Lacan, *Encore*, p. 50). 'For a long time I have scanded what constitutes the first step in this undertaking with a certain "There's such a thing as One" (*Y a d' l'Un*). This "There's such a thing as One" is not simple – that's the word for it. [. . .] If the unconscious is truly what I say it is, being structured like a language, it is at the level of language (*langue*) that we must investigate this One' (ibid. pp. 66–7).
24. Ibid. pp. 119–20.
25. The point is developed in more detail in Seminar XIX: 'the Real affirms itself by an effect which is in no way the least, by affirming itself in the impasses of logic. I will explain. The fact is that at the start, in its all-conquering ambition, logic proposed for itself nothing less than the network of discourse in so far as it is articulated and that by being articulated, this network ought to close itself into a universe that is supposed to embrace and cover like a net anything that was involved in what was offered to knowledge. Experience, the experience of logicians, showed things to be different [. . .] The remarkable thing [. . .] is that it is not starting from the values of truth that Gödel proceeds in his proof that there will always be in the field of arithmetic something that can be stated in the proper terms that it involves, which will not be within the grasp of what posits itself as a means to be held as acceptable in the proof. It is not starting from truth, it is starting from the notion of derivation. It is by leaving in suspense the true or false value as such that the theorem is demonstrable' (Lacan, Jacques, *Seminar XIX: . . . ou pire . . .*, trans. Cormac Gallagher from unedited French manuscripts, available at <http://www.lacaninireland.com/web/wp-content/uploads/2010/06/Book-19-Ou-pire-Or-worse.pdf> (last accessed 5 April 2016), pp. 38–40). The issues about totality, unity and completeness raised here also have obvious relevance to the significance and derivation of Lacan's so-called formulas of sexuation, which involve distinct forms of

non-totality indicated by a specialised use of logical quantifiers. For an illuminating discussion, see Chiesa, Lorenzo, *The Not-Two: Logic and God in Lacan* (Cambridge, MA: MIT Press, 2016).

26. For a fuller discussion of the meta-formal application of these ideas in connection with a realism predicated in part on Lacan's register of the Real in the specific way it is formally available through the development of formal impasses, see Livingston, Paul M., 'Realism and the Infinite', *Speculations: A Journal of Speculative Realism*, 4 (2013), pp. 99–117.

27. Deleuze, *The Logic of Sense*, p. 35.

28. Ibid. pp. 39–42.

29. See Livingston, *The Politics of Logic*, especially ch. 10.

30. Badiou, Alain, *Being and Event* (London: Continuum, 2005 [1988]), pp. 1–3, 431–5; Badiou, Alain, *Theory of the Subject* (London: Continuum, 2009 [1982]), p. 22. For discussion, see Livingston, *The Politics of Logic*, pp. 188–92.

31. See Livingston, *The Politics of Logic*, ch. 9.

32. For this line of critique, see Livingston, *The Politics of Logic*, chs 9, 10.

33. The problem is evident in passages such as this one, where Žižek, commenting also on Badiou, takes up the implications of Lacan's motto about formalisation and the impasse: 'For Lacan, the Real can only be demonstrated through formal logic, not in a direct way, but negatively, through a deadlock of logical formalization: the Real can only be discerned in the guise of a gap, an antagonism. The primordial status of the Real is that of an obstacle, the absent cause of a failure, a cause which has no positive ontological consistency in itself but is present only through and in its effects. To put it succinctly: one tries to formalize the Real, one fails, and the Real *is* this failure. That is why, in the Lacanian Real, opposites coincide: the Real is simultaneously what cannot be symbolized *and* the very obstacle which prevents this symbolization. And this coincidence, the coincidence of a Thing with the very obstacle which presents our access to it, in other words this overlapping of epistemological failure and ontological impossibility, is profoundly Hegelian' (Žižek, Slavoj, *Less Than Nothing: Hegel and the Shadow of Dialectical Materialism* (London and New York: Verso, 2012), p. 841). As we have seen, however, the *identification* that Žižek here proposes between the failure 'to formalize the Real', and the Real itself, is nowhere suggested by Lacan (or Deleuze) and is moreover highly problematic in itself. Lacan does not say that the Real *is* the impasse or failure of formalisation, but just that it can *only be inscribed on the basis* of such an impasse. Whereas the inscription *of* the impasse or paradox – as for instance in the writing of Russell's paradox, or the inscription of Gödel's theorems – *is* in a certain way a 'direct' symbolisation *of* the Real, this writing is itself not to be understood as either an impasse or a positive obstacle to this symbolisation Moreover, the kind of impasses or paradoxes (not 'failures') that show up here are in no simple sense epistemological *or* ontological, and so cannot be used, as Žižek suggests, to license a 'Hegelian' transformation of (critical) epistemological limitation into ontological (dialectical) positivity. It is rather (as for instance in Gödel's theorems) the case that a formalisation of the *possible* formalisation of the symbolic (which has nothing to do with epistemology) here yields, not the ontological production of a new thing, but the inscription of a new undecidable at the formal limit of the symbolic structure itself.

34. For a fuller development of these points, see Livingston, Paul M., 'How Do We Recognize Strong Critique?', *Crisis and Critique*, 3 (2014), pp. 85–115.

Notes on Contributors

Lorenzo Chiesa is Director of the Genoa School of Humanities and Visiting Professor at the European University at St Petersburg and the Freud Museum of the same city. He was previously Professor of Modern European Thought at the University of Kent, where he founded and directed the Centre for Critical Thought. He also held visiting positions at the University of New Mexico, the Istituto di Scienze Umane of Naples and the Institute of Philosophy of Ljubljana. He has published volumes on Lacan (*The Not-Two*, MIT Press, 2016; *Subjectivity and Otherness*, MIT Press, 2007; *Lacan and Philosophy*, Re.press, 2014) and on political theory (*The Virtual Point of Freedom*, Northwestern University Press, 2016; *Italian Thought Today*, Routledge, 2014; *The Italian Difference*, Re.press, 2009). He has edited and translated books of Agamben and Virno into English and of Žižek into Italian.

Guillaume Collett is a Research Fellow in the Centre for Critical Thought at the University of Kent. He is the author of *The Psychoanalysis of Sense: Deleuze and the Lacanian School* (Edinburgh University Press, 2016), and co-editor with Masayoshi Kosugi and Chryssa Sdrolia of the special issue of *Deleuze Studies* 'Deleuze and Philosophical Practice'.

Adrian Johnston is a Professor in the Department of Philosophy at the University of New Mexico at Albuquerque and a faculty member at the Emory Psychoanalytic Institute in Atlanta. He is the author of *Time Driven: Metapsychology and the Splitting of the Drive* (2005), *Žižek's Ontology: A Transcendental Materialist Theory of Subjectivity* (2008), *Badiou, Žižek, and Political Transformations: The Cadence of Change* (2009) and *Prolegomena to Any Future Materialism, Volume One: The Outcome of Contemporary*

French Philosophy (2013), all published by Northwestern University Press. He is the co-author, with Catherine Malabou, of *Self and Emotional Life: Philosophy, Psychoanalysis, and Neuroscience* (Columbia University Press, 2013). His most recent book is *Adventures in Transcendental Materialism: Dialogues with Contemporary Thinkers* (Edinburgh University Press, 2014). Moreover, he currently is finishing two new book manuscripts: *Prolegomena to Any Future Materialism, Volume Two: A Weak Nature Alone* and *A New German Idealism: Reflections on Žižek's Dialectical Materialism*. With Todd McGowan and Slavoj Žižek, he is a co-editor of the book series Diaeresis at Northwestern University Press.

Peter Klepec is a Research Adviser at the Institute of Philosophy, Scientific Research Centre of the Slovenian Academy of Sciences and Arts, Ljubljana. His main areas of research are French contemporary philosophy, German Idealism, Lacanian psychoanalysis and critique of ideology. He has published two books in Slovenian: *On the Emergence of the Subject* (2004) and *Capitalism and Perversion, 1. Profitable Passions* (2008).

Paul M. Livingston is the author of three previously published sole-authored books drawing on analytic and continental philosophical approaches; the most recent of these is *The Politics of Logic: Badiou, Wittgenstein, and the Consequences of Formalism* (Routledge, 2012). His manuscript, *The Logic of Being: Realism, Truth, and Time* (Northwestern University Press, forthcoming) examines the relationship between truth and time from a position drawing centrally upon Heidegger's thought of ontological difference as well as recent analytic philosophy of language and logic.

Boštjan Nedoh is a Research Assistant at the Institute of Philosophy, Scientific Research Centre of the Slovenian Academy of Sciences and Arts, Ljubljana. In 2015 he obtained his PhD in contemporary continental philosophy from the postgraduate school at ZRC SAZU with the thesis title: 'The structure and role of perversion in contemporary philosophy and psychoanalysis'. His primary research interests lie in Lacanian psychoanalysis, Italian biopolitical theory and contemporary French philosophy. He has published articles in *Angelaki, Filozofski vestnik, Paragraph* and *Journal for Cultural Research*.

Laurent de Sutter is Professor of Legal Theory at Vrije Universiteit Brussel. He has been Visiting Researcher at Benjamin N. Cardozo School of Law, Yeshiva University; Käte Hamburger Kolleg 'Recht als Kultur', Universität Bonn; and Waseda Institute for Advanced Study, Waseda

University. He is the Managing Editor of the Perspectives Critiques series at Presses universitaires de France, and Theory Redux at Polity Press. His most recent books are *Magic. Une métaphysique du lien* (Presses universitaires de France, 2015), *Vies et morts des super-héros* (Presses universitaires de France, 2016) and *Théorie du kamikaze* (Presses universitaires de France, 2016).

Samo Tomšič is researcher at the Humboldt University in Berlin. He obtained his PhD in philosophy at the University of Ljubljana, Slovenia, where he also worked at the Institute of Philosophy, Scientific Research Centre of the Slovenian Academy of Sciences and Arts, Ljubljana. His research areas comprise continental philosophy, psychoanalysis and epistemology. Recent publications include *The Capitalist Unconscious: Marx and Lacan* (Verso, 2015) and *Jacques Lacan Between Psychoanalysis and Politics* (ed. with Andreja Zevnik; Routledge, 2015).

Tadej Troha is a Research Fellow at the Institute of Philosophy, Scientific Research Centre of the Slovenian Academy of Sciences and Arts, Ljubljana. Author of two books in Slovenian: *Neither Miracle Nor Miracle* (2010) and *Intervening into the Irreversible* (2015), and numerous articles on psychoanalysis, politics and literature.

Scott Wilson is a Professor of Media and Psychoanalysis at Kingston University, London. He is on the Board of *The Lacanian Review* and is a regular contributor to the *Lacanian Review Online*. With Eleni Ikoniadou he edits the series Media Philosophy (Rowman & Littlefield International). With Professor Michael Dillon he edits *The Journal for Cultural Research* (Taylor and Francis). His latest books are *Stop Making Sense: Music from the Perspective of the Real* (Karnac, 2015) and with Eleni Ikoniadou *Media After Kittler* (Rowman & Littlefield International, 2015).

Andreja Zevnik is a Lecturer in International Politics at the University of Manchester. Her research interests include theories of subjectivity, political violence and resistance, aesthetic politics, law and psychoanalysis. She is a convener of the Critical Global Politics research cluster and a member of the editorial board for the *Journal of Narrative Politics*. She recently published *Lacan, Deleuze and World Politics: Re-thinking the Ontology of the Political Subject* (Routledge, 2016) and *Jacques Lacan Between Psychoanalysis and Politics* (ed. with Samo Tomšič; Routledge 2015).

Alenka Zupančič is a Research Adviser at the Institute of Philosophy, Scientific Research Centre of the Slovenian Academy of Sciences and Arts,

Ljubljana, and professor at the European Graduate School, Switzerland. She is the author of numerous articles and books on psychoanalysis and philosophy, including *The Odd One In: On Comedy* (MIT Press, 2007), *Why Psychoanalysis: Three Interventions* (NSU Press, 2008), *The Shortest Shadow: Nietzsche's Philosophy of the Two* (MIT Press, 2003) and *Ethics of the Real: Kant, Lacan* (Verso, 2000).

Index

58–9, 80, 86, 88, 101, 107, 122n, 155, 167–8, 171, 173
power-relation, 126
sexual, 52, 57
symbolic relation, 47
see also non-relation
Renaissance, 144–5, 152
repetition, 4, 9, 21, 50, 86, 93, 101, 163–73, 176, 178n, 179n, 181, 186–7, 190–5, 197
representation, 3, 9, 29n, 72n, 78, 81, 125, 133, 136, 152, 196–7, 203, 205, 207
repression, 3–6, 12n, 46–7, 49–54, 54n, 58, 94, 99, 117, 142, 164–5, 176
resistance, 206
    primal repression (*Urverdrängung*), 3
Revault d'Allones, Olivier, 63
revolution, 21, 29n, 131, 149, 155, 173
Russell, Bertrand, 204, 212–13; *see also* Russell's paradox

Sacher-Masoch, Leopold von, 5, 11n, 14, 35–8, 41, 42n, 43n, 45–6
Sade, Marquis de, 5, 32–8, 41
sadism, 5
Saint Teresa (Bernini's sculpture), 136, 153, 155
Saint Thomas Aquinas, 23, 89, 152, 215
Sartre, Jean-Paul, 20, 26
Saussure, Ferdinand de, 2, 125–7, 130–1, 205
Schelling, F. W. J., 182, 197–8
schizoanalysis, 1, 6, 59
schizophrenia, 26, 58, 66
Schreber, Daniel Paul, 7, 94–6, 100–3, 103n
science, 25–6, 60, 123, 125–9, 132–6, 138, 139n, 151, 155, 175, 184, 198–9, 216
Scott Fitzgerald, Francis 170
Sellars, Wilfrid, 197
sense
    common, 18, 108, 192
    Freudian, 85, 198
    Lacanian, 4, 75, 85, 173
    linguistic, 203, 213
    non-sense, 8, 59–60, 65, 86, 94, 103n, 107, 111, 113, 115–17, 181, 213
    psychoanalytic, 176
sexuation(s), 6, 50–2, 54, 172, 195, 219n
    formulas of sexuation, 6, 50–2, 54, 219n

signification, 6–7, 74–6, 78–9, 83–4, 113, 132, 177, 203–4, 206, 208, 210–18
signifier, 4, 6, 10, 18–20, 22, 29n, 49, 51, 53, 55n, 57–8, 60–1, 68, 72n, 75–6, 80–1, 84–90, 106, 116, 131–4, 139n, 143–5, 176–7, 187, 189, 191–3, 205–7, 211, 213–15, 219n
signifying chain, 4, 49–50, 55n, 75, 77, 79, 83, 91n
Silverman, Kaja, 79
singular, 8, 13, 21, 34, 41, 52, 83, 93, 95, 106–9, 111–13, 117–18, 119n, 151, 168, 170, 174, 187, 209, 211, 216
singularity, 3, 8, 38, 106, 108–9, 117, 136, 150, 209
Snark, 7
Soler, Colette, 68, 70
Sollers, Philippe, 32
sovereign, 7, 32, 37, 76
speaking, 13–14, 19–20, 46, 55n, 65–6, 113, 115, 136, 141–3, 145, 153–4, 193, 205
    body, 24, 59, 136
Spinoza, 24, 113, 119n, 170, 182, 196–8, 215
Stalin, Joseph, 133
structuralism, 1–2, 4, 8, 40n, 45, 53, 83, 106, 108, 110, 123, 125, 127–30, 132, 134–5, 137–8, 139n, 194, 203, 205, 207–8, 218
    baroque, 8, 123–40
    history of, 43n
    hyper, 2, 4, 132
    post, 2, 45, 53
    weak, 4
structure, 2–6, 8–9, 18, 36, 39–41, 47–50, 57, 76, 81–3, 85–6, 88–9, 95, 98, 106, 112, 116–17, 119n, 123–5, 125–30, 132–4, 136–8, 143–4, 146, 149, 164, 174, 176, 203, 207–17, 220n; *see also* language; perversion
subject, 1, 3–7, 13, 18, 23, 25, 29n, 39–41, 46–7, 50–1, 53, 57, 61, 70, 74–88, 90, 93, 97, 99–101, 103, 109, 111, 114, 119n, 123, 126, 132, 135, 138, 142–50, 163, 176, 179n, 180, 182–3, 196–8, 204–6, 214, 217–18
    of cognition, 135
    Lacanian, 76
    of the signifier, 214
    supposed to know, 25
    of the unconscious, 87–8, 123, 132

EU Authorised Representative:

Easy Access System Europe Mustamäe tee 50, 10621 Tallinn, Estonia

gpsr.requests@easproject.com

Printed and bound by CPI Group (UK) Ltd, Croydon, CR0 4YY

15/05/2025

01873226-0002